MEMORIES OF *TIMES* PAST

MEMORIES
OF *TIMES* PAST

by

Louis Heren

Hamish Hamilton · London

HAMISH HAMILTON LTD
Published by the Penguin Group
27 Wrights Lane, London W8 5TZ, England
Viking Penguin Inc., 40 West 23rd Street, New York, New York 10010, U.S.A.
Penguin Books Australia Ltd, Ringwood, Victoria, Australia
Penguin Books Canada Ltd, 2801 John Street, Markham, Ontario, Canada L3R 1B4
Penguin Books (N.Z.) Ltd, 182–190 Wairau Road, Auckland 10, New Zealand
Penguin Books Ltd, Registered Offices: Harmondsworth, Middlesex, England

First published in Great Britain 1988 by
Hamish Hamilton Ltd

British Library Cataloguing in Publication Data
Heren, Louis
Memories of times past.
1. Heren, Louis. 2. Foreign correspondents
—Great Britain—Biography
I. Title
070′.92′4   PN5123.H38
ISBN 0-241-12427-1 OM

Typeset, printed and bound in Great Britain by
Butler & Tanner Ltd, Frome and London

Contents

Acknowledgments

Memory fades, and I am grateful to the archivists of *The Times* for helping me to refresh it; and to Times Newspapers Ltd and Times Books for permission to use the paper's official histories and files. Lady Haley and Mark Barrington-Ward kindly allowed me to refer to her husband's correspondence and his father's diaries. I also thank Simon Jenkins and Michael Leapman and the literary agents of Claud Cockburn and Donald McLachlan for allowing me to quote from their books.

1

More Than a Newspaper an Institution

Queen Elizabeth II has a number of good bars, and the one preferred by drinking men is the Midships' Bar. The bartenders know their business, and when to leave a customer alone. That was one reason why every evening during a crossing from Southampton to New York in the late summer of 1981 I had a couple of their martinis before going into dinner. I am a gregarious man but had a lot to think about on that trip, and it came down to this: should I quit *The Times* after working for the paper, boy and man, for more years than I cared to remember.

The question would have been ridiculous a year earlier, before Rupert Murdoch bought Times Newspapers Ltd. Not that I had anything against the Australian; that he owned the *Sun* did not bother me. Northcliffe had published *Answers* and *Comic Cuts*, but had been a great proprietor before going mad. Murdoch was a born newspaperman – his father was a distinguished war correspondent – and had a reputation for knowing how to deal with the print unions. He was also the best of a bad bunch – the other men who wanted to buy the company were less acceptable for a number of reasons. Early rumour that he was in the running shocked some of the journalists; Patrick Brogan, the Washington correspondent, resigned and others threatened to leave but I supported Murdoch's bid at an editorial conference. Not that the journalists had any say in the matter, for all our professional pretensions we were hired men, but probably the editor had been asked about the attitudes of the assistant editors. They were of little interest to William Rees-Mogg, who had earlier announced that he would resign the editorship. As deputy editor, I was asked first and said Murdoch and the others agreed.

Murdoch's arrival in the office was not exactly propitious. About half of the advertisement staff was fired, and given only a few hours to clear their desks. Murdoch had already demanded huge reductions in the production departments, which were definitely feather-bedded, and then announced that he wanted a number of editorial men and women to take early retirement. Some of the older people were happy to go, redundancy payments were generous, but one could feel a cold wind blowing through the editorial floor. Then I was asked to see Murdoch in his office on the top floor.

He was friendly enough, we were soon calling each other 'Lou' and 'Rupert'; then he suddenly said, 'You are not going to be editor, Lou. You're too old.' At least, that is how I remembered it. I was disappointed of course, but the editorship was in his gift and I had heard that he intended to appoint Harold Evans, the editor of the *Sunday Times*. Murdoch added, 'You are 61, and I want an editor who will last at least ten years.' That proved to be a bit of a joke.

Murdoch then suggested that I should become an associate editor. I could travel the world and choose my own stories. He also wanted me to be the first journalist member of the board of the holding company. I accepted if only because I had never thought of leaving the paper until they put me out to grass, but it was an unhappy arrangement. Evans largely ignored me, treating me as an unwanted passenger. Hence the moody drinking of martinis in the Midships' Bar.

On the second night out I realized that I should have left with Rees-Mogg, who correctly saw the sale of the company as the end of a chapter. He was surprised when I told him that I intended to soldier on – especially as my redundancy entitlement was bigger than his. I should have known that the new editor would want his own men about him, but life without the paper was unthinkable. I loved *The Times* as most soldiers love their regiments. Indeed, for me *The Times* was a good fighting regiment with more battle honours than the Brigade of Guards, and which I had joined as a boy soldier.

Before the war it had been part of the tradition to recruit likely young lads whose fathers had served, or were still serving. My father, a printer, had died when I was four years old, but the connection was not broken. A widows and orphans party was held every Christmas in the staff restaurant in Printing House Square, and we were also invited to Hever Day, a splendid occasion. Everybody came, from the editor and manager to the charladies and messengers, and with their wives or friends travelled in six special trains to Hever castle, the proprietor's country seat in Kent. A posh lunch was served with claret cup in vast marquees, and beer tents were erected in the grounds. Some of the men spent most of the day in them, but there was tennis, swimming and rowing on the lake, and in the early evening dancing on the lawn. The day ended with a speech made by the chief proprietor, the then Major J.J. Astor. I cannot remember what was said, but am fairly certain that the honour of serving *The Times* was the main theme. Astor had lost a leg in the First World War, but with his trim figure and close-clipped moustache still looked every inch the soldier. He was the perfect colonel-in-chief of the regiment and Geoffrey Dawson, the editor, was of course the commanding officer.

The company secretary, Charles Hoar, was the recruiting sergeant. He kept the list of potential boy soldiers, and interviewed them when a vacancy occurred. My turn came in the autumn of 1933 when Hoar wrote to my mother requesting her to report with me to the office. She was to bring a medical certificate, and our GP duly certified that I was in good health and of sound constitution. She also brought my father's indenture papers issued when he was apprenticed as a printer. It said that he was to serve his master for seven years, and 'he shall not commit fornication nor contract matrimony during the said period. He shall not play cards, dice, tables, or any unlawful games ... haunt taverns, or playhouses, nor absent himself from his said master's service day or night unlawfully'. For my mother the papers represented my claim to an apprenticeship, but Hoar was in no position to give promises or encouragement. The unions decided who was to be apprenticed, and he must have known that sons of live printers would be chosen before me. He could only promise that I would begin as a messenger. I would be paid 17s. 6d. a week for the probationary first month, and then £1 a week with two weeks holiday a year. Annual pay increases of 7s. 6d. were guaranteed, and my eventual wage would depend upon the department I was promoted to. He was sure that I would do well if I worked hard and behaved myself.

Hoar did not ask about my education, probably because *The Times* had its own ideas about training its recruits. I was required to attend a night school off Kingsway two nights a week, where I learned typing, shorthand and simple bookkeeping. Later I transferred to Goldsmiths' College in New Cross for courses in French and what was described as the art of writing, but the real training – indoctrination is perhaps the better word – took place in the office. With three other boys I was under the command of the chief commissionaire, first Sergeant Brooker and then Mr McCluskie. We were inspected each morning for cleanliness and neatness. Jackets and neckties were obligatory, as was a respectful demeanour. At the end of the first month Hoar wrote asking if Messenger L. Heren had 'given satisfaction in the performance of his duties'. Brooker answered: 'Sir, This lad has given every satisfaction'. I had passed my first test, and was on my way to becoming a *Times* man.

My duties were simple – delivering messages and accompanying visitors. Only then was I allowed to use the lift, an antique cage which could only carry three people and then very slowly. A notice under the control panel said that messengers would be instantly dismissed if they used the lift when not accompanying visitors. Britain was of course a deferential society in those days, but everybody who worked for *The Times* was supposed to be a member of one big happy family known as the Companionship. We were not employees or hands, but Companions joined in a mystical union dedicated to producing *The Times*. Astor was the Chief Companion. It was taken very seriously, and those who thought it a joke – there must have been some – kept quiet if only because of the advantages. They were considerable. For instance, the Companionship ran the staff restaurant – not the usual canteen but a real restaurant with linen tablecloths, fresh flowers, uniformed waitresses and a licence to sell beer, wines and spirits most hours of the day and night. It also ran the sports ground in Ravensbourne, Kent, and a number of clubs ranging from cricket and golf to music and amateur dramatics. I joined the boxing club, but was not very good. I always closed my eyes when I saw a straight right aimed at my face, but the showers attached to the well-equipped gymnasium were wonderful. We did not have a bathroom at home, and those showers were sheer luxury.

To that extent, *The Times* was more than a job from the beginning. It paid me, fed me, educated me, entertained me and provided creature comforts. (It also played Cupid. Many of the men married girls employed as secretaries and waitresses.) It sounds paternalistic, but the print unions were already powerful and negotiated with management on equal terms. In retrospect, it seems that the paper was also more than a job for most of the staff. For instance, when the General Strike was called in 1926 Astor met the fathers of the chapel, or shop stewards, and was applauded when he said that they parted as friends and hoped to meet again as such before long. He added, '*The Times*, being above party and class, does not recognize the right of anyone to dictate policy or course of action and will carry on – so far and as long as possible. Goodbye and good luck.' The paper did not cease publication, but was got out by pensioners, apprentices and volunteers, and the circulation was more than doubled by the tenth and last day. Two duchesses helped to deliver copies by car and Lady Diana Duff-Cooper ran the subscription department. The pickets were sustained with beer and sandwiches from the staff restaurant, and saluted Astor when he walked through the picket line.

When I was still living in the East End, *The Times* was also a completely different world. I lived in a vast slum unrelieved by a big house and other manifestations of conventional society. The few doctors were socially invisible, and the school teachers commuted in from outside. I did not know I was poor because everybody was poor, but every working-day morning I not only crossed the frontier into that other world but into a bastion of the Establishment. Dawson, the editor, was one of its pillars and was treated as such. His arrival at the office was a daily triumph, and three messengers were generally involved in the exacting ceremony. The first stood outside to signal the approach of the editorial Rolls from the Victoria Embankment, the second opened the front door and the third rang down the lift. The commissionaire, who had earlier inspected our shoes and haircuts, ejaculated 'Morning, sir!' and saluted smartly. We all stood to attention as Dawson gravely returned the salute with a slight inclination of the head or a flourish of his walking stick, and stepped into the lift. We remained at attention as he slowly disappeared from view.

I cannot recall my feelings at the time, except that I knew that I was lucky to have a job and was proud to be working for the world's greatest newspaper. I was only peripherally involved in its production, but being a messenger was rather like being a stage hand in Chinese opera. I moved about unseen and, not being overworked, wandered unhindered through most of the departments. Occasionally after boxing I would go into the composing room, and stand enthralled by the disciplined bustle of newspaper production. The only constant noise was the clatter of the Linotype machines which set the editorial matter. I had been brought up to believe that the Linotype operators were the aristocrats of Fleet Street, and they were certainly the highest paid apart from the senior editorial men and managers. Most of them wore collars and ties, and little aprons to protect their waistcoats and trousers. The stonehands, the men who made up the pages from galleys of type, earned less but were more interesting to watch. They worked under a subeditor, who always wore a jacket, but did not appear to need much direction. They made a few editorial decisions. The sub chose and laid out the big stories, but left it to the stonehands to fill up the bottom of the page with 'shorts', generally of one or two paragraphs. Smoking was not then allowed in the composing room, and when waiting for more galleys or corrections they would take out their snuff boxes which they also offered to the sub.

Without haste they got the editions out on time and without typographical errors. They seemed to share my excitement when the page formes were locked up; they certainly enjoyed pushing the formes to the foundry, but they were probably longing for a pint and a smoke in the staff restaurant. They would disappear when the whistle was blown, but occasionally I would wait while the formes were moulded in the foundry. A few minutes later the building seemed to shake when the presses in the basement were started. They rotated slowly at first, but were soon accelerated and within a few minutes their roar, muted by two floors, filled the room. Only then did I walk up to Ludgate Hill to catch the no. 15 bus home. The fare was two old pennies, half the cost of the Underground ticket. The pennies saved were spent the next morning on a packet of five Woodbine cigarettes dispensed from a machine in the entrance to Blackfriars station opposite the office. As at school, we smoked in the lavatories.

In those days the paper was peppered with Latin and Greek tags – *The Times* must have been the only paper in Britain to stock Greek type and employ compositors capable of setting it. One evening I went into the room of an assistant editor, C.W. Brodribb, and found him discussing a Greek quotation with the head reader. If I had not known the reader, I could have mistaken him for a leader writer, such was his demeanour and scholarship. This convinced me that *The Times* had the finest printers in the world. The readers, or correctors of the press as they were once known, did not have to be convinced. They had a high opinion of themselves, and always wore evening dress at the annual departmental dinners.

Brodribb was the then archetypal *Times* man, a classicist and poet who devoted the last years of his career to maintaining the high editorial standards of the paper. He was said to read every word that went into it. He had joined in 1904 and was one of the black friars, so named and ridiculed by Lord Northcliffe who became the proprietor four years later. (The office stood on the site of the medieval Blackfriars monastery.) My mother remembered the press lord with gratitude because he raised the printers' wages. The black friars were no less grateful at first. He had revived and modernized the paper, but they resisted his efforts – he was going mad at the time – to impose his political views and idiosyncrasies. As the paper's official history says, Northcliffe could not learn the lesson that on *The Times* personal power, whether of the proprietor or the editor, must be limited; that the quality that gave the paper its distinction was not conferred by one man but was the collective contribution of the staff. Northcliffe would have defeated them if he had lived but died before he could do any more damage.

My interest in the production departments began to wane during my second year. One reason may have been the realization that I would not get an apprenticeship. Two of the other mess-

7

engers would obviously be the lucky recipients; in any case, the editorial department had begun to exert a powerful attraction. I suppose that I was a romantic. As a kid, I used to lie in bed and listen to ships dropping down the river, their horns sounding mournfully, and dream of all the faraway places they were bound for. Four dioramas in the front hall of *The Times* similarly fed my imagination. They depicted great events in the history of the paper, and one that especially impressed me showed the great war correspondent, William Howard Russell, in his tent in the Crimea. Another showed a cutter landing dispatches from France during the Revolution, with a horseman on the beach waiting to rush the news to London. I had no idea how a messenger could become a journalist of *The Times*. In the 1930s it really was the top people's paper, and the senior editorial men looked Olympian. Their offices on the first and second floors of the main building were rather grand. At least I thought so – book-lined and with handsome fireplaces. In winter an elderly messenger replenished the coal fires from a polished brass scuttle. He had a knack of raking ashes without making a noise. The senior men sat at large desks, at most two or three to a room, lighted by green-shaded lamps. According to Claud Cockburn, one of his colleagues in the foreign room translated a passage of Plato's *Phaedo* into Chinese for a bet. Another, who had written the definitive grammar of an obscure Polynesian language before becoming a professor of Chinese metaphysics at the University of Tokyo, spent some hours deciding how to spell Kuala Lumpur. He is reported to have said, 'There are eleven correct ways of spelling Kuala Lumpur, and it is difficult to decide which should receive the, as it were, imprimatur of *The Times*.' (Claud Cockburn, *In Time of Trouble*, 1956.)

Younger men such as Graham Greene had written or sketched out novels while working as subeditors. Peter Fleming walked across the roof of the world from China to Kashmir. One of the photographers took the first aerial pictures of Mount Everest. George Steer was the first to report the bombing of Guernica during the Spanish Civil War. I watched Charles Morgan, the drama critic, return from the theatre resplendent in white tie and tails to write his notice against the clock. The sports writers spent their days watching cricket, golf or football and some of their evenings drinking in the Baynard Castle next door until they were drummed out after playfully drenching the landlord with soda water. I occasionally had to go down and remind them that the subs wanted their copy. They were characters out of Surtees, and had nicknames like Beau. They all seemed to be captains, and wore regimental or club ties, cord trousers with narrow cuffs and old tweed jackets. Then there was Dermot Morrah, a leader writer who was a Fellow of All Souls and one of the kings-of-arms, and once came into the office wearing his medieval uniform; and a mysterious bald-headed Russian émigré who wore a long coat with a fur collar and was always followed by a couple of borzoi hounds. He looked like a master spy out of Sherlock Holmes, but was apparently a purveyor of diplomatic news.

Room 6, where the early evening editorial conference was held, was always crowded, and this gave me the opportunity to stand by the door and watch. A couple of the lesser men sat by the fireplace apparently enjoying the comfort of easy chairs but possibly resentful because they were not senior enough to sit at the large mahogany table where the decisions were supposed to be made. If they were, the process was beyond my comprehension. The editor presided in an impatient or preoccupied manner as if he had more important things on his mind. On his right sat his deputy, Robin Barrington-Ward, who looked keen, and on his left Brodribb looked distracted presumably because of all those proofs he would have to read before going home. Only Herbert Russell, the night editor, and the chief foreign and home subeditors were businesslike. They had to get the paper out, and generally it was one of them who had called for a messenger. He would finally see me standing by the door and then peremptorily wave me over to take some copy to the subs.

Brodribb was the first black friar to show any interest in me. I was sitting on a windowsill in an alcove near his room, and he asked me what I was reading. I held up a library copy of Conrad's *Lord Jim*. He said that I must read *Nostromo*, Conrad's greatest book, and asked for my name. One evening a few weeks later, coming out of the editorial conference with the editor and William Casey, another assistant editor, he drew their attention to the literary messenger; I was reading *Nostromo*, and thinking that I preferred *Lord Jim*. The great man dutifully smiled and without a word sauntered on, but Casey was delighted. He asked about the origin of my name, and grinned when I said that my father's father was a French Basque. Extraordinary people, he beamed; you might make a good journalist because the Basques are against authority. When he became editor after the war, and some ambassador complained about my reporting, he would benignly explain that I was a Basque and against all governments, not only his.

Casey was a wonderful Irishman who, I discovered long afterwards, loved good claret, conversation at the Garrick Club, books and the theatre. While still practising at the Dublin bar – he once said that he was given only one brief for which he was paid one guinea – he wrote two plays for the Abbey theatre. He also managed it for a while before seeking his fortune in London where he was invited to write reviews for *The Times Literary Supplement*. His career on the paper began in the sporting room as a subeditor, and he was a foreign correspondent in Washington and Paris before becoming a leader writer and one of the assistant editors. As such he kept an avuncular eye on the younger editorial men and was said to be a good talent spotter, but Stanley Morison and not Casey was responsible for my initial advancement. I had been transferred from the messengers to the publicity department as an office boy. I did not much like the idea, but the publicity people were nice and encouraged me to try my hand at a number of jobs. Within a few months, and still being paid 35 shillings a week, I was writing advertisement copy, designing publicity pamphlets and helping with the monthly *House Journal*. This was edited by William Binne, who taught me the rudiments of typography and layout and asked me to design the weekly double-crown posters for the *TLS*. Morison had to approve the designs, and helped me in more ways than one.

The fifth volume of the paper's official history (*The History of the Times*, 1984) describes Morison as a scholar with little formal education. His father was a drunken commercial traveller who deserted his mother, and Morison left school at fourteen to earn a few shillings. He was an office boy and clerk until he read a printing supplement of *The Times* in 1912. King's Cross railway station, where he bought the supplement, proved to be his road to Damascus. He was enthralled by printing, and after working for Burns & Oates, the publishers, joined the Monotype Corporation where he was eventually recognized as an outstanding typographer. Unlike some men who later became Roman Catholics after being disillusioned by the Communist party, he was converted to Roman Catholicism and remained a political radical but apparently not a member of the party although he designed the titlepiece of the *Daily Worker*. He was imprisoned during the First World War as a conscientious objector.

It says something for *The Times*, and indeed for the period, that he was invited to design a new type for the paper, to write the first four volumes of its official history and later to edit the *TLS*. He also became the *eminence grise* to the proprietor, two editors and one manager, and was resented by some of the senior men because they did not know where his responsibilities began and ended. He was another member of the Garrick, where he was known as a connoisseur of wine and a lively companion, but looked like a priest with his wire-rimmed spectacles, black suit and what I thought of as a Father Brown hat.

His extraordinary influence began with the first volume of the Official History (published 1935). Everybody knew that the paper had a great and glorious history, but little concrete was known about its early days. Morison established that Thomas Barnes, the first editor, was a compaigning journalist who was as much responsible for the 1832 Reform Bill as any politician or reformer. In digging out the facts on which the paper's reputation rested, Morison strengthened the loyalty and pride of the editorial staff. He himself had a near-religious faith in *The Times* and its place in the world. He was said to light candles to it in his flat in Whitehall Court; apocryphal no doubt, but his Roman Catholicism may have explained the intensity of his feeling for the paper. A number of senior editorial men were also Catholics. *The Times*, like the old foreign office, presumably attracted them because of its authority and assumed infallibility. When I was deputy editor, the editor, chief leader writer, features editor and I belonged to what is known as the true church.

The man most impressed by Morison's researches was not a Catholic. Barrington-Ward, the then deputy editor, was the son of a Church of England parson. After reading the first draft, Barrington-Ward wrote that Morison 'has had to dig Barnes out almost completely, from the substratum of anonymity and oblivion, and he promises to succeed brilliantly in establishing the identity of the real formula of TT and of independent, professional journalism'. Nicolas Barker, Morison's biographer, wrote,

> It was a remarkable achievement, and not merely as a piece of historical research, for in clearing away the undergrowth and rubble from the early days of *The Times* Morison had discovered – as Barrington-Ward was quick to recognize – its *genius loci*. Barnes, with his preference for anonymity, was far more a man after Morison's heart than the self-assertive Delane. As well as Barnes, he had discovered Barrington-Ward: one to share his ideal of *The Times* as a greater force than the words in any issue, greater than the men who staffed it at any time. It was a vision of the paper that now drew them closer together, and to which they held through the difficult days of the war. It was the same vision that Morison sought to preserve after Barrington-Ward had gone. (Nicolas Barker, *Stanley Morison*, 1972)

This 'vision' explained much of Morison's influence on the paper, and it lasted long after Barrington-Ward's death. When it was seen to be faltering in 1958, he wrote a memorandum to the proprietors worth quoting in part:

> The prime responsibility of the Chief Proprietorship is to organize the office so that the tradition, authority and leadership of the paper are maintained in the present, and safeguarded for the future. The national interest clearly demands it. It is difficult for any outside critic to deny this. Obviously Great Britain cannot function without a strong, educated, efficient informed governing class. *The Times* is the organ of that class.... As long as free political discussion is the necessary prerequisite of legislation this is obvious. Secondly, the due discussion of the country's affairs cannot be adequately conducted in Parliament alone so long as it is elected quinquennially and sits only for a few months in the year.
>
> The existence of a competent governing class is rightly said to be absolutely dependent upon *The Times* because no other newspaper attempts to rival it in self-respect, impartiality, independence, range of significant news, and capacity to reason

upon the matter printed. No other newspaper possesses the space in which adequately to discuss in leading articles and letters to the Editor the topical and national problems of today and tomorrow. This was true a hundred years ago and it is true today. A country like Great Britain depends for its administrative efficiency upon its politically intelligent and professional men; these in turn depend upon *The Times* for the material upon which to reflect, and, ultimately, act.

This was romantic nonsense, and did considerable damage to the paper when it was written. *The Times* was a unique newspaper under the editorships of Thomas Barnes and John Delane who between them created the first genuinely independent newspaper. It became indispensable by providing the first comprehensive news service, and the best for many decades. 'Politically intelligent and professional men', including successive prime ministers and their cabinet colleagues, did indeed depend upon it, but its uniqueness began to be eroded in 1855 when the Stamp Act was repealed and newspapers such as the *Daily Telegraph* became rivals. By the 1950s Britain did not have a governing class but political parties increasingly divided along ideological lines and competing groups such as the trade unions with political clout undreamed of in the previous century. Some preferred the *Telegraph* or the *Guardian*, others the *Morning Star* or the *Daily Express*. The *Daily Mirror* was the establishment paper when Labour was in power. *The Times* remained a very good newspaper, one of the best in the world, but no longer unique or indispensable. Nevertheless, Morison's faith in *The Times* remained absolute to the end.

Not that he discussed it when he took me under his wing. I was still an office boy allowed by an indulgent employer to stray into an area which properly did not concern me. It could be said of course that I was exploited in that I was paid an office boy's wages for doing a skilled man's job. The truth was probably somewhere in between; in any case the great typographer treated me as an assistant. He lent me fount books and introduced me to St Bride's library which had one of the best collections of books on printing in the world. I enjoyed the work but still wanted to be a reporter, and again Morison was helpful in suggesting that I could help to cover the coronation of King George VI. Dermot Morrah

13

reported the actual coronation, but full treatment was given to the day's festivities and I was asked to cover the street parties in the East End of London. They must have been short of copy because my short story was published more or less untouched, and the home news editor did not forget me. I continued to work in the publicity department, but from time to time was asked to do a story when the reporters' room was shorthanded.

I also looked outside for freelance work which was available as long as I kept my sights low and knew where and what to look for. The East End was a mine of stories, from tarantula spiders coming ashore with the bananas in the old West India docks to a murder in Limehouse. I was usually paid five shillings an item, but got a lot more when Oswald Mosley tried to lead his fascists through the East End. I acted as a 'leg man', that is I gathered information for a Fleet Street journalist who was born in the provinces and was completely out of his depth east of the Tower. Occasionally, very occasionally, the freelancing doubled my *Times* pay.

James Cameron, the journalist and friend of blessed memory, once wrote that I was born old. He exaggerated a bit, but in my day East End kids had to grow up very quickly. I grew up in the depression years when men were lucky if they got two or three half-day's work a week in the docks. The dole, or unemployment pay, was not much, and nearly everybody was poorly clothed and ill-fed. The tenements and little terrace cottages were old and crowded, and in some tenements many families shared a lavatory. I was lucky. I was one of the few who ate well because my mother ran a café, or what was known as a coffee shop although the only coffee served came out of a bottle of Camp extract. Working for *The Times* also made a great deal of difference, but the toughness of the neighbourhood rubbed off on me. I was streetwise at an early age, and could take care of myself. The isolation of poverty bred a strong tribal spirit and nurtured working-class solidarity. We were suspicious of authority and wary with the police. To sanitize the tribal rallying cry, our attitude to authority was 'muck'm all'. Not that life was grim. The schools were good as was the Carnegie library, and in summer we swam in the river. I enjoyed life, especially after going to work. I gave most of my wage to my mother, but had enough left over to discover the theatre. I regularly walked across Waterloo bridge to the Old Vic, and lined up for seats in the gods of West End theatres. It cost only six old pennies. Covent Garden cost more, but I once heard part of the Ring cycle and with Wagner thundering in my ears walked all the way home because I had no money for the bus fare. I also discovered that girls were interesting.

I was a political animal almost since I learned to read because one of my duties at home was to read newspapers, the old *News Chronicle* and the *Star*, to my uncle who had been blinded in the war and lived with us. He had an insatiable appetite for news, and we also listened to the radio. While still in my teens, I had some idea of the economic and political reasons for unemployment and poverty, and a fair grasp of the conditions in Europe which had produced Hitler and Mussolini. If I had been old enough I might well have gone to Spain to fight in the International Brigade, and I almost joined the Communist party. Thank heavens I did not; it would have blighted my subsequent career as a foreign correspondent, especially in the United States. I became increasingly critical of *The Times*, or rather of the editor. Dawson's appeasement of Hitler and Mussolini infuriated me. I bought a copy of the Official History at a reduced staff rate, and Barnes became one of my abiding heroes. Dawson, I decided, was a traitor to the principles of journalism established by the paper's first editor.

The Times, under the masthead *The Daily Universal Register*, was launched by John Walter in 1785, the year Barnes was born, but did not have an editor until his appointment in 1817. In its early years the paper was indistinguishable from London's other eight morning papers. Walter took bribes and received a government subvention. He was also awarded a printing contract in return for giving general support to the government. It was a seedy beginning, and the circulation was down to about 2000 when his second son, John Walter II, took over in 1803. He may not have been the first British publisher to recognize that the press could not be free unless it was financially independent, but was the first to do something about it. He developed his own news service, appointed the first foreign correspondent, Henry Crabb Robinson, and installed the first steam press. There was still no editor in the modern sense until Walter retired to the country. He was at first doubtful of Barnes, his drama critic and political reporter, because he was regarded as a radical, but eventually appointed him and gave him complete editorial independence.

Barnes was a strange choice in that he was well known for wining and wenching, kept raffish company and lived with another man's wife. He was not a radical, but a reformer and practical idealist. He battled doggedly for political reform, and supported the underdogs of his age – the Roman Catholics, the Dissenters and the new industrial working class. He insisted upon anonymity, but demanded forcible writing with 'a little of the devil in it'. He was rightly sceptical of the ability of aristocratic politicians to understand what was happening beyond their great town and country houses, and of parliament, unreformed and unrepresentative. They appeared not to understand or care about the misery and hunger brought about by the slump after the Napoleonic wars and the rising food prices due to the 1815 Corn Law, especially in the new industrial towns which were not represented in parliament. The paper's report of the Peterloo Massacre was a sensation. The cause of parliamentary reform became a national issue overnight, and Barnes a power to be reckoned with. The nickname 'The Thunderer' was earned by a leading article urging the country to 'thunder for reform', and it stuck when Barnes successfully campaigned for other causes. He was said to have become the most powerful man in Britain, but modestly maintained his anonymity to the end. There was no obituary notice.

Dawson could also have been a hero of mine. Appointed editor by Northcliffe in 1912, he resigned seven years later because the press baron threatened the paper's editorial integrity. He returned to the editorial chair in 1923 on condition that the new chief proprietor, Astor (later Lord Astor of Hever), reconfirmed the independence of the editor. Astor agreed that the proprietors had only the right to hire and fire the editor; that once appointed the editor alone would be responsible for the contents of the paper and 'for the selection of his assistants at home and abroad, and for the allocation of their duties'. This was a unique achievement. John Walter II gave Barnes editorial independence because he wanted to live in the country and pursue a parliamentary career. It was a matter of personal convenience and not of principle. It was more or less honoured until the arrival of Northcliffe, but

Dawson entrenched and codified it in an exchange of letters. All *Times* men who came after were grateful to Dawson. Many years later, when as deputy editor I was frequently in the editorial chair, I never had to look over my shoulder. I, a hired man, was completely in charge of the editorial content and could throw out any advertisement I considered unworthy of the paper. To that extent, it was my newspaper.

But Dawson was not another Barnes. He did not stand aloof, but was an intimate friend of the Tories who controlled the country's destiny for many years, and obviously believed that he had the God-given right to share their responsibility. Educated at Eton and Magdalen, Oxford, and a fellow of All Souls, he was a landowner and had been accustomed to being at the centre of power from his early twenties. In 1901 he went to South Africa as private secretary to Lord Milner, the high commissioner, and joined an élite group of young men known as Milner's kindergarten. Their main task was the reconstruction of the country after the Boer war, and this proved to be a training ground for some of the future leaders of Britain. Dawson became a journalist only because Milner asked him to edit the *Johannesburg Star*. He learned the trade, but saw his main function as supporting Milner and the newly-created administration. He was part of the local establishment, and not an independent editor. This explained his approach to the job when, after contributing to the paper from South Africa, he was appointed editor of *The Times*. Sir Basil Liddell Hart, who was military correspondent for four years, wrote in his memoirs that Dawson 'sought to make *The Times* the "submerged half" of the government, or the cabinet behind the cabinet, instead of giving priority to its function as a newspaper' (*Memoirs*, 1965).

Dawson had never been a reporter or foreign correspondent. He had entered the craft of journalism at the top, first in Johannesburg and then London. When he returned to Britain he knew little about the condition of the country he had left as a young man, and nothing about continental Europe. Apart from Barrington-Ward, he had few friends in the office although he could be affable and easy-going. They moved in different worlds; when he was not hobnobbing with the great and powerful he was playing the part of the country squire in Yorkshire. Nor did he depend upon the advice of his 'assistants at home and abroad'. To that extent he was as bad as Northcliffe; he did not learn that the quality that gave the paper its distinction was not conferred by one man but by the collective contribution of the staff.

His main friends and advisers belonged to the Round Table, a group including other former members of Milner's kindergarten. Many had made their way in the world of government and politics, and they were imperialists to a man, truly believing that the British Empire was a civilizing and stabilizing force. They wanted to create the British Commonwealth which did not formally exist when Dawson returned to Britain, and some of them hoped that it would evolve into a federation with centralized institutions controlling defence and foreign affairs. They had enlightened ideas about India and the colonies, and assumed that they would evolve into independent members of the Commonwealth.

The Round Table often held its 'moots' at Cliveden, the country house of Waldorf Astor, who owned the *Observer* and was the older brother of the more socially modest proprietor of *The Times*. His wife, Nancy, was a well-known political hostess and gave house parties for the rich, famous and powerful. The Dawsons stayed at Cliveden on other occasions and were drawn into this exclusive world. Later he became a member of what was known as the Cliveden Set. I only read about the set in the popular papers which portrayed it as a cabal which ran the country. They made it sound very sinister, which annoyed Dawson, but there was little doubt that the policy to appease the dictators was discussed and formulated at such gatherings. Dawson accepted it in part because of his devotion to the Commonwealth ideal. He really did not want to involve Britain in the quarrels of Europe, and unlike Casey and other senior *Times* men had no affection for France. This was to prove disastrous for the paper and the country. There were other reasons why *The Times* supported appeasement, and they will be discussed in the next chapter, but more than any other editor he transformed the creation of Barnes and Delane into the Establishment newspaper. Being the man he was, I doubt that Dawson realized that he betrayed the paper and its traditions. He may well have thought that he did no more than Delane, who spent much of his time with the titled ruling class, but Delane kept his distance editorially; he sought news to be used against the government or a minister if necessary and not to defend those who regarded themselves as the natural ruling class. Both men became powerful and influential, if for different reasons. In Dawson's case, this became evident in Edward VIII's abdication crisis. Lord Beaverbrook, the proprietor of the *Daily Express*, wrote that apart from the prime minister Dawson was the most important factor in compelling the king to abdicate, and that he did it by methods many could condemn, pursuing his quest with a vigour that seemed more like venom. That was not altogether true, but Dawson acted more like a member of Baldwin's cabinet than as the editor of *The Times*.

Edward first met the Simpsons in 1931, when he was still Prince of Wales. They were wealthy American socialites, who fitted easily into the prince's circle of raffish friends, and by 1934 Mrs Simpson was his mistress. Fleet Street was well aware of this, but remained silent. She was not his first mistress, and in those days the press was more deferential or perhaps more grown up. Mrs Simpson was regarded as a passing fancy who would be abandoned when Edward became king and had to chose a suitable consort. There appeared to be no doubt that he would do his duty when the time came, but the affair was serious. The archbishop of Canterbury told Dawson of the distressing talks he had had with King George V. He thought that it had definitely shortened the king's life. Baldwin must also have known, and on the occasion of the old king's jubilee in 1935 said:

> If in any cataclysm the crown vanished, the empire would vanish with it. It is a link which once broken can never be repaired, and so long as the tradition to which we have been accustomed, the tradition which guides those who sit on our august throne, so long as that tradition lasts, it will be blest to our country and no power can break it.

If that was a coded message it was ignored by Edward, and Mrs Simpson did not make a gracious exit when he ascended the throne in January 1936. The American press reported the continuing affair with increased gusto, and one New York paper said that they would marry after she had been granted her second divorce. The British press still remained silent, hoping that the king would come to his senses before the coronation, but Dawson decided that the king would have to go if he married his mistress. The evidence is compelling. Many readers with connections in the United States knew about the affair, despite Fleet Street's self-censorship, and wrote to the paper. Not one letter was published, and after the abdication Dawson asked one of the senior men to read them and write an analysis. It showed that at the beginning of the crisis the majority were on the side of the king, and at the end the majority opposed the marriage. The official history records this without comment, perhaps because it suggests that by with-holding the earlier letters Dawson had manipulated public opinion.

One early letter was not filed away. Dawson called on Major Alexander Hardinge, the king's private secretary, at Buckingham Palace and gave him a copy of a long letter from a British reader living in the United States. Signed *Britannicus in Partibus Infidelium*, it said that American press publicity had transformed Britain, as envisaged by the average American, from a sober and dignified realm into a dizzy Balkan musical comedy. Admitting the presumption of a person far removed from the centre of events to suggest a remedy, the writer nevertheless suggested that the king should abdicate before calling in question the institution of the monarchy. Dawson asked Hardinge to pass the letter to the king.

This was certainly a strong hint of what Edward could expect from *The Times* if he did not behave. In return, Hardinge showed Dawson the draft of a letter he was writing to the king warning him that the British press could not remain silent much longer. It also included a statement on the constitutional position and an appeal to get Mrs Simpson out of the country as quickly as possible.

Edward was shocked, and Baldwin went further when he met the king a week before the divorce suit was due to be heard at the Ipswich assizes. He said that the criticisms of the American press were endangering the monarchy, and that in his opinion the case should not proceed. It did, and *The Times* and other papers reported that a decree *nisi* had been granted but without comment or mention of the king. Edward had six months – the period then imposed by law before the decree was declared absolute – to make up his mind, and he did not wait long. Three weeks later he told

Baldwin that he intended to marry Mrs Simpson even if he had to abdicate. The prime minister passed this on to Dawson, whose worst fears were confirmed by Barrington-Ward. *The Times* had a foot in both camps in that the deputy editor was an old friend of Walter Monckton, the king's legal adviser, who told him that Mrs Simpson was unlikely to 'retire'.

Dawson became a regular visitor to Downing Street; he afterwards claimed that Baldwin did not discuss the crisis with him, but they certainly discussed the constitutional position. Dawson afterwards wrote a leading article stating that it was clear enough. The king was the only member of the royal family who could marry whom he chose, provided that she was not a Roman Catholic. The political situation was no less clear. The cabinet, the leaders of the opposition and the Commonwealth governments were opposed to the marriage, not because she was a commoner or an American but because she had two living husbands.

There was another obstacle; the archbishop of Canterbury could not officiate at the coronation if the king married Mrs Simpson. Nevertheless, the king was immensely popular and Dawson suspected that Winston Churchill and his press friends, the Lords Beaverbrook and Rothermere, were ready to rally in support of the marriage. This soon became evident when the king visited economically depressed areas in South Wales, and *The Daily Mail*, Rothermere's paper, contrasted the royal solicitude for the unemployed with government indifference. Rothermere also privately suggested to the king the idea of a morganatic marriage. His argument was that such a marriage would be acceptable because Mrs Simpson and any children of the marriage would not share or inherit the rank and possessions of the king. Baldwin told Dawson that it was to be discussed by the cabinet and referred to the dominion governments. Dawson knew that the crisis would soon break but, to use his word, the floodgates were opened not by the king, prime minister or himself but an obscure provincial bishop.

On 1 December Dawson went out to dinner as usual, and returning to the office was shown a news agency report of an address delivered by Dr A.W.F. Blunt, bishop of Bradford, to his diocesan conference. It expressed the hope that the king was aware of his need for God's grace at his coronation and wished that 'he gave more positive signs of this awareness'. There was no mention of Mrs Simpson – the bishop, it was established later, was unaware of her existence – but the report also quoted a leading article which was to appear in the *Yorkshire Post* that night revealing the whole course of the affair as reported in the American press. Dawson was in a quandary, it was too late to get in touch with Baldwin who always went to bed early, and he decided to publish the bishop's address without comment. The other national papers were similarly cautious, but the following day Dawson twice went to Downing Street. He noted in his diary that Baldwin was going to see the king at six, and had nothing to tell beyond reporting a solid front in the dominions and parliament.

So much for his protestations that the prime minister did not discuss the crisis with him, and later that evening Baldwin rang him twice. He first said that the king understood that *The Times* was to publish an attack on Mrs Simpson, and had instructed him to forbid it. He had protested that the British press was free, and that he had no control over *The Times* or any other newspaper. The second time Baldwin said that the king would be satisfied if he could read the leading article for him. For all their closeness, Dawson was not prepared to reveal to anybody what was to appear in the paper. He waited until midnight, when the presses were running off the first edition and Baldwin was in bed, before sending a proof to Downing Street.

Dawson's first leader on the crisis was restrained. Knowing that most of the readers were unaware of the king's intention, he wrote informatively about the American press coverage; the silence of the British press was described as 'a common self-restraint, inspired by the hope that some authoritative act or statement would enable them to put an end to it once for all'. Mrs Simpson was not named, but the marriage was dismissed as 'incompatible with the throne'. The institution of the monarchy, the leader concluded, was greater than the individual, and a reassuring statement was required from the monarch if the institution was not to be damaged. Readers were left in no doubt as to the position *The Times* had taken up.

The arguments against the marriage were rehearsed in a series of articles. Parliament and not the monarch was supreme, and the king had to accept the cabinet's advice in everything including his private life. Royal opposition to the established government could only end in monarchical dictatorship or abdication. Mrs Simpson was unfit to be the king's consort because of her two divorces. Barrington-Ward wrote a savage leader when Baldwin announced in parliament that morganatic marriage was unknown to English law, and that neither the British nor the dominion governments were prepared to change the law. The leader said that it was inconceivable that 'the empire should accept a permanent statutory apology for the status of the lady whom the king desires to marry. The constitution is to be amended in order that she may carry in solitary prominence the brand of unfitness for the queen's throne.'

The Times was accused of kicking a man when he was down. It was indeed rough stuff, but Dawson and Baldwin were anxiously watching the efforts to organize a so-called King's party. Dawson described the organizers in his diary as 'mischief makers, a curious alliance of Churchill, Beaverbrook and Rothermere with all their papers, the *News Chronicle* representing the liberal intellectuals ... reinforced by Oswald Mosley's fascists, who were organizing demonstrations in the streets'. He drove round town one evening and watched the processions of fascists with their banners and the bewildered crowds standing outside the Palace and in Whitehall. It must have looked ominous, and the Beaverbrook and Rothermere press still appealed for delay, for reference to the people – for anything that would keep a once popular king on the throne and remove a prime minister they, the press lords, did not like. Churchill denied that the king and parliament were in conflict, and hinted that the government wanted to get rid of the king who was forced to remain silent. Whatever persuaded the great man to intervene can only be guessed at, possibly his romanticism, but it damaged his political reputation and further delayed his return to power. Baldwin disposed of his charges in parliament, as did Dawson in *The Times*, and Edward abdicated and left Britain forever in HMS *Fury*.

Knowing that the instrument of abdication was being drafted, Dawson prepared a leading article, entitled 'King Edward's Choice', which appeared on 11 December, the day of his departure for France. After expressing regrets over the king's decision and repeating that the initiative came from him, it went on:

23

Above all let us have no talk of 'romance' about what is indeed a drama, but a drama of the deepest tragedy. King Edward has most of the qualities that would have made him a great constitutional monarch. He has shown himself brave, completely free from pompousness, chivalrous where his affections were engaged, conscientious in his everyday public duties, attractive to a crowd, genuinely interested in the condition of the poor as he went among them. He was unfortunate, no doubt, in some of his intimates ... too largely composed of men and women, some of them of high birth and all of them remote from 'the people', who cared less for his welfare than for their own amusement.... That, amid all his great qualities, there was also something lacking in himself is sufficiently shown by the unprecedented decision recorded this morning.... What seems almost incredible is that any man who was born and trained to such high responsibilities, who had clearly the capacity to undertake them, and who had in fact begun to exercise them with the complete good will of the nation, should sacrifice it all to a personal preference for another way of life. *Omnium consensu capax Imperii nisi imperasset* – the well-worn quotation from Tacitus is irresistible. It can hardly have been a better verdict upon the Emperor Galba than it is upon King Edward that all men would have judged him worthy of the throne if he had never ascended it....

The leader was a *tour de force*, and after sending his hand-written copy down to the printer Dawson went to a dinner party to celebrate. That was his word, and his diary shows that he was very pleased with himself. He had decided at a very early stage that the king must go if he did not behave himself, and had duly warned him by sending him a copy of that reader's letter. He had probably influenced the reports of the Commonwealth high commissioners to their respective governments, whose veto of the marriage was decisive once Baldwin, again with his help, had decided against compromise; and he had manipulated and guided public opinion to accept the abdication of a popular king. That was power, real power. Clearly the king had to go, but *The Times* was to pay dearly for Dawson's loyalty to the establishment which made victory possible.

2

The Arch-Appeaser

Geoffrey Dawson was in one way similar to John Delane; every door in the kingdom was open to him. Delane was frequently the only commoner at aristocratic occasions when the country was still largely run by aristocrats. The most prominent people sought him out in public, and he was seen one day riding his horse down Whitehall with a duke walking on either side. Dukes played more modest political roles in Dawson's day, but prime ministers and foreign secretaries were intimate friends and he knew everybody worth knowing. Otherwise they were very different. Delane was married to the paper; his wife was mentally ill and lived apart under strict medical supervision, and he had no other interest. Dawson was happily married, and had many outside interests apart from the Round Table, his Yorkshire estate, Eton and All Souls. He enjoyed country pursuits, was a clubman and took long holidays. He happily left his deputy to run the paper for weeks at a time.

Delane normally rose at noon, and rode in Hyde Park after an austere lunch. Then he spent two or three hours at his desk planning the next issue and briefing his leader writers. Many of his scoops were written as leaders, using the secrets, information and rumours he had picked up the night before. The evening was spent at social functions or dining with politicians or ambassadors, and he returned to the office after 10 p.m. When other men were thinking of bed, he became night editor, reading, rewriting and subediting foreign dispatches and parliamentary reports, and selecting letters for publication. He rarely left the office until the last edition was being run off at 5 a.m., when he walked to his flat in Serjeants Inn. He once remarked that in the course of his career he had seen more sunrises than most men.

Dawson was no slouch. Iverach McDonald, who worked under him for many years and had reason not wholly to admire him, nevertheless wrote in the fifth volume of the Official History that Dawson 'worked much harder than his easy, unflurried manner suggested, and took a direct concern in most parts of the paper. He could do most things better than anyone else in the office, whether drafting leaders, or writing headlines, or doing picture captions, or seizing on news and playing it up.' Every day he had what are now known as working luncheons and dinners, and invariably returned to the office after dinner to check up on the news, read or change leaders written in his absence and inspect the main news page. His weekends at great country houses such as Cliveden were occasions for gathering information and exchanging ideas with other members of the Establishment, although Lady Nancy Astor apparently had the annoying habit of playing musical chairs after dinner.

Delane was the greater editor, however, because he remained true to the principles he articulated in a famous leader. He believed that 'the press lives by disclosures, that its first duty is to obtain the earliest and most correct intelligence of the events of the time and instantly to make them the common property of the nation'. He refused to accept any limitation on his freedom to report, and if he lived today would be the subject of innumerable complaints to the Press Council. Mowbray Morris, the manager of *The Times*, reflected Delane's principles when called before a parliamentary committee to substantiate a report that some members were receiving bribes. He said that the press had the right to do whatever it chose and was not required to explain to anyone. Asked if he was willing to offer any explanation or justification of the charge, he answered, 'I am not.'

Lord John Russell, the Whig statesman, told Queen Victoria that the degree of information possessed by *The Times* with regard to the most secret affairs of state was mortifying, humiliating and incomprehensible. Humiliating or not, the very men who complained provided information in the hope of securing Delane's goodwill. Because so many were eager to cooperate he was in fact independent of any one of them. He wrote to one supplicant: 'I don't care to have confidential papers sent to me at any time because the possession of them prevents me using the information which from one source of another is sure enough to reach me without any condition of reserve.' The queen complained to Lord Palmerston about his 'atrocious articles' but when Delane criticized her for withdrawing from public life after the death of the prince consort she wrote a letter to *The Times* explaining the reasons. Under Delane, *The Times*' coverage of the Crimean war brought down the government. This was power, but Delane was not corrupted; he only wanted news, and had no ambition to run the country.

Times change, Delane's Britain was more robust than Dawson's, but that does not explain his editorship. He was irritated by the widespread assumption that *The Times* was the faithful voice of the government, but his rebuttals were not persuasive. First, he argued that the paper should give an incoming government the benefit of the doubt. When the paper felt called upon to criticize it should be moderate and constructive, and display a full knowledge and understanding of the problems facing the government. In other words, it should write less as an outside critic and more as a judicious, informed and independent-minded member of the governing group. In fact, *The Times* normally conformed with the official line because Dawson was a member of the Establishment. He was a close and loyal friend of many leaders of the Conservative party, and the paper often anticipated official policy because he had helped to formulate it.

There is much to be said for new governments, democratically elected, being given at first the benefit of the doubt; but the paper would not have been mistaken for the official mouthpiece if Dawson had adhered to Barnes' and Delane's principles of independence and outspokenness. Both men responded to events no matter where they and the paper were led. One wonders what Dawson would have done at the time of Peterloo or the Crimean war.

They were also better editors than Dawson because they trusted and worked with their staffs. They lived long before *The Times* Companionship was established, but they and their correspondents at home and abroad were genuine companions who worked together for the greater glory of the paper. Dawson and Barrington-Ward preferred the official version of events and the advice of their establishment friends.

The fundamental change in the old system of policy-making in respect of foreign affairs became evident after Harold Williams, the foreign editor, died in 1928. Continental European affairs, of which Dawson knew little, were beginning to dominate the news, but Dawson did not appoint a new foreign editor. He made all kinds of excuses, none of them persuasive, and it soon became clear that despite the paper's traditions he and Barrington-Ward were determined to keep editorial policy in their own hands. The Official History said:

> The paper's intelligence, independence and leadership were permanently lowered. This declension was most conspicuous and disastrous in the department of Anglo-German affairs. No responsibility attaches to the correspondence, for the two resident correspondents who successively from 1920 to 1937 represented the paper in Berlin were the equal of their predecessors....Neither nourished any bias in favour of Nazism; both recognized the dangers of German rearmament before Nazism became a force. One was expelled. The reason why *The Times* failed to provide the country with the basis for sound judgment on the real objectives of German foreign policy is that the foreign correspondence was not made, as hitherto, the basis of the policy expressed in the leading articles.

Opposition in the office to this fundamental change was considerable. The assistant editors pressed Dawson to appoint a new foreign editor, but he rejected the idea that foreign policy required an expert who could give his whole time to its complexities. Barrington-Ward argued that the job of a foreign correspondent was to report and that policy was the prerogative of the editor and his deputy. More than that, he believed that 'if *The Times* decided that the policy towards Germany – or any other country – should be conciliatory, then it was expected that the correspondent should bear this in mind'. (Donald McLachlan, *In the Chair: Barrington-Ward of The Times*, 1971) This was monstrous in that it suggested that correspondents were not to report events which contradicted the paper's editorial policy. Dawson went further in a letter to H.G. Daniels in May 1937. Daniels, a former Berlin correspondent, returned to the German capital for a few weeks while Norman Ebbutt, who was then in charge, took a vacation. Dawson wrote:

> It really would interest me to know precisely what it is in *The Times* that has produced this new antagonism in Germany. I can really think of nothing that has been printed now for many months past to which they could possibly take exception as unfair comment. . . . I shall be more grateful than I can say for any explanation and guidance, for I have always been convinced that the peace of the world depends more than anything else upon our getting into reasonable relations with Germany.

The significance of this letter is still disputed. Philip Howard, the paper's literary editor, recently wrote, 'It is clear that Dawson is referring to comment in leaders, not news'. (*We Thunder Out: 200 Years of* The Times, 1985). Howard is a splendid journalist and a loyal *Times* man, but the letter referred to the paper's report of the bombing of Guernica during the Spanish Civil War which indicated that Dawson was not excluding news. The Official History says:

> The editor undoubtedly felt that, having gained an unprecedented degree of control and responsibility at Printing House Square, he would see that *The Times* ran no risk, even indirectly, of contributing to another collision like that of 1914. This hope for relations, 'reasonable' in the British sense, strongly and ably supported as it was (by Barrington-Ward) after 1928, that provided the continental policy of *The Times* was now becoming highly dangerous. *The Times* correspondents in Europe felt bothered by the practice of excluding anything that the Germans might choose to regard as 'unfair' from both the leader- and the news-columns of the paper. It looked to them as though correspondents' messages were being 'trimmed' to fit a policy. In fact, messages were cut or omitted from time to time in accordance with what was accepted by the editor as the requirement of diplomacy.

Bearing in mind Morison's exaggerated respect for the paper, and his intimate friendship with Barrington-Ward, it was unlikely that he would have written this without establishing beyond doubt that Dawson was guilty of managing the news. Ebbutt, who was eventually expelled from Berlin and suffered a stroke from which he never recovered, told me later that he had been censored. This was denied by the chief foreign subeditor, Geoffrey Pearson, who said that Ebbutt often overwrote and had to be cut for reasons of space. Thomas Barman, who was stationed in Paris at the time, remembered otherwise (*Diplomatic Correspondent*, 1968). An experienced journalist who became the BBC's diplomatic correspondent, Barman wrote that Dawson and Barrington-Ward often suppressed news that militated against their appeasement policy. W.F. Casey, D.D. Braham, one of the senior leader writers, and Iverach McDonald, then the diplomatic correspondent, held diametrically opposite views on appeasement and did their best to get them into the paper in spite of Dawson. 'McDonald was so upset at times that he could be heard muttering to himself words of Old Testament vengeance as he came out of the office.'

Almost certainly one such occasion was in 1939 when McDonald heard that Hitler and Stalin were about to sign their infamous pact. It was a superb scoop, and might have changed history if acted upon, but was not published. McDonald later wrote:

> Later in the evening I was staggered to learn from Herbert Russell, the night editor, that Geoffrey Dawson, just before rushing off somewhere, had said it must not appear – 'not at any price'. Dawson had been talking to Halifax [the foreign secretary]. Our own negotiations with Russia were at an especially delicate stage. We must not rock the boat. (*A Man of* The Times, 1976)

In fact, Chamberlain was reluctant to negotiate with the communists, and when he finally agreed the negotiating team travelled by slow boat to Leningrad. When they finally reached Moscow it was found that they were not empowered to table concrete military plans for action in the event of war and Stalin agreed to the pact with Hitler.

McDonald presumably felt obliged to be diplomatic when he wrote the fifth volume of the Official History many years later. A loyal *Times* man with a distaste for washing dirty linen in public, he wrote that this and other stories did not appear because Dawson disliked having in the news columns anything which he called 'waffle' or 'idle speculation' even though the writers had been trying to convey confidential or sensitive information by hints rather than flat statement. McLachlan said much the same about Ebbutt. His stories were often late because he wanted to be 'cautious and balanced in his judgments of a situation in which it was hard to trust sources and even harder to guess what was happening behind the scenes'. The subeditors must have known what Ebbutt was trying to do, and that he was working under very difficult conditions, including the threat of expulsion. I did what Ebbutt did when working in difficult areas such as the Middle East, and the subs understood. The only difference was that Dawson was not the editor.

Dawson's appeasement policy was doubly disgraceful; when he wrote that revealing letter to Daniels the persecution of the Jews and the campaign against the Christian churches were well under way, but he was unmoved. He may have thought in terms of *Realpolitik*, and saw Hitler as a bulwark against the Soviet Union, but there was little evidence to suggest that he did. He may have been an unconscious anti-Semite, as were many members of his class at the time. By all accounts he was a conventionally decent man and a devout churchman, but the persecution of German Lutherans, including Pastor Niemöller, did not persuade him to reconsider his policy. Certainly he was not prepared to antagonize the Nazi regime by publishing a series of articles on concentration camps.

Hermann Goering ordered the construction of six camps in 1933. Their use, first as detention centres for political enemies and then as extermination camps, was kept secret, but Ralph Deakin, the foreign news editor, learned the following year about their true nature. The worst was said to be at Dachau outside Munich, and Deakin asked Simpson, the local correspondent, to investigate. The assignment was dangerous, but Simpson, who had lived in Munich for years, established that Jews, communists and social democrats were held in the camp and that some had died while being tortured by Gestapo interrogators. He also acquired a map of the camp, which he hid inside the frame of a picture until it could be smuggled to London. A friend agreed to take it, but washed it down a lavatory when the Gestapo searched the train. Simpson eventually finished the series, based on the testimony of widows and relatives of murdered prisoners, and smuggled it to Printing House Square. He had scored a notable scoop, but it was not published. Dawson, who was supposed to have had the true journalist's respect for hard news presented straight, killed it.

Throughout this shameful period – for that is how I still see it fifty years later – Barrington-Ward was a loyal deputy to Dawson although the two men were very different. Dawson was financially independent, and Barrington-Ward came from an impecunious professional family. His father was an inspector of schools who took holy orders after retirement, and he was one of nine children. He won scholarships to Westminster School and Oxford, and during his first year at Balliol decided that the presidency of the union was more important for a young man who had to make his own way in the world than scholastic honours. This was not unusual for undergraduates with political ambition which Barrington-Ward did not have; instead, he calculated that as president he would meet people in a position to further his career when he went down. In fact he met Dawson who later hired him as editorial secretary despite his third class degree.

Barrington-Ward had a strong Ulster strain in him, and the puritanism and tension which went with it showed. At Westminster he was said to have been a strict prefect, something of a martinet, and he was an excellent and much decorated infantry officer. He volunteered when war was declared in August 1914, and it had more influence on him than Westminster or Balliol. His light infantry battalion suffered terrible casualties, and he never forgot the horrors of Flanders. He was willing to pay almost any price to save the next generation from the fate that had overtaken his. McLachlan wrote, 'The conviction in later years that the fighting had not been worth while because the peace had been bungled was burnt deep in him. It was at the root of his determination that war between the same contestants – the return match that some Germans dreamed of – must be avoided.' It also made him anti-French if not necessarily pro-German. He afterwards wrote in his diary that 'the peace was essentially vindictive and vulgar, bred by French blindness and ruthlessness out of British party politics'. He never forgave the French, and during the early years of appeasement held them responsible for some of Hitler's actions.

Barrington-Ward did not return immediately to *The Times* after demobilization because of the conflict between Northcliffe and Dawson, who resigned soon afterwards. He thought of the law, but Edward Grigg, later Lord Altrincham, introduced him to J.L. Garvin, the editor of the *Observer*, whose deputy editor he became before the age of thirty. For a young man with few connections his advancement seemed almost as effortless as Dawson's, but he had written for the quarterly magazine of the Round Table of which Grigg was a member. His contributions to the magazine had also led to the occasional weekend at Cliveden. That Waldorf Astor owned the *Observer* probably helped to make up Garvin's mind.

Barrington-Ward returned to *The Times* in 1927 as an assistant editor. Dawson needed a younger man to write leaders and be responsible for the administration of the editorial department. It was an onerous job, and Dawson disliked getting too involved with the staff. Even the senior men were kept at a distance. Claud Cockburn, that wonderful fount of irreverent stories about the paper, recalled meeting Dawson in his room to confirm that he had been posted to New York:

> It was difficult to find out, because Mr Geoffrey Dawson had perfected a technique for not telling people anything much, and yet appearing all the time both approachable and communicative. His room had two doors. When you had been announced, and had entered, you found him standing in front of his desk, poised always on the same mark on the carpet, both hands lightly outstretched and his whole attitude that of one who has been unable to prevent himself bounding from his chair and rushing forward to meet you. Already touched and impressed, you were further overwhelmed by the warmth of his greeting and the voluble geniality of his conversation as he put his hand on your shoulder or took your arm.
>
> There you were, pacing the floor of the sanctum of the editor-in-chief of *The Times*, and he concentrating on you while his secretary, you could imagine, told anxious cabinet ministers and bishops over the telephone that the editor was in conference. The effect was practically hypnotic, and in this state of partial hypnosis you were scarcely aware that with one arm across your shoulders the editor was with the other hand

opening the door at the far end of his office and pushing you gently into the corridor, bidding you a warm farewell after an interview which had lasted approximately eighty seconds. (Coburn, *In Time of Trouble*, 1956)

Cockburn was poking fun, but affectionate fun, and many of his colleagues who were also opposed to appeasement could not but admire Dawson's genial urbanity and what appeared to be his casual, even off-hand approach. Moreover, unlike some editors jealous of their authority, Dawson wanted a deputy to hand over to when he withdrew to Yorkshire to shoot. Barrington-Ward was just the man. He had been very much in charge on the *Observer* because Garvin lived in Buckinghamshire and only came to the office once or twice a week. Their views of Germany were also similar if for different reasons.

Dawson had been too old to fight in the war, and his approach to Germany, if not casual, was certainly not the product of careful analysis. He was pro-German, although obviously not pro-Nazi, because for much of his life he had shared the affinity many Britons felt they had with the country before the rise of German imperialism. His was probably stronger than most. He was a trustee of the Rhodes trust which also awarded scholarships to Germans because Rhodes had believed that 'an understanding between the three great powers (Britain, the United States and Germany) will render war impossible'. Dawson shared this view, as his letter to Daniels indicated.

One reason why he had fallen out with Northcliffe in 1918 was that he was against imposing harsh terms upon the defeated enemy, and he had been party to a transparent stratagem to prevent it before the armistice. Milner, his old mentor, gave an interview to the *Evening Standard* in which he said that there were good as well as bad Germans and that peace would be secured if Prussian militarism was destroyed. The interview was republished in *The Times* a week later and without comment. Northcliffe was furious, and publicly attacked Milner, already suspect because of his German blood and education, for wanting to 'let the Hun off'. Northcliffe spoke for the majority of the British electorate, as he often instinctively did, and for France which he admired. The peace treaty they wanted was imposed on the Germans at

Versailles, and a year later Dawson resigned. When he returned to *The Times* in 1922 he was already committed to the revision of the treaty.

Whether or not the treaty was unduly harsh is arguable. Reparations did not bring about the collapse of the German economy. Germany borrowed twice as much from the United States and then defaulted on most of the loans. After 1919 Germans were taxed much less than Britons and Frenchmen. What ruined the German economy was four years of war during which the government floated loans amounting to 98,000 billion marks, about four times the amount paid in reparations. Moreover, the treaty was never fully applied and was quickly modified or revised. The counter argument is that the allies lost all chance of reconciling Germany to the treaty provisions when their failure to enforce them encouraged the Weimar republic and then Hitler to nullify them. Only from that point of view can the Versailles treaty be considered the cause of war in 1939.

Neither Dawson nor Barrington-Ward was convinced; the latter could not forget his war experiences and the former was too interested in Commonwealth affairs to have second thoughts. They denied themselves expert opinion by refusing to appoint a new foreign editor or listening to their correspondents in central Europe. Dawson asked his deputy to take care of Anglo-German affairs, and gave much of his attention to the constitutional development of the Commonwealth. To be fair to Dawson, it was then of the greatest importance. The dominions, which had not been recognized as independent states at Versailles, were growing up quickly, and Britain was no longer the acknowledged leader of a world-wide confederation but merely the first among equals. The full significance of this evolutionary development was not immediately recognized, but Dawson realized that Britain could no longer assume Commonwealth support should it once again become involved in a European conflict.

Dawson's response to King Edward's determination to marry Mrs Simpson was explained by his position within the establishment, but he understood better than other editors that Edward was also king of each of the dominions and that their governments had an equal right to decide on the king's future. He also believed with Baldwin that the monarchy was the lynchpin of the Commonwealth, and that one could not survive without the other. Throughout the abdication crisis he kept in close touch with the Commonwealth high commissioners, and arguably he was better informed on the views of their governments than the old Dominions Office. The same could not be said of his knowledge of Germany. He was clearly not emotionally and intellectually involved, but his position on the Versailles treaty remained unchanged even when Hitler's territorial ambitions began to threaten the peace of Europe. He defended his appeasement policy by claiming that Britain was powerless to intervene without Commonwealth support. He believed that this would not necessarily be forthcoming until 1939 when every dominion, including pro-German South Africa, declared war.

Most of the senior *Times* men found Dawson's behaviour inexplicable. As for Barrington-Ward, his belief that every effort should be made to establish whether the Nazis wanted reasonable change in Europe or complete domination made some kind of sense in the early years; but not after 7 March 1936, when Germany reoccupied the demilitarized Rhineland and denounced the Locarno treaty. Earlier breaches of the Versailles treaty, such as the reintroduction of conscription, were bad enough; but Locarno, which provided mutual guarantees of frontiers, had been freely negotiated by Germany, France and Belgium and was supported by Britain. It had nothing to do with the Versailles Diktat and Germany's denunciation was seen as proof of Germany's future aggressive intentions.

In Britain and France it was widely believed that Hitler had created a pretext for allied military intervention, perhaps the last opportunity for the two countries to stop him. According to McLachlan, there was a spontaneous gathering of senior men in Barrington-Ward's room who wanted Britain to 'stand up to Hitler'. They included Casey, the assistant editor, Arthur Baker, the diplomatic correspondent, and two leader writers, D.D. Braham and Colin Coote. As Baker remembered it, they argued that this was the time to stop Hitler. His troops had crossed a prohibited line which Britain had guaranteed in the Locarno treaty. Acquiescence would give Hitler a resounding success that would make him virtually unassailable in Germany; whereas, if he was compelled to withdraw, the reaction at home might well be fatal to him. *The Times* still had the chance for a few hours more to give the lead that had been lacking. Let there be no excuses in the next morning's paper for Hitler's action, no suggestions of settling for verbal assurances while accepting a *fait accompli*.

It was a powerful argument. Baker, who had served as a correspondent for many years in Vienna, Warsaw and Geneva, knew what Germany's neighbours thought of Hitler's revisionist claims. Casey had served on the paper longer than Barrington-Ward, and his shrewdness was respected. Braham, the oldest man present, had served in Berlin, and was also head of the imperial and foreign news department before the First World War. Coote was a senior leader writer. They were men whose opinions could not be lightly dismissed, but Barrington-Ward finally said that he did not share their view of Hitler, and that he still had hopes of evoking constructive statesmanship. Late that night, he noted in his diary: 'Wrote and enjoyed writing a difficult leader trying to ensure, while condemning her breach of the treaty, that [Germany's] offer to negotiate a full settlement should not be rejected'. The leader was entitled 'A Chance to Rebuild'. In the following year Baker left the paper in despair.

Barrington-Ward was an intelligent man, and later proved that he could respond to change better than most editors, but there was no fundamental change in his thinking about Germany between 1919 and 1939. He was shocked by Hitler's brutal invasion of Austria, but still thought that the *Anschluss*, or annexation, was inevitable. He was still convinced that the years of alleged injustice had brought Hitler to power in Germany, and that he would be removed from office if the Versailles treaty was scrapped. As late as 1938, he still believed that Hitler's main aim was to break the French encirclement of Germany – a reference to the Franco-Soviet, Franco-Czechoslovak and Soviet-Czechoslovak pacts – and that the dictator should be helped to achieve it if it could bring a general European settlement closer. The horrors of the First World War were still fresh in his mind when Neville Chamberlain flew to Munich. He wrote a leader in which he said that 'a few days' delay in 1914 would have saved eight million lives. England then had lost control of its policies. One country carried another, like climbers roped together, into the abyss. The same rope binds nations today but it is choice and not blind necessity that governs possible catastrophe'.

His fear of another war led him to appease Hitler, but he actually believed that Germany had a special role in reshaping eastern Europe. He was prepared to accept Hitler's *Drang nach Osten* as long as he did not resort to war. After a discussion about eastern Europe with von Scherpenberg, the son-in-law of Schacht, Hitler's economics minister, he noted in his diary: 'Von S. anxious to know whether it was worth while continuing to hope for an understanding with England. I told him it was, but Germany must refrain from action which would precipitate war. *If she goes slowly she will get all she wants in any case*.' (Author's italics.) They are damning words which his biographer failed to explain, but to be fair they only reflected his belief that Germany could become the predominant economic power in eastern Europe without resort to force. In many ways Prague had long been a German city, but it seems not to have occured to him that his assurances could be received as further proof of abject appeasement.

The same conclusion could have been drawn from Barrington-Ward's refusal to condemn the persecution of the Jews. Kurt Hahn, the headmaster of Gordonstoun, an old friend, could not persuade him to take up the cause of German Jews. Nor could Hahn's brother, Rudo, who had recently been released by the Gestapo when they met in Berlin in 1936. He described his experiences to Barrington-Ward, and told him that hundreds of Jews in the arts and professions had lost everything, but to no avail. Barrington-Ward refused to jeopardize the influence he believed *The Times* had in Berlin although Hitler refused to see him. Instead, he was fobbed off with an interview with Rudolph Hess, Hitler's deputy, who had nothing to say.

After all these years, Barrington-Ward's contributions to the paper also remain inexplicable. His impressions of Germany, which he confided in his diary after the Berlin visit, reveal an ambivalence:

A splendidly vigorous, magnificently capable people but flawed with the odd strain of atavistic emotionalism. The forest tribes. Mentally enclosed. All their best and worst qualities evoked and stiffened by the stupidities of the victors after the war. They seem set in thought and deed, collectively, for war again. But, individually, as everywhere, few or none want it. We can only go on trying to make civilization prevail. But can democracy and these regimes [he was also thinking of Mussolini's Italy] coexist successfully?

A good question, but he never tried to answer it in his leaders. Nothing that happened in Europe could budge him from his preconceived notions. As already mentioned, when German troops reoccupied the Rhineland in 1936, he ignored the advice of senior colleagues and welcomed it as 'a chance to rebuild' a peaceful Europe. In 1938 when Hitler seized Austria, the Vienna correspondent, Douglas Reed, wrote that he had not foreseen anything so perfectly and ruthlessly organized. 'When this machine goes into action it will blight everything it encounters like a swarm of locusts. The destruction and the loss of life will make the World War look like the Boer war.... Their real hatred is for England.' He did not convince Barrington-Ward who had already written in his diary: 'Deeply sorry for the Austrians, but allied impolicy in the past has brought this upon us and them, and there is nothing we can do about it.' A few days later, Iverach McDonald, then the special correspondent in Prague, interviewed Eduard Beneš, the Czech prime minister, and privately reported: 'I am convinced that Nazi Germany has a long-term programme which she is determined to carry out – however peaceful her declarations are between bursts of action – and that she means both to break up this country [Czechoslovakia] and to challenge the British empire.... At what point are we going to cry "halt"?' Barrington-Ward decided that there was nothing to be done.

Not that he remained silent. Still obsessed by the belief that the allies were beastly to the Germans at Versailles, and ignoring German troop movements near the Czech frontier, he wrote in the spring of 1938 a leader advocating the secession of the Sudetenland to Germany.

For the rectification of an injustice left by the treaty of Versailles the Sudeten Germans have an undoubted case ... the Czech government might not willingly agree to a plebiscite likely to result in a demand for the transfer of the Sudetens and the loss of their territory for the republic. Nevertheless, if they could see their way to it, and to granting a similar choice to the other minorities, Hungarian and Polish, the rulers of Czechoslovakia might in the long run be the gainers in having a homogeneous and contented people.

This was really outrageous, and John Walter IV, co-proprietor of the paper, protested to Dawson. 'In contemplating the dismemberment of Czechoslovakia as a measure of justice to the Sudeten Germans, our leader writer made no allusion to the flood of injustice and cruelty that would certainly overwhelm the minorities thus handed over to the tender mercies of Messrs Hitler, Goering and Goebbels.' Dawson airily replied that his own impression was that neither Hitler nor Henlein, the Sudeten leader, wanted a revision of frontiers. He did not explain how he had acquired the impression, but von Scherpenberg conveniently popped up again and assured Barrington-Ward that this was the case.

Germany waged a war of nerves throughout the summer. Troop movements and army manoeuvres were accompanied by a violent press campaign. At this stage Henlein's demands did not go beyond autonomous status for German Sudetens within Czechoslovakia, but *The Times* published two more leaders suggesting secession: 'No solution should be too drastic.' On 29 July the British government sent Lord Runciman, an elderly peer with no knowledge of foreign affairs, to Prague as a mediator and adviser. On 29 August the French manned the Maginot line, and on 4 September Beneš, now president, met the Sudeten leaders and offered them a settlement which conceded most of their demands including full autonomy within Czechoslovakia. This was the position when *The Times* published, on 7 September, the leader which everybody opposed to appeasement condemned as infamous.

Whether or not the Czech's offer would have been accepted by Hitler or his stooge Henlein, it did not go far enough for Dawson as he made clear in the leader. The offending paragraph was as follows:

No central government would still deserve its title if it did not reserve in its own hands defence, foreign policy and finance. There does not appear to be any dispute about this principle in the minds of the government or of Herr Henlein; and if the

Sudetens now ask for more than the Czech government are apparently ready to give in their latest set of proposals, it can only be inferred that the Germans are going beyond the mere removal of disabilities and do not find themselves at ease within the Czechoslovak republic. In that case it might be worth while for the Czechoslovak government to consider whether they should exclude altogether the project, which has found favour in some quarters, of making Czechoslovakia a more homogeneous state, by the secession of that fringe of alien populations who are contiguous to the nation with which they are united by race. In any case the wishes of the population concerned would seem to be a decisively important element in any solution that can hope to be regarded as permanent, and the advantages to Czechoslovakia of becoming a homogeneous state might conceivably outweigh the disadvantages of losing the Sudeten German districts of the borderland.

The leader was a sensation, and the assumption that it reflected British government policy reverberated round the world. 'There was a hubbub, as I fully expected, over the morning's leader,' Dawson jotted in his diary, but hubbub was hardly the word. The Foreign Office issued a statement denying that it represented the view of the government. Runciman, still hoping that Henlein would accept the Czech offer, telegraphed to the Foreign Office that the leader had added to his difficulties. A few hours later, after Henlein had refused Beneš's offer, Runciman told McDonald, who must have been terribly embarrassed, 'This is a black day for us.' Lord Halifax, the foreign secretary, agreed with Maisky, the Soviet ambassador, that the article had had the worst possible effect.

Dawson stood his ground, and in a leader published two days later wrote:

It is really grotesque that so much righteous indignation should be expelled on the mere suggestion, which has frequently been made in these columns before, that a revision of boundaries should not be excluded entirely from the list of possible approaches to a settlement.

41

Secession had indeed been suggested before, but not when most of Henlein's demands had been met by the Czechs and there was a possibility, however slight, that an agreement would be reached. To those who did not know him, Dawson must have appeared to have been a fool or a knave, or even a German stooge. It must be said that Hitler did not need any encouragement from *The Times* to continue with his *Drang nach Osten*. Historians subsequently established that he had already made up his mind to dismember and then occupy Czechoslovakia. The *Wehrmacht* had been ordered to prepare for action some months earlier. Despite the Munich agreement, Czechoslovakia was invaded in March 1939. Hitler obviously believed that he could move with impunity because he knew that the British and French armies were in no condition to fight. The embassy in London had kept him informed about the apparent strength of pacifism in Britain. The Oxford Union's vote against fighting 'for king and country', and the massive peace ballot organized by the League of Nations Union, seemed to prove that opposition to war recognized no class barriers.

There was no sinister motive behind Dawson's leader. Rather was it the inevitable consequence of the elitism which influenced his editorship. He and his deputy had isolated themselves by ignoring their foreign correspondents and their senior colleagues in Printing House Square. They also invited disaster when they took their summer vacations at the same time. Both left on 8 August, Dawson for Yorkshire and Barrington-Ward for a family holiday in Pembrokeshire. Brodribb, who had been reduced to a proof-reading functionary, was left in charge. Barrington-Ward returned for a few days, and saw Halifax at the Foreign Office. He found Halifax more impressed than formerly by reports that Germany had decided to settle the Czech problem soon, and by force if necessary. Halifax asked him if Britain should guarantee the integrity of Czechoslovakia, and he answered in the negative. They agreed that Germany must be made to see that Britain was not complacent, and that this should be done without encouraging Prague or embarrassing Runciman. Coming out of Halifax's office he met the French *chargé d'affaires* who said that his government was much more disturbed than it was prepared to admit publicly.

One would have thought that Halifax's news and the Frenchman's comment would have rung alarm bells, but Barrington-Ward remained convinced that Hitler was less interested in dismembering Czechoslovakia than in breaking her alliance with France and Russia. He wrote to Dawson saying that he did not think Hitler would take all the risks implicit in forcible action, and the editor agreed that he should resume his vacation. Before leaving for a shooting holiday in Scotland he asked Leo Kennedy, a leader writer, to prepare another leader on Czechoslovakia. He did not tell him about his conversation with Halifax, and Kennedy prepared a rough draft, a common enough practice of journalists who often have to write at short notice. Having nothing new to say, he rehashed previous leaders no doubt hoping for a new development before he had to complete it.

Dawson returned to the office three days later, 6 September; he arrived late in the afternoon and had been out of touch for a month but was determined to have a leader that night. He read Kennedy's uncompleted draft, made some deletions and ordered it to be rewritten while he had dinner at the Beefsteak. The Official History takes up the story:

> When the editor came back, rather late, and read the corrected draft in proof, he began to doubt his decision earlier in the day to print it as that night's first leader. . . . It was about 11.45 p.m. when misgivings assailed Dawson. He sent a proof of the entire article to the one senior member of the editorial staff still in the office. Casey, who was a Francophile, knew that his judgment on foreign matters carried little weight, and would have preferred to pass over the request in silence. Twenty minutes before the first edition was due to go to press the editor sent for him and asked his opinion of the article. Casey said that he did not care for it as a whole, and particularly disliked the hints with which it was closed. The editor was so little influenced by Casey's point that at 12.05 a.m. he sent out to the composing room a revised version of certain passages. (Vol. IX, 1952)

What he did in fact was to harden up the passages which Casey disliked and suggest that the secession proposal had official support. At the same time the leader was calculated to have the maximum impact on the government which was divided at the time. Dawson was determined to shape events as he and Milner had tried to do in 1918. They had failed then because public opinion was demanding that Germany must be punished. In 1938 he was certain that the country did not want to go to war over a faraway country. His misgivings that night can be explained by dissatisfaction with the wording of the article; it had been drafted by another man, and the first rewrite had been unsatisfactory. He probably assumed that Casey, who over the years had accepted Dawson's and Barrington-Ward's monopoly of the foreign policy of the paper, would help him with a few felicitous phrases instead of criticising the thrust of the leader.

There is enough evidence to establish that Dawson knew what he was doing. He was always convinced, before and after, that he was right. He knew that Chamberlain was like-minded, and had got rid of Sir Robert Vansittart, the permanent head of the foreign office, because he had advocated a stronger line against the dictators. In a letter to Chamberlain written in November 1940 long after he had resigned as prime minister, Dawson congratulated him on having done his utmost to avert war. He went on:

> I shall always be an impenitent supporter of what is called the 'Munich policy'. No one who sat in this place, as I did during the autumn of '38 with almost daily visitations from eminent Canadians and Australians, could fail to realize that war with Germany at that time would have been misunderstood and resented from end to end of the empire. Even in this country there would have been no unity behind it. We know now that it was inevitable sooner or later; but we owe it all to you that it was later rather than sooner.

The 7 September leader was, nevertheless, an unmitigated disaster for *The Times*. As Oliver Woods concluded, Munich was the outcome of a long period during which the British had tried to opt out of their international responsibilities by refusing to make the sacrifices necessary if they were to shoulder them. The government, the opposition and the electorate all bore their share of the blame, but in retrospect the government leaders naturally became the scapegoats. The 7 September leading article identified *The Times* in the most dramatic way with the 'guilty' leaders in the eyes of contemporaries and posterity.

It was the stooge of government, the creature of the 'Cliveden set'. The image of *The Times* as the arch-appeaser was carried into the post-war era and proved impossible to cast off. *The Times History* (volume IV), published in 1952, put on sackcloth for its sins. All this was a very heavy burden to carry for a paper which was to be launched into the merciless newspaper competition of the 1950s and 1960s and explains to some extent the severity of its struggle for survival. (Oliver Woods, *The Story of* The Times, 1983)

That is undoubtedly true, but equally painful for the editorial staff at the time was that Dawson had betrayed the principles of the paper. He was not appointed editor for the greater glory of the British empire but to report the news. To quote again from the 1852 leader written under the direction of Delane:

The press lives by disclosures: whatever passes into its keeping becomes a part of the knowledge and history of our times; it is daily and for ever appealing to the enlightened force of public opinion – anticipating, if possible, the march of events – standing upon the breach between the present and the future, and extending its survey to the horizon of the world.... The duty of the journalist is the same as that of the historian – to seek out the truth, above all things, and to present to his readers not such things as statecraft would wish them to know but the truth as near as he can attain it.

Most of the *Times* men aspired to this ideal. If Dawson had presented readers with the truth as near as his foreign correspondents could attain it and not such things as statecraft wished them to know, it is possible that the electorate would have been awakened to the dangers before it was too late. Even if it had been ignored, we would have remained faithful to the principles of Barnes and Delane. This is what rankled at the time, and which led some men to leave the paper.

I was still on the periphery, an occasional reporter of no consequence. When the navy was mobilized in 1938 I was sent down to Portsmouth to see what was happening. I saw very little, but I enjoyed my first experience of travelling on expenses. They were modest: 12s. 6d. for bed and breakfast and 10s. for lunch and dinner, but I took a girl out one evening and still made a tiny profit. 1939 was an unsettling year. War seemed inevitable and military conscription was introduced in the spring. I was young and physically fit, and knew what was coming. It came when Hitler invaded Poland, and I marched off to the war.

3

The Threepenny Pravda

I had my first taste of foreign travel in the army. I served in countries as far apart as Iceland and Borneo, and after nearly seven years was mustered out in Singapore with the substantive rank of captain. A lowly rank compared with the heights achieved by another *Times* messenger, Admiral Sir Raymond Lygo, Vice Chief of the Naval Staff. Six years and ten months was a long time to be in uniform, but I would not have missed the last year. The Japanese surrender suddenly opened up Southeast Asia, and after India and Burma I was happy to swan through Malaya, Thailand, Indo-China, the then Netherlands East Indies, Sarawak, the other Borneo territories and the periphery of China. The struggle for independence had already begun in Indo-China and the NEI, and promised plenty of good copy for a bright reporter. I was also half promised a job in Australia, and I returned to Britain determined to become a foreign correspondent or emigrate.

London was a shock. The victory celebrations were a distant memory, the shops were half empty and the people looked shabby and wan. I can still remember travelling in a crowded suburban train to see my mother. I had forgotten that commuters switch off when travelling, and the impassive faces were grey. They looked as if they had been raised on weak tea and baked beans on toast, and had bought their clothes second-hand in church bazaars. I had dined and drunk well on the trooper coming home. My skin was yellowy-brown from anti-malaria tablets, I was dressed in well-tailored SD with Sam Browne, and my back was as straight as the proverbial Pomeranian grenadier's. Like one of Kipling's time-expired men, I was suddenly homesick for somewhere, anywhere east of Suez.

Printing House Square was no better. I had once thought of it as the centre of the world, but on that autumn day in 1946 it seemed drained of life. It was very disheartening for a young man eager to follow in the footsteps of William Howard Russell and other famous foreign correspondents. I wondered how long it would take to emigrate to Australia.

The office and those grey-faced people in the train reflected the condition of Britain at the time. The older men who had stayed at home to produce the paper had worked under dreadful conditions. The main building had been bombed, and the air raids had driven them underground where after a night's work they slept on campbeds until the early trains and buses began running. They had not missed a single issue, and the night when the bomb dropped the presses stopped for only eighteen minutes and the full print run was delivered on time. They never forgot that they were *The Times*. Dawson did not go home before the air raids began, and soldiered on with his troops working and sleeping in an opera cloak. Men who had despised him for his appeasement policy grew to respect him. Astor became the commanding officer of the press battalion of the Home Guard and his Rolls-Royce, painted with his racing colours of light blue and black, was converted into an armoured car. It was parked in the square ready to stop the Hunnish hordes if they dropped by parachute to seize Printing House Square. The staff restaurant remained open, if without the daily change of flowers, and so did the bar. There is a photograph in the Official History Vol. V of the two proprietors, Astor and Walter, and Dawson and Barrington-Ward in an air-raid shelter dining off fine plate, crystal and linen sent over from Astor's house in Carlton House Terrace.

All this helped to maintain morale, and I discovered that many of them had rather enjoyed the war. In retrospect at least, they only resented having to produce the paper during one of the most newsworthy periods in history with rationed newsprint. The size of the paper was cut to twelve, ten and then eight pages. Other newspapers went down to six or four, but *The Times* reduced circulation to print more pages. That was bad enough, but a year after the end of the war the paper was still struggling with too little newsprint, though the flow of news had not slackened.

An interview I had with the manager, C.S. Kent, added to my

impression of greyness. All companies were obliged by law to re-employ ex-servicemen for at least six months although there was not enough work for those who had stayed at home. I was an embarrassment. Moreover, Kent was not a friendly man. He belonged to an obscure puritanical sect practising self-denial, and he seemed to enjoy denying me any hope of advancement. I was to return to the publicity department with a salary of £6. 1s. 0d. a week. This was a double disappointment; with war service increment, Japanese campaign and special service pay I had been earning more than £30 a week, and only paying Indian income tax. Fortunately there were more generous men in the office and I was soon transferred to the reporting staff with a salary of £9. 9s. 0d. a week. The minimum pay for an experienced reporter in Fleet Street was then £12. 12s. 0d., but it was a start.

I owed it to three men. George Pope, the advertisement manager, remembered me as a likely lad who had wanted to be a reporter. He mentioned me to Frank Waters, the assistant manager, knowing that Kent was too mean-spirited to do anybody a favour. Waters had led a commando during the war, and was probably decent to me because I had been in the army for so many years. He recommended me to Donald Tyerman, the day editor, who agreed to give me a three-month trial on condition that I stayed on the publicity department's payroll during that period. At least, this is what I was told afterwards. At the time I was just told to report to the home news editor on the following Monday morning. I had made it. I was a *Times* journalist, but a lowly one as I quickly discovered.

At the apex of the editorial pyramid was of course the editor, then the deputy and assistant editors, and the foreign correspondents and leader writers. Most of them were Oxbridge and club men, and in the hierarchy of the paper, gentlemen. Then came the night editor, news editors and subeditors. Most of them had been recruited from Scottish and provincial newspapers, and apart from a few university graduates working as junior subs while waiting to become leader writers or foreign correspondents sounded as if they had been to grammar schools. Their status was indeterminate, but the reporters at the bottom of the pyramid were definitely regarded as players and not gentlemen. We did not work in book-lined rooms with coal fires but were tucked away in a tatty office block connected to the main building by a bridge. The reporters' room looked like a tailor's sweat shop, and we wrote on benches constructed by the office carpenter. There were not enough typewriters and telephones.

It was a rather sad room. The miserable furnishings and the location, the building was mainly occupied by advertisement and subscription clerks, indicated our lowly status. There had been no recruitment for years, and most of my colleagues were middle-aged and frustrated. During the war they had covered the blitz and other stirring events. No doubt life had been grim much of the time, but they had been doing something worth while. One of them had been a war correspondent, and another had flown over Europe in RAF bombers. There were still good stories to be covered, the consequences of war and the painful adjustment to a peacetime economy yielded many, but Barrington-Ward, who had succeeded Dawson as editor, was not interested unless they were of political significance. Unlike parliamentary and foreign news, they were not considered essential reading. It was a terrible mistake. Home news sells newspapers whatever those who set themselves up as critics of the press have to say about its responsibilities. Some of the older reporters retreated into themselves or became time servers. It was also a sad waste of talent.

Barrington-Ward appeared not to be interested in their predicament, and the paper was to pay dearly for this narrow view of the function of the press. The *Daily Telegraph* devoted more space to home news and achieved an enviable circulation. There were other factors of course. *The Times* printed only in London, which helped to explain why few copies were sold in Scotland and northern England. The *Telegraph* also printed in Manchester, which made easier the distribution of the last editions with the latest news. For Scottish readers *The Times* must have looked like yesterday's paper. Another fact was the cautious management of Kent, an accountant by training, who preferred to restrict expenditure instead of increasing turnover.

That said, the influence of *The Times* was still considerable, and Barrington-Ward used it to good effect. His editorial authority and his new thinking were evident long before Dawson had retired. As early as December 1940 a leader entitled 'The Two Scourges' indicated the direction he was to take the paper. Arguing that unemployment was as great a scourge as war, it was both imaginative and courageous:

> Prosperity can be regained (after the war) only by new policies adapted to new and sterner conditions ... we must plan for peace as consciously and deliberately, and with the same common readiness for sacrifice, as we now plan for war. It must not be said that we are more ready to risk our lives than our vested interests, or that peace – unlike war – holds no purpose worthy of sacrifice of things we prize for a greater common good. The British people will shrink from no sacrifice for a purpose in which it believes. In war it has gladly accepted – indeed demanded – leadership which asks for sacrifice from all. The planning of peace calls for a leader who will have the courage and the vision to make the same appeal.

The writer was E.H. Carr, a former foreign office official and a future professor of international politics; Barrington-Ward had recruited him to expound his own views. This extraordinary man who had advocated appeasement remembered not only the sacrifice of the First World War but also the shabby treatment of the survivors who had been promised a land fit for heroes. He was as single-minded as ever, and to some extent still blinkered. The leader mentioned was published when Britain was still losing the war, and some of the staff must have wondered if it could be won. Within the establishment, especially among former appeasers who disliked Churchill, the smell of defeat was apparently obvious. Grigg, a member of the Round Table who advocated a revolt in the cabinet to be led by Stafford Cripps, said he had been talking to Waldorf Astor and others and asked for the support of *The Times* (Donald MacLachlan, *In the Chair*). Barrington-Ward would have none of it. He was critical of Churchill's personal conduct of the war and his reluctance to think of postwar reconstruction, but he was a patriot. Moreover, Churchill decided that he needed *The Times*, and after one luncheon, a boozy one according to Barrington-Ward, was persuaded to broadcast a forty-five-minute speech on domestic policy. The elated editor wrote in his diary, 'Nevertheless, we must continue independent and critical, but not hostile.'

Barrington-Ward had more than full employment in his editorial sights. According to his diary, *The Times*, almost alone in the press and certainly the first, was trying to get the 'right answer to Hitler' in showing that the country was fighting for a new Europe and not the old, a new Britain and not the old: planned consumption, abolition of unemployment and poverty, drastic educational reform, family allowances and economic organization. His policies were not universally popular, and the paper was dubbed the 'Threepenny *Pravda*'. Three articles by W.H. Beveridge on his social security report infuriated some of the larger advertisers who believed that the paper was unsympathetic to private enterprise. A number of advertisements were withdrawn. Complaints were heard on the editorial floors; the senior men disliked Carr who had been appointed an assistant editor over their heads. They did not want the paper to be used as a platform, especially for radical programmes that had nothing to do with the war. They were wrong; the morale of the troops and working population had to be maintained, and the promise of a better future was as important as the prime minister's stirring oratory. They were correct, however, in concluding that Carr was not a journalist.

Their ire was understandable. Carr had all the arrogance of the intellectual of the period, and his years at the Foreign Office had reinforced his belief that only his kind knew what was best for the human race. Unlike journalists, he had had little experience of, and no patience with, its foibles. Admittedly the senior *Times* men also thought that they knew best, but at least most of them had been disciplined by the requirements of their trade. That said, Carr was a brilliant writer and was more aware than most that the war was generating forces that would change the world out of all recognition. His critics said that he was always on the side of the big battalions because he believed, correctly as it turned out, that the future would be dominated by the United States and the Soviet Union. He was dismissive of most British institutions and of the paper's editorial system – or, as he saw it, the lack of system. He wanted to reorganize it along the lines of a government department with a delegation of control which, in Barrington-Ward's eyes, would be incompatible with an editor's duty and interest.

Carr was deeply interested in the Soviet Union, and after leaving the paper completed a many-volumed history of the Bolshevik Revolution, but his civil service background and his intellectualism inclined him towards central planning and permanent state intervention. Barrington-Ward had become somewhat disenchanted by the end of the war in Europe when it seemed that Carr was appeasing Moscow by assuming that Soviet forces would remain in eastern Europe. Barrington-Ward agreed that the Russians would have influence in and over eastern Europe, but wrote in his diary:

> I would have preferred to let Britain and the other western countries argue each case without *The Times* announcing that the conclusion was inevitable and that argument was useless. Where Carr would jump into the final position, I would have dragged my feet. Whether it would have made any difference in the end result I do not know. . . . Carr tended to write what he thought without regard to the country's diplomatic needs of the day.

Barrington-Ward had apparently forgotten that he and Dawson had been similarly guilty of 'announcing that the conclusion was inevitable' when Hitler was on the rampage. He frequently modified Carr's leaders, but the paper did not escape charges of appeasing Stalin, betraying Mihailovich in Yugoslavia and generally being a red rag. The final break between the two men became inevitable when Carr failed to see the significance of the atomic bomb attack on Hiroshima. The editor was in the country that weekend, and hearing the news on the radio decided to return to London the following morning. He discovered to his dismay that Carr had ignored the bomb and had written a leader about Europe's need for food. Afterwards Carr said that there was nothing to say apart from reporting the attack in the news columns. Hiroshima was covered by an impenetrable cloud of dust and the extent of the damage would not be known for days. That was true, and of course very few people at the time knew about the atomic bomb. Nevertheless, had he had any journalistic instincts he would have guessed that the reported impenetrable cloud of dust could only have been created by a new and terrible weapon.

Carr left the paper soon after the war to seek an academic

appointment and write his book. There were sighs of relief but
Carr had been more influential than his reluctant colleagues chose
to see. He had articulated Barrington-Ward's hopes for postwar
Britain, and in so doing had helped the editor to move *The Times*
to the left. In turn, Barrington-Ward made it a very much better
paper. Not only was he determined to avoid if possible the unemployment and widespread deprivation after his war, but he sensed
the mood of the country. He was not surprised by the Labour
Party's overwhelming electoral victory in 1945, and may well have
been secretly relieved. He had been instrumental in his leading
articles and private conversations in persuading Churchill to pay
attention to postwar reconstruction as already indicated, and in
that 1943 radio talk the great war leader had declared himself 'a
strong partisan of national compulsory insurance for all classes,
for all purposes, from the cradle to the grave'. That phrase was
to live on longer than anybody's memory of that remarkable
speech, and he went on to say that there was a broadening need
for state ownership and enterprise especially in relation to monopolies. He also called for the expansion of existing health services,
adding that there could be no finer investment than 'putting milk
into babies'.

It was an example of the influence *The Times* could still wield
in those days when edited by a man who understood the mood of
the nation. Barnes and Delane also shared an instinctive awareness of the national mood; in their case that of the then rising
middle classes, the entrepreneurs, factory owners and merchants
who had led the first industrial revolution and made Britain great.
Barrington-Ward clearly understood that the children of that
revolution, the lower-middle class, which Northcliffe's *Daily Mail*
had been the first to recognize as potential readers and a collective
political force, and the working class, to which the *Daily Mirror*
then addressed itself with considerable success, wanted and
deserved a better life. He was also impressed by the Labour leaders
who had been members of the wartime coalition: Ernest Bevin,
Herbert Morrison and of course Clement Attlee, the old Hailey-
burian who had won an MC in the First World War and was
one of his own.

He saw them as well-tried men and old-fashioned patriots –
Churchill could not have won the war without them – and his

diaries indicate that he did not believe that Churchill could lead the country to the brave, new world it deserved. While admiring Churchill as a war leader, it is clear that he did not trust him as a politician. Notwithstanding Churchill's past political follies, it's possible that Barrington-Ward still resented the altercation over Greece.

Late in 1944 the paper had criticized the use made of British troops sent to Greece after the German retreat. The editor had been reluctant to criticize largely because of his own army experience. Charges that he had stabbed the troops in the back horrified him, but he had strongly believed that Britain's role in Athens was to impose law and order and give Greeks the opportunity to elect a government. It was not their job to prepare for the return of the king or become involved in a civil war. Churchill, who wanted to restore the monarchy, was furious, and attacked the paper in the House of Commons. Barrington-Ward was in the House at the time, as was Astor, who was then the Conservative member for Dover. The entry in the editor's diary that night read:

> This – a direct and obvious reference to *The Times* – immediately touched off the loudest, largest and most vicious – even savage! – cheer that I have heard in the House. It must have lasted a full minute or more. I went on with my notes and did not inspect the demonstration, but there could be no doubt it was almost wholly Tory.... It was a vent for the pent-up passions of three years, a protest against all that has, wrongly or rightly, enraged the Tories in the paper during that time.... This open onslaught by Winston must have put a strain on the support which John [Astor] gives me.

He need not have worried. His independence as editor was guaranteed and his relations with the chief proprietor were excellent, but in the following year he heard that one of the company's directors, David Bowes-Lyon – Eton, Magdalen, merchant banker and a relative of the queen – disliked his policies, and had argued that the board had the right to pass judgement. Astor, who regarded Bowes-Lyon as a 'bit of a diehard', told him that it did not, but to placate him and Walter, the junior co-proprietor, who was worried about the paper's attitude to the Russians, invited the directors to meet the editor at dinner in his house in Carlton

House Terrace. Barrington-Ward was not happy when Astor told him about Bowes-Lyon, but the conversation over the dinner table only departed from a general political discussion when he pointed out what independent journalism meant and the kind of criticism it was likely to attract. Barrington-Ward later wrote in his diary of his admiration for Astor, 'the most truly modest man I have known, he is essential to *The Times* on its present line'.

At the time, independent journalism for Barrington-Ward meant the expression of views and the support of policies which the people he met at dinner parties and in his clubs might regard as threats to their interests and privileges. It did not mean, as many claimed, a conversion to socialism but he believed that men and women of the moderate Left must play a part in running the country. *The Times* was an independent paper, it had always given new governments the benefit of the doubt, and his approach to the new Labour government was benign but cautious. The leader published after the 1945 election expressed the hope that it would not depart too far from the consensus established by the wartime coalition, and went on:

However the electoral choice had gone, the issues before the government and the policies required would not have differed in essence. There is at home the paramount obligation to make the most of the nation's physical and human resources by conscious and calculated partnership between the organizing power of the community and the full and enterprising vigour of the people, individual and corporate, so that the amount and distribution of national wealth may steadily advance. There is a special duty to make war against inefficiency and restriction in all their manifestations, and to permit no established interest, whether of employers or of trade unions, to impede the technical and managerial revolutions in British industry and trade which modern necessity dictates. For the Labour Party in particular there is the prime task of demonstrating to the workers' organizations which make up the faithful core of their following that no real benefits can accrue to their members in wages or conditions of living without a corresponding increase in national output and individual productivity. The task for the new government will be to increase and not simply to reshuffle the national income, and to secure the abolition of poverty and inequity, not by doles, but by a practical and expert policy which will aim unremittingly at full employment and the continuous expansion of the national dividend. There are no short cuts, socialist or otherwise, to the better life, no panaceas, in the form of wholesale public ownership, no mere devices which will avoid the complex and technical processes of reconstruction, each to be regarded and decided on its merits. Any indifference to these truths will bring with it its own inexorable penalties ...

There is no evidence that Barrington-Ward realized at the time how prophetic that leader was, but he had recruited special writers experienced in industrial and trade union affairs to broaden the scope of the paper. It was competent enough to report and comment upon the changing world, and he was clearly confident. The paper was selling well, if not nearly as well as the *Daily Telegraph*, and profits had never been higher. This was the situation when he suddenly asked to see me.

I was ushered into the office where Dawson had performed his disappearing act to avoid discussion with staff members, and was asked to sit down while he finished some work. I had seen him often enough in the corridors, but this was the first opportunity to study him at close quarters. He looked very dapper in a striped suit, stiff white collar and what could have been a college tie. A black homburg and rolled umbrella hung from a stand in the corner. He could have been the manager of a bank in the City, but his back was as straight as mine and although I could not see his face he seemed to be very intense. I was wondering if this was my imagination when he looked up and his dark eyes, made brilliant by the pale skin and domed forehead, were intense. There was no handshake or preliminary small talk, but he was friendly enough. He asked me where I had served, and his eyebrows were raised in almost comic surprise when I reeled off the countries. He wryly said that he had only got as far as France in his war, and then asked me about India whose independence was very much on the horizon. I said that I had been impressed by the Indian army officers I had met, that I had only read about Pandit Nehru and Mahatma Gandhi in the newspapers but that they were clearly popular among the Hindu majority. I welcomed independence, and asked if I could help cover the transfer of power when it came. I also said that I was interested in Southeast Asia.

Barrington-Ward said that I must not be impatient, Civvy Street was very different from the wartime army and in any case I still had a great deal to learn about my craft. He then asked me if I enjoyed reporting, and I said that I would if I had more to do and if home news was given extra space. I still doubted that he was interested in general news, and have since wondered if Morison had told him of Delane's interest in crime stories and that the paper had devoted four columns to the trial of the murderer of Maria Monk in the red barn. I did not ask of course, but he said without explanation that there would be more to do when winter came and then stood up and wished me well. Only afterwards did I realize that he looked desperately tired.

My work continued to be undemanding and unsatisfying. Unless I had been assigned to a story the night before, I was expected to report to the home news editor, Alan Pitt Robbins, at eleven. He was a large affable man, who had once been a fine journalist, but his appetite for news had diminished with the lack of space. I was rarely asked to do any real reporting, and often left Printing House Square at six feeling that I had not earned my keep. Fortunately I had met my future wife, and life outside the office was wonderful, but as winter approached I had more than enough work to do. I had no idea of how the editor had earlier known that the fuel crisis was looming, but it brought down upon the country, in the words of one leading article, 'a degree of dislocation that not even the most savage efforts of the enemy in the recent war could impose'.

Fuel for industry, offices and homes was drastically cut, and I was assigned to cover the consequences. In one way it was miserable; accustomed to tropical heat I shivered in my old army trenchcoat, but there was plenty to write about and I was given the necessary space. The old Ministries of Labour and Fuel and Power suddenly became vital news centres when factories were closed or put on half time, and labour unrest was widespread. I covered strikes and, indeed, voted for one when a militant punched me in the back and said, 'Put your f . . . . . g hand up'. Surrounded as I was by angry truck drivers in what was supposed to have been a closed meeting, I put up my hand instantly. I scored a few scoops; on one occasion by reading upside down the draft of a directive on the desk of the permanent secretary of the Ministry of Fuel and Power. I got thousands of words into the paper, and was learning my craft at last. The industrial correspondent of the old *Daily Worker* was a mentor. When I asked him for some advice before interviewing a senior official, he said, 'Always ask yourself why these lying bastards are lying to you.'

I worked all hours of the day but, as I discovered, not as hard as Barrington-Ward. On two or three occasions he asked to see me when I returned to the office late in the evening. He could depend upon the experience and advice of Eric Wigham, the paper's industrial correspondent, but he would ask me about the mood of the people I had met that day. The central heating had been turned off, and the fire in the grate was banked. We sat in his cold office, he in his dark overcoat and me in my trenchcoat, and talked. One evening we shared some scotch. He was a good questioner and listener, and at one meeting told me that he had met the permanent secretary at his club and was asked how *The Times* had heard about the plan to stop the publication of magazines during the crisis. My little scoop had caused a political rumpus because what were then known as organs of opinion – *The Economist*, *The New Statesman* and *The Spectator* – were included. He looked shocked when I told him how I had read the draft of the directive upside down, and then laughed. Just like de Blowitz, he said.

Henri Stefan Opper de Blowitz, one of the paper's great foreign correspondents, had a photographic memory. As Paris correspondent, he was acquainted with statesmen all over Europe and was as at home in Berlin and in Vienna as in the French capital. His greatest scoop was the 1878 treaty of Berlin, which redrew the frontiers of the Balkan countries and ceded Cyprus to Britain. Blowitz's coverage of the congress was, despite official secrecy, so comprehensive and accurate that Bismarck, the German chancellor, was said to have lifted the cloth covering the conference table 'to see if Blowitz is underneath'. He finally acquired a copy of the treaty, and because he was being followed by the Prussian police smuggled it out of the country sewn inside the lining of the coat of another *Times* man.

I came to the conclusion that Barrington-Ward worked quite as hard as Delane. He was editor for only seven years, but as deputy editor had administered the editorial department during the day and written leaders in the evening. The war years were demanding, and when he became editor in 1941 he did not at first have a deputy to do the administrative work. He had to assemble a new staff after the war while propounding policies that affronted many of his establishment friends. He made mistakes; his lack of interest in non-political news was one, and he preferred to recruit experts, with no newspaper experience and often no news sense, instead of journalists capable of becoming expert in any field assigned to them. This was a grave mistake and took some years to rectify. That said, he willingly worked a 16-hour day.

Inevitably the pace wore him down and, as my mother would have said, he was his own worst enemy. Like Dawson, he nearly always had working luncheons, dined with the powerful and influential and returned to the office after dinner. Unlike Dawson, he could not switch off except for brief summer holidays with his family. Nor did he have any country pursuits, and tried to keep fit by walking back to the office from one of his clubs after lunch. His intensity, which must have been wearing, was the outward sign of an almost missionary zeal. Within his chosen field of politics and diplomacy, he wanted to know and explain everything, and what went into the paper had to fit and promote his world view. As editor, he was ruthless. He quickly got rid of Leo Kennedy, the foreign leader writer who thought that he had underestimated Hitler. Colin Coote, a senior home leader writer, had to go because he had tried to support Churchill in his struggle against appeasement. Coote was a very good journalist and went on to become managing editor of the *Daily Telegraph*. Other tried and true *Times* men also had to go because they had differed with him, including Thomas Cadett, the Paris correspondent, and his assistant, Thomas Barman; later both flourished at the BBC.

As editor he was of course entitled to appoint men he could work with comfortably, but Barrington-Ward could be as ruthless as a popular newspaper editor trying to survive in the Fleet Street jungle. He obviously would not have seen it that way. He was a man with a vision – witness the entry in his diary on his fiftieth birthday, a few months before he was appointed editor:

> My life was really in forfeit in 1914 and it is the merest, the least deserved of flukes that I have survived to enjoy so much of which war robbed the pick of my contemporaries. The more reason to remember the mission which August 1914 and survival have together set men like me – namely to strive for the creation and organization of peace, above all things, and for the liberating truths at home, at whatever cost to conventional opinion.
>
> Revolution cannot do it. It is to be questioned whether revolution as such has ever achieved anything *on balance*: but evolution, active and painful evolution must. On my own humble anniversary it is well to have this old resolution sharp and clear again.

I later found the reference to revolution intriguing; apart from the fact that the American revolution achieved a great deal and the French on balance did quite well, it suggested that Barrington-Ward saw it as the alternative to peaceful social change and himself as one of the architects. This was reinforced by another entry, dated 5 May 1941, written after Astor had asked him if he was ready to take over. He said that he was:

> I went on to say that I thought it the duty and the opportunity of *The Times* to prepare for the great social changes inevitable after the war. Its function, I said, at all times is to apply common-sense, without prejudice, to issues as they arise and to gain acceptance of novel but necessary moves by getting them rationally expounded. He most warmly agreed to all this and spoke particularly of the excellence of Carr's articles last year. All of which was good. We left it that he would see [Dawson] and see me again. Throughout the talk he was his generous and understanding self.
>
> I imparted all this later to Stanley Morison, my sole confidant, as we walked through burnt-out Holborn and battered Gray's Inn to dinner.

This entry was also a reminder that whatever Barrington-Ward achieved it could not have been done without the approval of Astor. The arrangement Astor had come to with Dawson guaran-

teeing the independence of the editor from proprietorial interference also gave him the right to select his successor. After that
conversation he could have decided that the then deputy editor
was not his man. He was after all one of the richest men in the
country and it would have been understandable if he had decided
that his newspaper should not be used to reduce his wealth and
privileges. There were more conservative alternatives in and
outside the office. Colin Coote was one. He also had a fine record
as an infantry officer in the First World War, which was important
to Astor, and had been an MP for five years after being invalided
out of the army. He was on good terms with most senior politicians
as well as Churchill, which was why his leaders were always well-
informed.

Astor remained an enigma until his death. His great-great-
grandfather was John Jacob Astor who emigrated from Germany
to the United States in 1783, and established the American Fur
Company, the first American monopoly. Lurid tales have been
told of how he organized the fur trade among the American
Indians from the Great Lakes to the Pacific and acquired property
in New York. He died in 1848 worth over $25 million. His great-
grandson William Waldorf Astor, inherited $100 million and was
the American minister in Italy where he collected vast quantities of
antiquities. He had presidential ambitions but was not a political
success and emigrated to Britain and acquired a viscountcy. His
younger son, our John Jacob, was an aide-de-camp to the Viceroy
of India, the earl of Minto, and later married his daughter. The
major, as he was always known until he was promoted to colonel
in the Home Guard, bought a majority of the shares in The Times
Publishing Company after Northcliffe died in 1922 for £1,580,000.
The return on his investment over the years was modest, and there
must have been another reason for buying the paper. Clearly it
was not political; he would not have granted Dawson complete
editorial independence otherwise, and he afterwards wrote that
he wanted 'to secure as far as possible the continued independence
of one great journal, and through it the perpetuation of the highest
standards of British journalism'. He went on: 'It also seemed that
The Times could best fulfil this purpose if it stood aloof and free
from the necessity of having to consider any interests external to
Printing House Square.'

Such altruism is unusual to say the least, and as far as I know he always respected the independence of the editor. Nor is there any reason to believe that he had become a secret socialist or what Americans call a 'limousine liberal'. He held the parliamentary seat for Dover for 'enlightened conservatism'. In his quiet modest way he enjoyed the trappings of vast wealth: Hever castle, the mansion in Carlton House Terrace, the ocean-going yacht, horses, fine cars and, I suppose, ownership of *The Times*. That clearly meant a great deal to him although the editor reaped the glory. He was frequently in the office, and liked to be kept informed. He entertained the senior editorial staff, including foreign correspondents with whom he liked to discuss the affairs of their assigned country when they were in the office. I often met him and was always left wondering if he ever read the paper. That said, Astor must have known the talent available, and presumably he appointed Barrington-Ward to the editorship because he had been deputy for so long.

Morison was also a factor. He was very close to Barrington-Ward, and lived with him in Regents Park after his flat was bombed in 1941. Dawson had postponed his retirement because of the war, and two years later showed no sign of leaving. Barrington-Ward was a loyal colleague, but not unnaturally became increasingly frustrated. Morison mentioned this to Astor, who suggested to Dawson that it might be unfair to keep his successor waiting indefinitely to step into his shoes. By his own account, Dawson was taken aback but agreed at once, saying that 'I ought to have thought of it sooner myself.' Morison piously wrote afterwards that Dawson was loth to go. 'I don't in the least blame him. Few, if any, leave PHS willingly.'

One reason why Dawson had been able to postpone his retirement was the shortage of senior staff. The old guard were approaching retirement age, and most of the younger men such as Peter Fleming had left for the war. Barrington-Ward had no willing workhorse to help him when he became editor. Carr did not see journalism as a career, and was only prepared to write leaders. Men in their thirties were considered unready for promotion. If this was the case, Barrington-Ward had only himself to blame; he and Dawson had dominated the paper far too long to permit the development of younger men. Casey was appointed deputy editor, but no longer enjoyed working night after night into the small hours.

Barrington-Ward had to work harder than ever, and maintained this killing pace for nearly three years before Morison found a suitable assistant editor, Donald Tyerman. For a change the staff had no cause to complain about Morison's mysterious influence, and Barrington-Ward had every reason to be grateful to him. He noted in his diary that 'he is the one man with whom I can discuss anything to do with *The Times*, its policy and its staff and be sure of a detached and instructive comment'.

Tyerman was indeed a find. A Yorkshireman and former grammar-school boy who won a scholarship to Oxford, his rise in journalism had been spectacular. Only eight years before joining the paper he had been a lecturer in economic history and politics at Southampton University College, as it was then. As secretary to its appointments committee, he was asked by *The Economist* if they had a graduate who wanted to enter journalism. The post was modest, junior editorial assistant, but he put his own name forward and was accepted. He quickly became deputy to Geoffrey Crowther, the editor and one of the most brilliant magazine journalists of his generation. Tyerman could not have had better training, and his capacity for work was such that a year before joining *The Times* he was also deputy editor of the *Observer*. He was relatively young, only 31 when war was declared, but could not serve in the armed forces because he'd had polio as a child. He had to wear heavy leg callipers, and could only walk with the aid of sticks.

Tyerman quickly settled in as day editor, doing much of the administrative work, writing leaders and editing the paper at night when Barrington-Ward was away or wanted an early evening. He was a blunt man, and it showed in his writing. He disliked artifice in writing and politics, and his leaders did not have to be read a second time. Their import leapt off the page, which was one reason why Churchill savaged the paper over Greece. Tyerman had written most of the leaders, and had not pulled his punches. He was also very good with young people on the staff as I discovered.

I had decided after a few months that the reporters' room had very little to offer. My middle-aged colleagues were pleasant enough, and helpful, but I realized that even with a more imaginative news editor and more space life there would not much improve. I did not want to spend the rest of my career covering official and royal events, political meetings, strikes and other manifestations of the trade union movement's resistance to Barrington-Ward's vision of the new Jerusalem. The world was being turned upside down, and I wanted to report it – not the wrangles then taking place over the future of Europe, but what was happening on the periphery in the Middle East and Asia.

There was another factor of course. Life in Britain in those days was austere and, I felt, mean-spirited. I did not want to join the ranks of commuters; I did want most things young men want – such as a good car instead of the clapped-out MG I had bought for £200. Above all, Pat and I wanted to get married, but we couldn't find a flat. We had a couple of dirty weekends, but it was an unsatisfactory way of loving. Eventually we decided to emigrate and chose Australia, I suppose because I had once the promise of a job there. The next day we went to Australia House to make enquiries, and I told the news editor who said that I would have to give four weeks' notice. He also urged me to stay, saying that there would soon be opportunities on the paper. Then Tyerman asked to see me.

He had just returned from lunch and was still sweating from the effort of walking from the lift to his room. He also looked as if he had been drinking, and the conversation was genial. He was certainly receptive when I said that I wanted to be a foreign correspondent and that the only alternative was to emigrate because I could not live on my pay. He said that he would see what he could do, and meanwhile would raise my salary by three guineas a week. I had proved myself, and it was time for a rise.

I did not have to wait long; India was to become independent in August 1947, a great deal of violence was expected and the decision was made to send me to Delhi as an assistant to Eric Britter, the resident correspondent. The first intimation of this momentous decision was a short memorandum from Ralph Deakin, the foreign news editor. It read: 'The Foreign News Editor presents his compliments and looks forward to meeting

Mr Heren at his early convenience.' I answered in a similarly oblique manner, and was received the following Monday morning.

Deakin was responsible for a large section of the paper, but because he was not foreign editor and did not write leaders his status was indeterminate. He was, according to the Official History, one of the paper's enigmas. He spoke excellent German, was widely read and travelled, and had worked in the Berlin office until Northcliffe appointed him foreign news editor in 1921. He had run one of the world's largest and most comprehensive news services for seven years when Harold Williams, the foreign editor, died in 1928 but was not promoted because Dawson wanted to control the newspaper's foreign policy. Barrington-Ward had also decided that he did not want a foreign editor, and Deakin soldiered on no doubt suppressing his grievance. Colleagues told me later that the grievance was not always successfully suppressed, but that morning he looked and sounded what he was – a confident news editor completely in charge of his department.

As I have written elsewhere (*Growing Up Poor in London*, 1973), he sat upright behind his desk wearing a grey alpaca jacket. Behind him his bowler hat rested on a small shelf, which must have been made for that purpose. I did not know what to expect, but I was excited and assumed that he would also recognize what a great moment it was for me. I was also departing for a fairly dangerous assignment and anticipated a little drama. The conversation went something like this:

'Mr Heren?'

'Mr Deakin?'

'Good morning.'

'Good morning, sir.' (I had been a subaltern too long not to address an officer of field rank otherwise.)

'I understand that you want to go overseas for us.'

'Yes, sir.'

'When do you think you could go?'

'Before the end of the week.'

'Come now. We don't have to be too precipitate. Surely you need time to wind up your affairs.' I told him that I was recently out of the army and had no affairs whatsoever, and very little else. There was quite a lengthy pause, and then he said: 'It is rather strange, I think, Mr Heren. It takes only ten or fifteen minutes to appoint a foreign correspondent of *The Times*, and yet it can take twenty years to get rid of him.'

Deakin went on to say that he confidently expected a long and fruitful partnership, but made no mention of the assignment, what was expected of me, or when and how I was to leave for India. Eventually I asked where I could get the airline ticket. He looked at me, lips pursed and eyebrows raised, and said, 'Try Thomas Cook's.'

His reply reflected the awesome simplicity of *The Times*. Deakin ran the foreign news service with a young assistant and a secretary, and ran it well because correspondence was kept to a minimum. Unlike other newspapers, we did not have an account with a travel agent. It was just assumed that correspondents would make their own arrangements. We were grown-up chaps able to move about the world without the help of the company. Similarly with news. We were left to decide which story to cover because we were the experts.

My departure was delayed so that I could familiarize myself with the production side. I spent four weeks with the subs and two with the night editor. Tyerman twice invited me to join him at lunches he regularly gave, generally in Soho, for young men working for the Sundays or weeklies. He obviously enjoyed their company and their Fleet Street gossip, but was always looking for fresh talent. He was changing the paper. Previously the editor and deputy editor had depended upon their friends at All Souls to indicate who was the best and brightest. It was rather like MI6. Now Tyerman was seeking talent in Charlotte Street. Casey took me to dine at the Garrick, and got me slightly tight. Again not a word was said about my assignment; instead, he asked about my Basque grandfather, and was tickled pink when I told him that my other grandfather was German and that both had married Irish women. Not a drop of English blood, he exclaimed. Just like Russell and Blowitz. He then said that there was more to life than politics, and I should tell the readers about the subcontinent; about Indian and Pakistani society, about the peasants as well as the leaders. Give them a smell of the place. I promised that I would as we finished our second glass of port.

Barrington-Ward asked to see me the day before my departure. I had lunched at Carlton House Terrace with the proprietor and ten other people, including Ernest Bevin, the foreign secretary. I had first met him when I was growing up in the east end of London, when as the then general secretary of the Transport and General Workers' Union he had come down to settle an unofficial strike. He sat on Astor's right and I on his left, and I thought that I had at last joined the gentlemen. I then remembered that the foreign secretary had also been a working-class boy, which put my elevation into perspective. Bevin discussed India and referred sombrely to the outbursts of violence in Bengal and the Punjab, and feared that it would get worse. Take care of yourself, lad, he said. It was a good lunch, and I walked back to Printing House Square by way of the Victoria Embankment. I needed the exercise, and I also wanted a last look at a part of London I loved. It may have been the sherry, hock, claret and port, but I was always sentimental.

I met the editor after the afternoon editorial conference, and we had tea together. Again little was said about my assignment except that, almost in passing, he reminded me that the paper was dedicated to the Commonwealth. I went afterwards to the reporters' room to say goodbye, and as I crossed the bridge between the two buildings remembered that neither Deakin nor Barrington-Ward had mentioned pay and allowances. A letter was awaiting me in the reporters' room from the manager. It said that I would be paid £700 a year plus a cost-of-living allowance of £2. 10s. 0d. a day. I would also receive £100 as a kit allowance.

4

In the Deep End

Kipling would have recognized Eric Britter, the Delhi correspondent, as country born. He was the fourth or fifth generation of his family to have been born in India, and was bilingual in Hindi. He could also read the script, which was unusual among expatriates, and it gave him an immense advantage over other foreign correspondents who could not read the vernacular papers. Not all of them were dedicated to the high principles of objectivity and fairness, but they were in touch with an India beyond the ken of local English-language newspapers such as *The Statesman*. He was very much at home, but I could not establish how he felt about the country. His life style was English, he rarely ate a curry, but was genuinely fond of Indians and had a wide circle of friends. Independence did not bring his world to an end as it did for tens of thousands of expatriates. Britain was not home. He had gone to school in India, and first went to Britain as an undergraduate at the London School of Economics. He then worked for *The Times of India* in Bombay, and had joined us at the end of the war.

Britter was a good journalist, who afterwards replaced me in Korea and worked successfully in Tokyo and New York, but not one who could give readers a smell of the country. He was curiously detached, perhaps because his sense of nationality was ambivalent. Independence was the biggest story in India since the mutiny, but he was due for his biennial leave and spent it in Britain during the newsworthy last two or three months of the *raj*. I thought it odd at the time as, I suppose, did Barrington-Ward and Deakin, but nothing was said. Ian Morrison, the Southeast Asian correspondent, was moved up from Singapore to Delhi as a temporary replacement.

Britter and I met briefly in London, and flew out to India together. Long-haul civil aviation was in its infancy in 1947, and the BOAC plane was a converted bomber known as the York. It was of limited range, and we stopped at places such as Castel Benito to refuel. We were served boxed meals except for breakfast, which was scrambled eggs kept warm in a large thermos flask. I was nevertheless impressed after my flights in the army. I had flown over the Hump, the mountain range between Burma and China, in a Dakota, unheated and with canvas bucket seats; and in a Sunderland flying boat from Singapore to Kuching in Sarawak which had no seats. I was excited, of course, at last I was a foreign correspondent, but Britter was unmoved. He had already made the trip from the other direction, and India had no surprises for him, but I gathered later that he was worried about his future status. He did not know whether he would be recognized as a British subject or as an Indian citizen. He had no Indian blood, but his concern was natural enough. His family had lived in India since long before passports had become important. The British Nationality Act was still in the future, and his status was uncertain. The prospect of becoming an Indian citizen in 1947, when eastern races were, alas, still regarded as somehow inferior in the west must have been worrying.

We saw pillars of smoke rising from villages as we flew the last leg from Karachi to Delhi, and most of the passengers were silent as they peered down at the devastation. The plane was not flying high, and what was soon to become the frontier area between India and Pakistan could be seen in sharp relief. I recognized the irrigation ditches criss-crossing the Punjab plain, which had transformed the once arid province into prosperous farmland. The vast irrigation systems were one of Britain's greatest contributions to the subcontinent – about 47 million acres were watered – but the fields were empty. Britter was expressionless behind his glasses, and remarked that the expected communal violence had begun. He added that I would be covering it very soon.

Delhi airport was crowded with well-to-do refugees, most of them Muslim, awaiting planes for what was to become Pakistan. The city was also crammed with refugees, poor Muslims in the Red Fort and various mosques and Europeans in the hotels.

Britter had a large apartment in the Imperial Hotel, and he had
booked me a room down the hall which I had to share with another
foreign correspondent. He was an Englishman who worked for
The Christian Science Monitor, and wrote under the ceiling fan
stark naked. That was the only discomfort; while the road beyond
the extensive gardens was full of refugees coming in from the
countryside it was very much business as usual in the hotel. The
bar, with its ridiculous motto – *In Vino Veritas* painted large on
one wall – was crowded with foreign correspondents and army
officers. The dining room and grill room were similarly full. Only
a string of horses tethered outside one of the ground floor apart-
ments indicated that something untoward was happening beyond
the gates. They belonged to Ralph Izzard, the resident correspondent of *The Daily Mail*, and his wife, Molly. Both were
keen riders, Ralph had been the whipper-in of the Delhi hunt,
and their verandah was stuffed with bags of feed. I discovered
later that he had scooped us all with a feature article headed,
'They are putting down the horses'. Human nature being what it
is, readers were apparently more appalled by the shooting of
horses than the plight of refugees.

The Izzards were kind to me, and later we regularly rode
together on the Ridge outside the city. I bought a former Indian
army horse, a raw-boned Australian waler known in those days
as hundred-chippers because they cost only 100 rupees. Mine was
called Seagull. She was docile and big enough to carry me, but
was occasionally disconcerting. Apparently she had carried the
drums in a cavalry band, and when trotting would suddenly side-
step and break into a waltz.

Ralph was tall, handsome and almost silent. He had learned
his trade before the war in Germany where his father, the then
gardening correspondent of the *Mail*, had sent him to learn
forestry. With good German, he found it easy to drift into journalism and covered the rise of Nazism until the war when he
joined naval intelligence under Ian Fleming. Ralph was a good
correspondent, and I learned a great deal from him. He belonged
to a sub-tribe of foreign correspondents who hated working in
the great capitals such as Washington and Paris. They saw no fun
in covering politics and being polite to politicians and diplomats,
and preferred to roam the world covering wars and crises. Other

members of the sub-tribe had flown into Delhi, and later I was to meet them again and again in other trouble spots in the Middle East, Korea, Southeast Asia and Africa. We were like a bunch of vultures flying in from all quarters of the compass when a crisis story broke. We did not emulate the dashing foreign correspondent of film and fiction, at least I don't think so, but we probably proved that he was not entirely a figment of some writer's imagination. We learned how to travel light, to adjust quickly to different countries, climates and languages and to find the bar which for some mysterious reason became the press bar as long as the crisis lasted. We were pleasant to each other, perhaps because that kind of foreign corresponding is essentially lonely, but rarely talked about the story because we were rivals. We were willing to put latecomers in the picture, but hungered for scoops and rarely hesitated before cutting each other's professional throats. It was great fun while it lasted, but ruined marriages. As I recall, Ralph Izzard and I were the only two of the original bunch who were not eventually divorced. Perhaps we were lucky.

I might have wondered at the beginning if the paper liked this kind of journalism, but for Ian Morrison. We met in Britter's apartment for drinks on my first evening. He was the son of China Morrison, the paper's once famous Peking correspondent. The father had been fabulous in every sense of the word. An Australian who decided to become a foreign correspondent when as a teenager he heard that Archibald Forbes of the London *Daily News* was allowed £5000 for expenses when he covered the Turko-Russian war. He set about it in unusual ways by walking across Australia alone, 2043 miles in 123 days, and writing about his adventures for a newspaper. That was only the beginning. Young George next joined a blackbirder, and sailed for the New Hebrides to recruit, or kidnap, islanders for work in the Queensland sugar plantations. His reports of this kind of slave traffic were a sensation. He then went with an unofficial and ill-equipped expedition to colonize New Guinea, and was speared twice when they were attacked by natives.

Only then did he agree to study medicine, his father's profession, and arrived in Edinburgh in 1884. He was 22, lame and in great pain and was immediately operated on. A tapering fragment of wood, the point of a spear, was removed from his thigh. Morrison graduated in less than three years, during which time he began to earn a reputation for being a womanizer, boasting that he slept with three women in one night. He went to the Far East after serving briefly as court physician to the Shereef of Wazan, and dressed as a Chinese travelled from Shanghai to Burma. This remarkable journey entailed a 1500 mile voyage up the Yangste and a further 1500 miles on pony or foot over the mountains to Rangoon. Deciding that he was now equipped to become a foreign correspondent, he went to London where his account of the journey was published, and was introduced to Moberly Bell, the manager of *The Times*. As Morrison recalled later, Bell said, 'I don't know where I heard about you but I have read your book. Would you care to go to Peking as our correspondent?'

It is nice to know that Morrison was recruited as a foreign correspondent as casually as I was fifty years later, but unlike me he wanted a salary of at least £400 a year, in real terms a great deal more than any correspondent was earning when I joined the paper. Bell told him, 'You will have at least that.' *The Times* then not only regarded its foreign correspondents as gentlemen but also paid them accordingly.

Morrison and *The Times* were made for each other. His occasional raffish behaviour was no worse than de Blowitz's. He was, the Official History said, 'scientific in his power of observation, scrupulous in his thinking, and equipped with a remarkable memory. He was expert with the gun and the canoe, uniquely self-reliant and invariably unaccompanied on his explorations. His mind was candid, his writing fluent and balanced.' Apart from his expertness with gun and canoe, that is an apt description of the ideal foreign correspondent, but not content the history concludes admiringly that he was a magnificent specimen of Australian manhood.

Looking at the grave, bearded faces of the men who ran the paper at the time, it is hard to believe that they were so romantic, but what impressed them was that Morrison, the colonial, was just as much an imperialist as they were. George Curzon, who later became viceroy of India and was given an earldom, had toured the Far East for the paper, and a book he wrote after the tour summed up their belief in imperialism. It was dedicated 'to those who believe that the British empire is, under Providence, the greatest instrument for good that the world has seen'. They had no doubts and were supremely confident, but were suspicious of Russia. The bear had long been seen to threaten India, and they were convinced that it was ready to devour the border provinces of China. Morrison was regarded as the best man not only to report what was happening in China but also to keep an eye on Russia. They did not say as much, but the Australian was also expected to play Kipling's great game. He accepted with enthusiasm.

Hugh Trevor-Roper, in his book *Hermit of Peking*, said that Morrison was not interested in China as such. What interested him was China as a theatre of competing imperialisms. From the moment of his arrival in Peking, he threw himself into the great game of imperial power politics. 'He did not intend merely to report events: he proposed them.... From the beginning, he worked openly to promote a Russo–Japanese war, and when that war came, it would be known as "Morrison's war".'

That was less than fair. Morrison was deeply interested in China. Unlike other foreigners, he did not live in the legation quarter but in a Chinese street afterwards called Morrison Street. He knew the country better than most because of his frequent expeditions into the hinterland and his superb sources. He loved China, and eventually left the paper to become political adviser to the first president of the Chinese republic, but when he first arrived the country was weak, badly governed and corrupt; ruled not by the Manchu emperor but his aunt the Empress Dowager Tz'u Hsi, a former concubine who in turn was dependent upon the court eunuchs. It did not have a navy, army, police force or a currency. The reality was that China was a theatre of competing imperialisms. Morrison was an imperialist, and knowing that Britain wanted only to maintain the *status quo* supported Japan against what he regarded as the dangerous enemy, Russia.

Ian Morrison did not look like the son of a man who, according to a friend, had escaped 'the perils of ten thousand poxes' and had defended the legation quarter during the Boxer Rebellion. Slim and darkly handsome, he was the product of Winchester and Trinity, Cambridge, and could have been mistaken for a British diplomat. At first, while Britter mixed the drinks, he looked supercilious and patronizing, but was friendly enough. I knew him by reputation and admired him. After teaching at a Japanese university and being private secretary to the British ambassador in Tokyo, he had worked in Shanghai where he began stringing – that is writing occasional pieces – for *The Times*. Two days after Japan attacked Pearl Harbour in 1941 he accepted a telegraphed offer to join the paper, and went to Malaya. He warned that Singapore could not be held, reported the British retreat down the peninsula and their last stand and surrender before escaping to Java. The assignment established him as one of the great war correspondents and he went on to cover the fighting in the Pacific and Southeast Asia. Now he was based at Singapore.

That evening I was fairly silent, listening as he brought Britter up to date. He spoke dispassionately about the awful things he had seen, and of his conversations with Pandit Nehru and Lord Mountbatten. Obviously I was fascinated, but as the evening wore on I began to feel more and more like a new boy. Morrison had also been born in the East – Peking. Asia was his home despite Winchester and Cambridge. What was I, an East-End Londoner, doing here?

The thought crossed my mind that I was perhaps the only British-born *Times* foreign correspondent, and I later realized that they were true sons of empire. They belonged to the generation which followed Dawson and the Milner kindergarten, and no doubt they would have served it as faithfully had it not been coming to an end. Clearly Indian independence was the beginning of the end, and when the conversation was continued over dinner downstairs no regrets were expressed. Instead, they turned the conversation in my direction. Morrison seemed relieved when I ordered dinner in Hindi, hesitantly but understood by the bearer, and heard that I had spent part of the war in Asia. It was agreed that I should take the company car, a large Canadian-built Ford, a bed roll borrowed from Britter, whisky, gin and some American army K-rations which were on sale in the bazaar. I said that I liked Indian food, but was reminded that food was scarce in the Punjab. I was told to stay at Faletti's hotel if I chose to operate out of Lahore and to stay in army cantonments elsewhere if possible. The next morning they came down to see me off, and while Britter's bearer stowed my gear in the car he told me how to get on to the road to Lahore. Morrison said not to worry;

75

despite the dreadful killings I would be protected by the colour of my skin. Then they waved good luck and I slowly turned the car into the stream of refugees for my first foreign assignment for *The Times*.

I have written about my adventures elsewhere (*Growing Up on The Times*, 1978), but one incident is worth recalling. It occurred during my second or third foray into the Punjab which millions of refugees were crossing in both directions, many of them being killed before they reached the safety of India or Pakistan. By this time I was accustomed to the heat, about 115 degrees in the shade, and inured to the killings – the final estimate ran into hundreds of thousands. Driving into Amritsar I had to stop on a bridge over the railway tracks because of a mob surging across. The car soon became insufferably hot, and cautiously opening the door to get out I collided with a young armed Sikh. His eyes were dilated with bloodlust, and I thought that my last moment had come, but seeing that I was English he apologized and ran on. I looked over the parapet of the bridge and saw that a refugee train, only a few miles from safety, had been shunted into a siding. Every man, woman and child on board was killed, about 4000 souls. I was physically sick, but drove to the central telegraph office in town and typed my report at the deserted counter. I found an Anglo-Indian telegraphist, who was badly frightened but sent the story to London.

I had to get out of those awful killing grounds, and three or four days later turned the car in the direction of Delhi. It was late, I was tired and thirsty, and driving through Umbala decided to spend the night in the military cantonment. I followed the signs to the officers' lines, stopped outside the bungalow of the commanding officer of the 1/11th Sikhs, and shouted '*Koi hai*'. (This had long been the customary salutation of travellers in India. They always shouted 'who's there' when seeking sustenance in strange places, which was why oldtimers were known as Koa hais.) A voice shouted to me to come in. It belonged to the CO who had just got out of the shower. We met in the hall, he with a towel round his middle and his long hair tied in a top knot. I was told to fix a drink while he dressed. He returned in a freshly laundered tennis shirt and slacks, and I explained myself. We had another drink, then he produced an airmail edition of *The Times* from the next room, and asked me if I had written the story about the massacre outside Amritsar. We were anonymous in those days, and I could have said no. But I admitted authorship expecting to be shown the door. I could see the dinner, bath and bed disappearing. He looked at me pensively, his handsome Sikh face expressionless, and said that the other side was also guilty of bloodshed. I said that I knew, and had written about them. He nodded, apologized for his wife not being present, and we went into dinner and talked about the old days.

His decent behaviour was still very much on my mind when Britter, Morrison and I were invited to dinner at Government House by the Mountbattens. About thirty people were invited to dinner, and we understood that the meal would be plainer than usual because of the suffering outside. My experience of high living was admittedly limited, but the food and service seemed very grand. The pomp was overwhelming, and we were shepherded into the presence by ADCs in full regimentals. Lady Mountbatten received the guests seated, and when it was my turn the ADC said that I had recently returned from the Punjab. She asked me what the Muslims were doing to her poor Hindus, and I told her of the 4000 Muslims massacred by Hindus and Sikhs. The ADC led me away – presumably in disgrace although I was allowed to remain for dinner.

Morrison laughed uproariously as we drove back to the Imperial, and even Britter smiled. We had a nightcap in his living room and Morrison, who was leaving next morning for Madras to look at southern India before returning to Singapore, raised his glass saying that I had proved myself worthy to be a *Times* correspondent, especially with my brief exchange with the vice-reine. I told him about the advice the *Daily Worker* had given me, and the conversation took a serious turn. Britter had been with the paper for only two years and had little experience outside India. He was almost as eager as I to learn from Morrison who had been with the paper much longer and was the son of a great correspondent.

Morrison said that there were distinct advantages in working for the paper. Even anonymity could be a help. In a way, the correspondent was as independent as the editor. He was not told how to do his job; the paper was interested in news, had very few preconceived notions on how stories were likely to develop or how the correspondent should cover them. He was left to get on with it, and his stories were never rewritten. Moreover, a *Times* correspondent had better access than his competitors. People in positions of power, men who had information, were more inclined to speak to him. Not that they necessarily told the truth, but it was an advantage. A correspondent could not want for more, but there were disadvantages. Apart from the pay, there were always the dangers inherent in the universal assumption that *The Times* was the voice of the British establishment and represented the official view. This could be an advantage, it explained the relatively easy access, but too often the correspondent was assumed to have the discretion of a diplomat. Discretion was occasionally necessary, sources always had to be protected, but the correspondent was interested in news and not confidences. There were ways of handling this. Morrison did not believe in hinting something in a story although it occasionally had to be done, but having got the news it was often possible to get it confirmed elsewhere but not always. In any case, attribution was important. The correspondent had, indeed, to ask himself why these lying bastards were lying to him. The correspondent had the advantage over a diplomat or spook (the intelligence man attached to most embassies) in that he could move more easily about the country or in circles denied to officials. It was an advantage to be fully used, it was also good fun, but how to report truthfully and unambiguously and retain the cooperation of presidents, prime ministers and other high sources was a problem that had to be faced eventually. Morrison said that it was easier when the correspondent was well established, which was why presumably *The Times* left its correspondents in countries or regions for long periods but that also had its dangers. Correspondents could go native or become reluctant to disturb the even tenor of their lives.

We probably had more drinks than were good for us that night, but it was part of my education. I had a lot more to learn, but was grateful to Morrison and next day drove him to the railway station. He was eager to be on the road again, as all good correspondents are, and as we walked down the platform behind the baggage coolie I noticed that he travelled light: a valise, his portable typewriter and a Shan shoulder bag for his passport and notebooks. He had acquired it when doing a story in the Burmese hill tracts, and later I got one in exchange for some cigarettes when I flew into the Shan states from Thailand in a plane carrying American arms for the Chinese Nationalist troops who had crossed the frontier to avoid capture by the communists. I was young enough to emulate a man I admired although it would have been faintly ridiculous to carry a brief-case when wearing a bushshirt and shorts. That was the last I saw of Morrison but our fates were entwined. He was killed in Korea during the first weeks of the war and I replaced him.

The refugees killed in the Punjab were not the only victims of the division of the subcontinent. Lashkars, or raiding parties, descended from the tribal territories and invaded Pakistan. The old Indian army was still being divided between the two new countries, and Pakistan was powerless to stop them as they poured out of the Khyber pass. Some reached as far south as Lahore, but most of them invaded Kashmir. The maharajah's troops broke and scattered, and the invaders could have seized Srinagar, the state capital, within forty-eight hours. There would have been no war had they captured the airfield; a major military operation could not have been mounted over the Banihal pass, the only land route from India. Instead, the tribesmen stopped in Baramula to loot and rape, giving the Indians just enough time to fly in a battalion of troops. They came in commandeered commercial airliners and with little equipment apart from infantry weapons, but they turned the tribal flow and held the airfield until a sizeable force was flown in. Pakistan then intervened, the tribal incursion became a war between the two Commonwealth countries and overnight I became a war correspondent.

It was a sad war. The two armies knew each other well. Only weeks earlier their units had been brigaded together, and many Indian officers spoke fondly of their Pakistani enemies. Both armies used the same equipment. Both wore the same uniforms, and both still owed allegiance to the crown. I was with a battalion on some mountainside the day the then Princess Elizabeth was married and we toasted her with issued rum in enamel mugs. The colonel then toasted the king, and we all stood to attention. I long treasured that memory as a reminder of what might have been.

Partition is always savage, especially when a country is divided along religious lines. Nehru and Jinnah also despised each other, but India should not have accepted the accession of Kashmir from the maharajah. The state, along with Hyderabad, had been given time to decide its future, and the subsequent charges and counter-charges could not disguise the natural justice of Pakistan's claim. An overwhelming majority of Kashmiris were Muslim and wanted to join Pakistan, but Nehru's family were Kashmiri Brahmins and he was determined that the land of his fathers would become part of India.

The war soured relations between the two countries, but I continued to work in both with little difficulty; and in both I learned that *Times* correspondents did enjoy easier access to sources of information than their rivals. Mountbatten was a master of public relations and generally ensured that he was portrayed in the world press as a superman who had achieved the impossible, but his senior staff did not share this view and were willing to talk to me. General Ismay, Mountbatten's chief of staff, was one of them. He began his career as a subaltern in an irregular Indian cavalry regiment in the far-off days when the men who enlisted brought their own horse, saddle and sword with them. Only the rifle was issued by the army. He had been Churchill's chief of staff during the Second World War, and after leaving Mountbatten was secretary-general of NATO. He was a wonderful source of information, and I looked forward to our occasional drinks although their quantity and strength were a hazard until I learned to pour at least half of them into a potted plant or leave untouched glasses under the chair.

Nehru was too busy to spend time with journalists; he also had a patrician's disdain for them, but many Indian officials were helpful. The permanent secretary of the External Affairs Ministry, a former member of the Indian Civil Service, went out of his way to help and lent me books to improve my knowledge of India. His opposite number at the internal affairs ministry was no less obliging, and V.P. Menon, who was responsible for absorbing the princely states into the Indian Union, was positively enthusiastic. A few of the princes were reluctant to join, and on one occasion he invited me to join him and a company of Jat infantry on an expedition to a recalcitrant state. The troops waited at the railway station while Menon entered the palace, and within a couple of hours we were having lunch with the maharajah who had been persuaded to join. Similarly in Kashmir where the commanding general took me in his jeep on a visit to the extended front and explained his dispositions.

In Pakistan, Mohammed Ali Jinnah, the governor general, invited me to accompany him on a tour of the tribal territories and Baluchistan. I was treated as a member of his entourage at feasts given by tribal khans, and later I stayed at Government House in Lahore when much of the old city was in flames. I am not suggesting that other correspondents did not get to know the people at the top, but it was easier for me because I wrote for *The Times*. I also learned that being a *Times* correspondent was not enough; it was assumed that I was well informed and I was expected to provide them with information. This was easy enough in India and Pakistan; western foreign correspondents were free to roam during the riots and massacres – Indian journalists were not protected by the colour of their skins – and knew the dimensions of the tragedy. For their part, they knew that they could not always trust the reports of their minor officials and I was welcomed as an independent and reliable source.

Presumably as the paper had intended, I learned my craft in India and Pakistan and a great deal of Morrison's advice proved to be sound. The one problem was how to report truthfully and unambiguously and retain the cooperation of the authorities. Morrison said that it was easier when the correspondent was well established; that was probably correct, but I was a transient and many Indians were perhaps not unnaturally sensitive. For most of the foreign correspondents news was news, whether it was good, bad or indifferent, but for literate Indians our reports of the massacres, the horror of which was impossible to exaggerate, were regarded as attacks on independent India. Pandit Nehru warned us not to abuse Indian hospitality, whatever that meant. Mountbatten also took offence over my estimates of the casualties in the Punjab. He had his own reasons for being sensitive; his decision to advance independence and partition from June 1948 to August 1947 undoubtedly led to an enormous increase in the violence. Admittedly both had to be brought forward because of increasing unrest and the mutual suspicions of the Congress Party and the Muslim League, but there would have been fewer casualties if there had been more time to organize the Punjab Boundary Force, which was to have policed the migrations of refugees in both directions. Instead, the divided province became one of the worst killing grounds in history. The killings continued unabated for weeks because there was little or no control.

My casualty estimates were arrived at after talking to many of the senior military officers involved, including Major-General T.W. Rees, the commander of the boundary force, the governors of East and West Punjab, and district commissioners. It was agreed that several hundred thousand had perished. There was no real way of knowing; the dead of the refugee trains could be counted, and the district commissioners could calculate how many had died in their jurisdictions but there were more than 18,000 towns and villages in the Punjab and tens of thousands of the dead must have been buried or cremated or left to rot in ditches unnoticed. Rees guessed that about 1 million had been killed or had died from wounds. Mountbatten must have known the approximate number of people who died in East Punjab, India's portion of the divided province, but he claimed that only 3 per cent of the subcontinent's population had been involved in the migrations and only a fraction had died. That was true as far as it went but 3 per cent of 420 million, the then combined population, was about 12 million and 1 million was but a fraction of that number. The Indian High Commissioner in London made representations to the paper. The editor was sympathetic but continued to publish my stories. That was reassuring; he had learned to trust his correspondents after the years of appeasement, but I had to learn to live with Indian resentment. It was not too hard; I had some good Indian friends, but I also learned that even in sensitive newly independent countries politicians and officials could, for their own good or questionable reasons, remain cooperative.

I had another and more painful lesson to learn, this time from the British popular press.

Foreign correspondents working for popular newspapers could be remarkably good, and arguably their job was more difficult than mine. They had to persuade their editors that their stories could sell newspapers when important foreign stories were not running. They had to write very readable copy which could generate eye-catching headlines. It was known as tarting up the story and giving it a couple of coats of varnish. This may sound cynical, but the good ones could satisfy their paper's demand for sensational headlines and still tell the story honestly and well. Their editorial integrity was beyond question.

My main popular rival in those early postwar years was the *Daily Express*, then the best mass-circulation newspaper. While not providing the kind of comprehensive coverage which would satisfy diplomats, it took pride in its foreign service and boasted of having an *Express* man on the spot. The claim was occasionally spurious, but its best foreign correspondents, notably James Cameron, Sefton Delmer and René McColl, could be superb. Its circulation crossed all class barriers, and in any case the foreign news editor and his subeditors in Printing House Square were not professional snobs. They knew a good story when they read one, generally late at night when they read the early editions of other newspapers. They would then send a cable asking 'why you uncovered query'.

Those post-war years were almost certainly the golden age of Fleet Street journalism despite newsprint rationing. Most of the nationals had foreign correspondents as well as star writers based in London who flew out to cover the big stories. Rivalry was intense. We were utterly ruthless with each other but this did not prevent us from enjoying each other's company. Late-night parties were frequent, and were always jolly and light-hearted. We had a collective gift of writing songs about the events and people we were covering. One example was when Sheikh Abdullah, known as the lion of Kashmir, decided not to hold a referendum to decide whether the state should join India or Pakistan; and we composed a lyric to the then popular tune of 'Oh, what a beautiful morning'. A couple of lines went: 'And to his remarks he added an addendum/That this year there'll be no referendum.' Not exactly of Broadway quality, but amusing enough.

We did rather better later during the last days of the Palestine mandate when Homer Bigart of the *New York Herald Tribune* had a poor opinion of the departing British. Like some other correspondents working in a strange country, Bigart had a stringer to help him; in his case, a delightful Israeli journalist named

Gabriel Ziffrony. The lyric, to the tune of Lille Marlene, went: 'Gabriel Ziffrony telephones the news/Of how the dirty British are beating up the Jews/Homer sits down to earn his wage/And writes a page of earnest rage/And then ten pages more/And then ten pages more.'

A newcomer to the trade – he did not last very long – was upset by our light-heartedness and accused us of insensitivity. It was nothing of the sort. As soldiers or war correspondents during the war most of us had witnessed various horrors, from vicious battles such as Montecassino to the liberation of Nazi extermination camps, and almost without a break had gone on to witness other horrors and be exposed to more shot and shell. Memories of the mass killings in the Punjab palled when compared to the holocaust, but they were still disturbing. We needed to relax among out own kind to remain reasonably sane. The camaraderie was both natural and essential, perhaps because we knew that we would try to do each other down the next day.

The rivalry certainly helped to explain the comradeship in that it put us on an equal footing. It mattered not which newspaper we worked for, *The Times* or the old *Daily Herald*; it was our performance that counted, especially for youngsters such as myself. The older men had an advantage in that they had long proved themselves and knew the tricks of the trade. Great war correspondents such as Alan Moorehead had gone on to bigger or more profitable things such as writing books or for *The New Yorker*, but a few still worked at the coalface. Sefton Delmer of the *Express* was probably the best known. Born in Berlin, he was bilingual in German, and had made a name for himself covering the rise of Hitler, the Reichstag fire when Dr Goebbels was his guide, and the fall of Warsaw. He was the acknowledged star of the strong *Express* foreign team, and behaved accordingly. Delmer moved about the world like a diplomatic special envoy, stayed at the very best hotels and before meals drank a champagne-based cocktail which he always mixed himself. I was introduced to it in the King David hotel in Jerusalem, where naturally he occupied a suite of rooms overlooking the old city. A waiter appeared with a trolley loaded with champagne, various liqueurs, ice, a punch bowl and silver tankards; and Delmer, like an alchemist preparing an elixir, produced his cocktail. It was remarkably good, but after

a few sips he excused himself; he had to write his story in the next
room, but kindly invited me to stay and have my fill. I estimated
that his abandoned brew cost more than a week's pay for me.

I owe a great deal to my colleagues of the early years, and
before leaving India I received my first 'best thanks' telegrams.
Known as herograms, *The Times* used them sparingly which made
them all the more welcome when they did arrive. I also received
a couple of nice letters which suggested that I had passed my first
test. Arguably it had been cruel, I had been thrown into the deep
end without being asked if I could swim, but that was in the
tradition of the paper. Delane was 23 when he succeeded Barnes
as editor, and with only one year's experience in journalism. It
must have been a wonderful surprise; after being told he burst
into the rooms of a friend saying, 'By Jove, John, what do you
think has happened? I am the editor of *The Times*!' I felt much
the same although my advancement was much more modest. I
was at last a tried and proven foreign correspondent, relatively
inexperienced but judged capable. My transfer from the players
to the gentlemen was permanent, pleasing but at first not easy
to comprehend. When I thought of Printing House Square I
remembered the black friars who had occupied those book-lined
rooms on the main editorial floor when I was a messenger –
Brodribb, Braham and other elderly men in rumpled three-piece
suits and college ties who looked more like classical scholars than
journalists. I had to remind myself that they were now brief
mentions in *The History of The Times*, the last of the many
generations who had served the paper for more than 160 years.
Barrington-Ward and Casey were still there, but they led a new
generation, men such as Tyerman, McDonald, Woods and of
course myself, the youngest recruit. Other new men had joined,
including experts on foreign affairs, colonialism, politics, the
economy and labour; and most of them had strong reformist
views, and it showed.

I carefully read the air-mail edition of the paper, with paper
clips attached to the top of the pages to stop them flapping under
the ceiling fan, and was more or less convinced that it was being
steadily improved. But not entirely. Barrington-Ward's belief that
experts could be trained to become good journalists also showed.
One of the new men who wrote about the nascent welfare state

clearly knew more about it than the responsible politicians, but you needed a good degree in sociology to understand him. Similarly with the men who wrote about finance, trade and industry; on any other serious newspaper they would have addressed themselves to the general reader as well as the court of the Bank of England and captains of industry, and they read like lectures. They may have been appreciated by the senior civil servants at the Treasury and other government departments, but not readers willing to learn about the intricacies of the harsh new world. Perhaps I was not clever enough to understand, but I wanted to learn as did many other members of my generation. We got little or no help from the columns of *The Times*.

Barrington-Ward was also too fond of preaching, which was not the first function of a newspaper. His intention was good, he was determined to make Britain more efficient and a better country; I was on his side, that went without saying, but believed that there were better ways of doing it. Despite the change of direction, he remained unchanged. The former infantry company commander, the parson's son with Protestant Ulster blood in his veins, advanced towards his private vision of the new Jerusalem with the same unbending convictions which had led him to appeasement. His sense of moral and intellectual superiority remained intact. He probably no longer saw the editorship of *The Times* as a kind of permanent portfolio in the apparatus of government; but he clearly believed that he had something important to say to the country's leaders. For him, the leader page was the heart and soul of the paper – indeed, the reason for its existence. The space given to general news, the arts and entertainment remained compressed due to newsprint rationing, but the leader page remained inviolate. Fewer readers read it than the sporting and foreign pages, but no matter; it was his views which counted.

Obviously I did not see it so clearly in 1948. I was a journeyman journalist with much still to learn. It also seemed that after Carr's departure readers and advertisers liked what Barrington-Ward was trying to do. The circulation had risen from its pre-war level of about 180,000 to 265,000. Advertising was buoyant, and the company was profitable to the tune of about £450,000. That was a great deal of money in those pre-inflation days, and the proprietors probably thought that God was in his heaven and all was well in Printing House Square.

If they did, they were wrong. Fleet Street was operating in a sellers' market, newspapers were cheap and many people bought two or more newspapers. There was little or no competition from other media; television was an expensive and not very entertaining novelty and radio was insipid. Other newspapers did not give as much space to parliamentary debates, the court circular, obituaries and other items regarded as essential. No other newspaper published formal law reports. They could give more space to general news although they had fewer pages. As a consequence, our main rival, the *Daily Telegraph*, was steadily selling more copies. The *Express* was selling more than 4 million a day, the largest circulation in the world at the time. It was not a rival, but demonstrated what could be achieved by a proprietor and editor of genius.

Then I heard that Barrington-Ward's health was failing, which was not surprising. Tyerman had taken over much of the administrative work, and Iverach McDonald, the senior leader writer on foreign affairs, was promoted to assistant editor to relieve him at nights, but Barrington-Ward continued to work an exhausting day. His condition worsened, and Morison pleaded with him to take a long holiday. He eventually agreed to take the round trip to Capetown aboard one of the old Union Castle boats, and on his way home died from cerebral malaria off Dar-es-Salaam. He was 57, and I remembered that Barnes had died when he was 56 and Delane was also worn out when he died at 62.

The prepared obituary was incomplete, and had to be finished in haste. It was suitably glowing, but the obituary writer chose his words with care when referring to the appeasement years:

> His keen sense of the errors of Versailles, and the logical nature of his mind, led him, even after 1933, to work hard for peace; as a soldier he knew what war was and was prepared to go far to prevent a repetition of its destructiveness and wastefulness.

The Official History later said that Barrington-Ward foresaw the social revolution at home, and an end to the middle-class dominance of society and industry which had shaped the Britain in which he grew up. The middle classes had had to make room for the new classes as the landed classes had had to make room earlier for them. He wished to be editor of *The Times* because he saw the job as a means of shaping events. The paper's special standing made his advocacy the more startling and the more effective. At the same time, in using the paper so, he altered that special standing. *The Times* under him could no longer be regarded as the voice of the establishment or, as it was once also called, the gazette of the ruling classes. It lost a little and it gained much. Barrington-Ward made it more exciting, more provocative, an organ for advancing ideas which at once shocked and educated its readers. Apart from the last bit about educating readers, the history summed up the man as I knew him.

Casey was appointed editor, and soon afterwards Deakin ordered me home before going to Palestine to cover the last days of the mandate and the establishment of the state of Israel.

5

A Stopgap Editor

Printing House Square looked unchanged when I returned for a few weeks before going on to the Middle East. To my initial embarrassment, I was treated as one of the gentlemen, but was young enough to enjoy it. McCluskie, the commissionaire, left his lodge to welcome me when I walked up the stairs from Queen Victoria Street and rang down the lift. Astor invited me to a black-tie dinner at Carlton House Terrace, where I had to play the part of the swashbuckling foreign correspondent for the ladies. Casey invited me both to lunch and dinner at the Garrick, and on both occasions I decided that it was safer to take a cab home. Nice things were said about my work, and the foreign subeditors were friendly.

I soon became aware that much had changed since the death of Barrington-Ward. The barriers between editor and staff had been lowered; to revive my earlier military comparison, the editorial floor was more like a friendly officers' mess than an army headquarters with the general officer commanding and his chief of staff dining alone. Casey was an affable man. The Official History describes him thus:

He was a quiet Irishman: even, it could be said, an Irish quietist. Much of his reluctance to take a strong line, or share Barrington-Ward's fervour over some topic of the day, came from a gentle pessimism. It was almost a Tolstoyean belief that no human act could make much difference to events, and this led him to express the gravest doubts as to whether journalism was a worthwhile occupation.... There was an odd paradox about his position in those years. He was the very heart of the office; his influence and his personality spread out to every editorial department. He was the leaven of the whole. Yet in a curious way he remained detached, almost as if he was an observer and a sojourner. Remarkably enough, although never over-eager to work (he recoiled in horror once when Barrington-Ward advised him to try 'a little application'), Casey managed to keep his brain as sharp as if he exercised it daily on higher mathematics. No one could confuse his easy-going manner with sloppy mindedness. He had the gift of glancing at a column of type and straight away spotting a howler which everyone had missed. He had the same faculty for quickly detecting a false argument in a leading article, and then he would go to see Dawson or Barrington-Ward in the attempt, not always successful, to have it put right. Better still, he was an unfailing judge of men and had a deep instinctive understanding of the play of world forces, without bothering to read all the documents or the speeches.... When he wrote a leader himself, which was rarely, it was a model of clear, direct, short-sentenced writing. Within the office he remained, as he had been throughout the Munich crisis, the wise friend and counsellor of the younger men; and he looked the part with his silver hair, his lined and kindly face, his hooded and very blue eyes, and his gentlemanly stoop.

Casey certainly gave me a great deal of his time and was eager to discuss my approach to journalism. Apart from the meals, we had a couple of conversations in his room, generally after the last editorial conference. This surprised me. The early evening was when the entire building was being geared up to produce the first edition. Copy was flowing into the office, and decisions had to be made. Leading articles had to be written and vetted by the editor. There was a hum in the air even in those book-lined rooms with their double-windows and subdued lighting. It was the time when Barrington-Ward would have been writing a leader to change the world or some part of it, but Casey sprawled in his chair like some kindly old uncle listening to the adventures of a young nephew. He seemed to have all the time in the world, and one evening I had cut the conversation short because I had a dinner engagement the other side of town.

We mainly talked about India, but the conversations were not what came to be known after the war as debriefings. If he did not read documents and speeches, he had obviously read many of my stories and congratulated me on giving the readers a smell of the country. He seemed to be fascinated by India, which surprised me. It was well known in the office that, unlike Dawson and some of the black friars of his generation, Casey had never been a fervent Commonwealth man. Being Irish, and educated in Dublin, he had remained the immigrant outsider, at least intellectually, despite all the years he had lived in Britain. I suppose that it helped to explain his detachment. It soon emerged that he was not so much interested in Indian politics as in the country and its people. He wanted to know what kind of man Gandhi had been, or the naked fakir as he recalled that Churchill had once called him. He was also interested in Nehru, and asked why I did not share Professor Rushbrook Williams' enthusiasm for the Indian prime minister.

Rushbrook Williams was the leader writer who specialized in Indian affairs. He had been foreign minister of the princely state of Patiala, and had held a university chair in Allahabad where he had become an intimate friend of the Nehru family. His leaders sometimes left the impression that he regarded Panditji as some kind of superman capable of dragging India into the industrialized twentieth century. I respected Nehru but the professor had not witnessed the Punjab massacres or seen him distraught with impatience and tiredness. Moreover, the problems of India were too numerous and fundamental for one man to resolve. Anyway, I told Casey, what good a government could do was limited, and that applied to well-established democracies with none of India's intractable problems.

Casey was obviously attracted by my outspoken scepticism. He said that he was glad that we thought alike, which I silently doubted. If he was a quietist – an unknown word for me at the time – I was certainly not. I was very much an activist and believed in progress, but he struck me as a wise old man, perhaps too old for the job but with vast experience of men and matters which would serve the paper well.

I liked him enormously, as did most of the others I had met on the editorial floors. He had delegated authority as well as generated the relaxed atmosphere, and both were welcomed. Tyerman had assumed all administrative responsibilities, and was in charge of home affairs. He was also deputy editor, and a powerful one. The paper still did not have a foreign editor, but Iverach McDonald was in overall charge of foreign leading articles. He was an experienced foreign correspondent and leader writer, and well informed on the Soviet Union, of whom more later. Oliver Woods was also brought forward, to everybody's delight. He was related to Garvin of the *Observer*, and was a born journalist. He had also been a legendary tank squadron commander during the war, fighting from the Western Desert through Italy and France to Germany, although few people would have guessed it. He looked more like an academic; glasses on the tip of his nose, somewhat scrawny and round-shouldered, with thinning hair and dandruff on his collar. He often spoke diffidently, but there was a glint in his eyes and he loved life. His parties at Acacia Road in St John's Wood were famous. Dry martinis were served in goblets the size of communion chalices, the food and wine were splendid and the conversation even better. He seemed to know everybody. Many years later I returned from Washington for a month to write a series of articles on the differences between the British and American forms of government, and he arranged interviews with all the people I wanted to meet. For good measure, he threw in the chief of the secret intelligence service, MI6, who gave me two hours and much dry sherry.

A new generation was moving into positions of authority, and some new blood had been brought in, mainly by raiding the *Manchester Guardian* which was then regarded as a nursery for men recently down from university. They were good writers. I did not meet all of them – I was married the day after my return from India, and was loth to spend too much time in the office – but was convinced that a new and bright era had begun, and was happy to go off to cover my second war in less than a year. Alas, my optimism was not widely shared.

It was not immediately apparent; the senior men obviously did not discuss the editor with me, and the younger men were not much help. It was made clear, however, that Barrington-Ward had wanted Tyerman to succeed him as had other people in the department. Moreover, before Barrington-Ward died Casey had let it be known that he did not want to be editor. He was 64, not in good health and had in fact asked for early retirement. No man, it was said, was more disappointed than Casey when he found himself in the editorial chair. He was a stopgap, that much was clear, but opinions differed as to why the proprietors had postponed the decision when Tyerman was available. One school of thought held that they charitably wanted to give the older man a year or so as editor to crown his long and loyal career, and that Tyerman was young enough to wait. He had only been on the paper for four years, and a period as deputy would prepare him for the editorship. Another was convinced that the proprietors wanted to find their own man; that Barrington-Ward had swung the paper too far to the Left and they believed that Tyerman would take it further in that direction.

I decided long afterwards that they saw Tyerman as a kind of alien. The *Economist* and the *Observer* were not regarded as foreign territory, Barrington-Ward had also worked for the Sunday paper, but Tyerman was not in the tradition of the black friars. The breed was dying out, the novices joining the paper were evidence of that, but I suppose the proprietors were slow to adjust. They wanted the editor to wear the habit – homburg hat, dark clothes and a grave demeanour – and to subscribe to their version of enlightened conservatism. Tyerman did not fit the part. He was too much of a Yorkshireman; despite his poor shrivelled legs, he was a bull of a man, pugnacious and forthright. His round face with its short nose and bold eyes did not suggest that he was a liberal Tory and an establishment man. It could redden with anger or exasperation when a leader writer or correspondent was unwilling to oppose the establishment view. His throaty voice also changed with his mood, but he could smile warmly and was generous with his congratulations when a job was well done.

Most people liked and admired Tyerman. He was a member of the Reform, but preferred to eat in Soho where the company and conversation were often boisterous and lubricated with lots of wine. Some people said that he drank too much, but there was no evidence of this in his writing. He was frequently found snoozing at his desk in the early afternoon, but he worked long hours. Nevertheless, when Casey retired after four and a half years, his drinking was said to be one reason why he was again passed over. Sir William Haley, who was appointed editor in 1952, was one of the paper's better editors, but more than four years had been wasted. *The Times* stood still while the rest of Fleet Street adjusted to the postwar world and exploited the circulation boom. The circulation actually dropped as did the company's profits.

To some extent this was the inheritance of the Barrington-Ward years; parts of the paper were still not easy to read, but no less important was Casey's failure to make his predecessor's break with its establishment past total. The lingering reputation of being the gazette of the ruling classes doubtless guaranteed an elite readership, it was required reading for government ministers, senior civil servants, diplomats and Oxbridge dons; but as in the 1850s, when the stamp tax was revoked, the opportunity to appeal to a larger intelligent readership was missed.

I am convinced that it would have been different if Tyerman had been appointed editor instead of Casey. The Irishman was a delightful man, but the Yorkshireman was a tough and talented journalist who would have exploited Barrington-Ward's partial break with the past. Tyerman could have been another Barnes if not a Delane; his physical disability prevented him from moving freely in political society, but Barnes had created the paper without moving far from his desk. Nor did drink affect his editorial judgement. *The Times* became the 'Thunderer' under him, and Tyerman was capable of thundering. His mind was open to new ideas, and his enjoyment of the company of the young kept him in touch with the rising generation. His interests and imagination seemed to be as limitless as theirs. This may have scared the proprietors; as did some of the bright young men he brought on to the paper, and who left soon after his eventual departure. On Tyerman's sixty-fifth birthday I attended a rather grand luncheon given by an admirer. It was a large party because most of the guests were men he had launched into successful journalistic careers. The paper would have avoided some of its troubles if he and they had not left it.

The Official History has little to say about Casey's editorship except that he was not the pilot to weather the storm, but the man to ensure that within Printing House Square there would be no storm to be weathered. The nature of the storm is not defined, but the editorial direction and content of the paper were not the only concerns of the proprietors. They were also worried about the management of the company. Kent was seen not to be the ideal manager to deal with the unknown challenges of the future. He was also in his early sixties, and Frank Waters had been brought in as his assistant in the expectation that he would be a suitable successor. By any standards, it was a sensible choice. After coming down from Cambridge, Waters had joined the *Daily Express*, had launched the Sunday edition of the *Scottish Daily Express* and had acquired the *Glasgow Evening Citizen* for the group. He had considerable executive talent and an imagination sharpened by working for Beaverbrook. He certainly knew more about newspaper management than Kent. Moreover, the former commando colonel had played rugby for Scotland – he was capped eight times – which was sufficient to persuade Astor and Walter that he was the right material.

Perhaps I am not an impartial witness in that he was very good to me, but other senior editorial men liked him. They disliked Kent for obvious reasons, and wanted a manager who could succeed by generating revenue and not holding down expenditure. A few were wary of powerful managers – on some Fleet Street newspapers the manager and not the editor ran the show – but Waters was their kind of man despite his years working for Beaverbrook; indeed, this was not held against him. His experience of the Fleet Street jungle was seen as a kind of bonus. Nor did they object when it emerged that he wanted to broaden the paper's appeal to increase circulation. While accepting that *The Times* must remain a newspaper of record, he saw the need to improve home news and introduce features which would appeal to intelligent men and women of all ages and classes. This was an editorial decision, but Waters was not resented by Tyerman who knew that Barrington-Ward had not gone far enough. Cooperation from the managerial floor was welcomed. He was, however, resented by Kent who thought that his authority was being challenged. This became evident when he was discovered to have sat on Waters' recommendations to improve the distribution of the paper. They were eminently sensible, but apparently the proprietors and the board decided that they had to support the manager. Astor was also a traditionalist who saw himself as the protector of a national institution. He was determined to preserve the character of the paper. This was the main reason why news was not printed on the front page until his son, Gavin, became chairman. Waters decided that he could not win, and resigned to manage the *News Chronicle* and its evening paper, *The Star*. He died in 1954 from polio.

I was unaware of these differences with the proprietors when Morison invited Pat and me to dine with him at the home of a friend of his before I left for the Middle East. No reason was given, but I had a sneaking suspicion that he wanted to vet Pat. After all, he still regarded me as his acolyte. Our host was to be Francis Mathew, and not knowing him I made some enquiries. He was the managing director of a large printing firm, who had learned the trade when working for the Linotype company in Spain, Latin America and London. He was also a Roman Catholic, educated at Downside and Grenoble University, and came from a distinguished legal family.

The dinner was a black-tie affair, and as there were only five of us I assumed that the Mathews always dressed for dinner when they had company. They had a large duplex apartment in a block of Edwardian mansions near the Albert Hall as well as a country house, and they lived well. Morison especially enjoyed the burgundy, and after Mrs Mathew had led Pat away we sat near the fire while Mathew warmed the brandy glasses. He was amusing as well as hospitable, and I was impressed by his appearance. A broad-shouldered man of medium height with black horn-rimmed glasses, his face first revealed a lifetime of good living. This impression, I suppose, was enhanced by the soft white shirt and well-tailored dinner jacket, but the mobile face was also shrewd and alert. As I discovered later, he was to be the next manager of the paper. Morison had done it again.

The two men had first met during the war, when Mathew was involved in secret printing of overseas and black propaganda. They liked each other, and when the preliminary search began for a new manager during Barrington-Ward's time Morison had listed his friend's qualifications in a memorandum:

Francis Mathew, the manager of St Clement's Press, has all the abilities required for the management without any temptation to meddle with the editorial part, great as his sympathy would be with it. I think he understands enough about advertising, but his real strength is, of course, in production, labour relations, costs and finances for he understands business and would have a plan ready if the paper ran into choppy weather. Had he been a protestant I would have mentioned his name earlier.

The last remark was unnecessary, as Morison must have known. Arguably it could have been seen as an advantage; Kent's brand of protestantism – he was a Plymouth Brother – was said to have explained his cheeseparing management. As a colleague once said, he seemed to think that we could live on our miserable pay if we gave up drinking and smoking. Moreover, Mathew was not an accountant but a printer. This commanded respect in Printing House Square where presses had been housed long before the original John Walter launched the paper. It was probably the oldest continuous printing site in the country.

The conversation was at first inconsequential but genial, touching on my experiences in India and the next assignment, but eventually turned to the paper. To my surprise it was not a new subject for Mathew. The two men had obviously discussed it before, and by the end of the evening I was convinced that they had long been engaged in planning future strategy. The expectation in 1948 was that newsprint rationing would be abolished in the foreseeable future, and Morison believed that with extra pages *The Times* would reassert its authority as the newspaper of the governing classes. There was no reference to the changes in British society which had concerned Barrington-Ward, or the need to broaden the paper's appeal. Mathew had his own reasons for agreeing that a large circulation should not be sought. He lost me with his calculations of newsprint costs and advertising revenue, but it went something like this.

The price of newsprint had quadrupled to £40 a ton during the war, and was steadily rising. This would prohibit the lowering of the cover price to attract a large readership. Similarly with advertising which had to cover the difference between overall costs and revenue from sales, and provide a profit. The paper's advertising rates were relatively high because the purchasing power of its well-to-do readers attracted advertisers of expensive products. For instance, Rolls-Royce was willing to pay more per thousand readers because potential buyers read *The Times*. It would be unwilling to pay proportionally more if the number of readers who bought small family cars was sizeably increased.

Mathew saw all this as sound commonsense, an undeniable commercial case for appealing to an elite readership. Morison agreed for different reasons, and I was uneasy but silent.

Throughout its history, the paper was always proud of its foreign news service, but the department did not fit easily into Printing House Square. One reason was that the editors I knew were rightly more interested in Westminster and Whitehall; their first duty was to report the activities and intentions of the country's political representatives and to make them more accountable. Another reason was that the foreign correspondents were seen as – well, foreign, and they were in more ways than one. A few were foreign-born, some had been detribalized and one or two had gone native.

Dessa Trevisan, who served in Belgrade and Vienna, was born in Yugoslavia. Gerald Norman, who was chief correspondent in Paris for many years, was half French, and his successor, Charles Hargrove, was born in Paris and was married to a French woman. He looked and sounded very English, but clearly preferred Paris and his house in Normandy to Britain. The Indian-born Eric Britter was not at home in London, and married Americans – three of them – and eventually retired to the Caribbean. Ian Morrison, originally Australian, preferred living in Asia, as did David Bonavia. A Scot of Italian descent, he was appointed to Peking after his expulsion from Moscow, and left the paper rather than return to London as our Asian expert. Jerome Caminada, a correspondent who was captured by the Germans in 1940 and subsequently had a distinguished career in the Middle East and Far East, was a South African. John Freeman, a Bonn correspondent, married a German and became a confidant of Konrad Adenauer. Peter Nichols refused to leave Rome, married an Italian actress and looked more Italian with every passing year.

Even those who remained solidly English were associated with the countries in which they had spent many years. I was regarded as an American after ten years in Washington, and not because I wore Brooks Brothers' suits and button-down shirts. In a way, I had become an American; I tended to think like one, and after being brought back to London visited the United States at least once a year. Landing at Dulles or Kennedy airport was always like coming home.

I did not become the eternal expatriate, but like other correspondents I was rather rootless after nearly twenty-five years overseas. I often wore two watches, one on local time and the other on GMT. I ate and drank the food and wine of the country, smoked its cigarettes and drove its cars. I spent more nights in hotels than I care to remember, and lived in about twenty different houses and flats. My family moved with me, although in the early years my wife and I lived out of suitcases. Our children were born in Singapore, India, West Germany and the United States, and attended local schools. Apart from my family, the one certainty was *The Times*. I was connected to Printing House Square by a kind of umbilical cord, down which came money and the occasional message in return for words, millions of words.

The foreign correspondents were privileged people, we were better paid and enjoyed extraordinary independence, but most of us worked hard and for some life could be dangerous. Ian Morrison was not the first *Times* correspondent to be killed. Frank Power was with General Gordon when the Mahdi's forces besieged Khartoum. A young Irishman, Power ran the blockade of the Nile with a message requesting troops. Somewhere below Berber he went ashore to buy camels for a dash across the desert and was murdered by tribesmen. He was 25. Another correspondent, Frank Riley, was murdered during the Chinese civil war in 1927. Walter Harris, the correspondent in Morocco before World War I, was captured by rebels and shared a windowless dungeon with a decapitated corpse for some months. He was eventually ransomed for a dozen captured rebels. Jerome Caminada, after his capture in 1940, tried to escape from German prison camps two or three times, and when he finally got away was on the run for more than two years before reaching the Middle East. Roger Toulmin, who succeeded me in India, was the only survivor of an air crash; and in Palestine I walked away from an aeroplane which crashed carrying a cargo of industrial alcohol. Fortunately it did not ignite.

Arguably *The Times* correspondents were lucky. William Howard Russell covered the Crimean war, the Indian Mutiny and the American Civil War. He frequently rode into battle and was caught up in the retreat after the first battle of Bull Run, and lived to a ripe old age. Ferdinand Eber, who also covered the Crimea, was with Garibaldi when he invaded Sicily to begin the Risorgimento. To the distress of the editor, he led a cavalry brigade into action between filing reports to the paper. Mowbray Morris wrote an agitated letter to General Eber, as he had become, saying: 'Surely you do not think that we sent you to Sicily to liberate the island.... If you desire the fame of patriot and liberator, and choose to fight for Italy in the service of Garibaldi, do so (but) I must call upon you to make your election between *The Times* and your other masters.' Eber continued to report and fight. At the time of writing, Robert Fisk was still risking his life in Beirut.

This is not to suggest that the lot of a war correspondent is worse than that of the soldier, although in Korea casualties among correspondents were proportionally higher than they were for the military. They have to do the fighting, and apart from Eber correspondents do not lead them into battle. Correspondents also choose to go to war, and soldiers, many of them unwilling conscripts, have no choice. Apparently this was the view of Ralph Deakin, the foreign news editor in my early years. One of the few letters I received from him in Korea merely informed me that I had been insured against death and injury. There was nothing more to be said; as he once told me: 'We always give our correspondents a good obituary.'

Not all foreign correspondents go to war, but their foreignness had advantages and disadvantages for them and the paper. Most of us enjoyed our years overseas, and the paper was blessed with a corps of men and women who collectively knew much of the world intimately. A possible danger was that after years overseas they could lose touch with Britain, and the objectivity of those who went native could be at risk. They could miss stories; what was familiar to them could be interesting for the readers, and what they regarded as important developments could have little meaning and relevance. Home leaves, which were expensive for the paper when families had to be flown half way round the world, helped; but when stationed outside Europe we generally came home once every two or three years, which could be a long time.

This foreignness probably explained why correspondents were

rarely if ever considered as eventual candidates for the editorship despite the world view some of them had acquired. Wickham Steed, a most opinionated man, was the last foreign correspondent of *The Times* to become editor, and he was appointed by Northcliffe.

The absence of a foreign editor before 1952 also contributed to our isolation. Ralph Deakin was in charge of correspondents, but as foreign news editor his status and influence were not comparable to that of a foreign editor. He resented being treated as a kind of superior technician, first by Dawson and then Barrington-Ward, as he had every right to be. His knowledge of foreign affairs was unrivalled in the office, but he was even denied the recruitment of correspondents. As if to demonstrate his inferior status, he worked in a cubicle in what was once the composing room instead of one of those comfortable offices in the main building.

Deakin was foreign news editor for thirty-one years, and was married to the paper. He came in early and went home late, and spent a good part of every Friday and Saturday, his two free days, in the office. He was very good at his job, and had a flair for anticipating events and moving correspondents to cover them. He rarely bothered them with requests for news, saying that anybody who needed such prompting was not up to the standards required by *The Times*. His infrequent messages were always short, often shorter than the minimum number allowed in foreign telegrams. Only when a correspondent transgressed did he allow himself a few more words, invariably pompous. I once received a cable begining 'great perturbations your missing ...' I suspect that one reason why he allowed us to get on with the job was that he had only a trainee journalist to help him, but he obviously trusted the judgement of the men in the field.

What I did not know at the time was that this apparently self-sufficient man longed for the recognition denied him. He lunched at his desk when the fortnightly board meeting and luncheon were held in case he was summoned to explain some point or other. The call rarely came.

Outside the office Deakin was highly respected, and his advice was frequently sought, but this was small compensation and towards the end he gradually withdrew into himself. His messages to correspondents apparently ceased; certainly I heard nothing from him for about a year. I was in Singapore at the time and was having trouble with the colonial government in Malaya. My pay, living allowance and expenses arrived regularly, as did copies of the paper and cuttings of my stories, but otherwise I could have been living on another planet. I was relieved when the occasional messages and herograms were resumed, but this was after Deakin had been retired at the age of 64. He had pleaded to stay on, and died soon afterwards in rather mysterious circumstances. His widow gave evidence at the inquest, and produced a sad letter he had written before his death. A pathologist said that he had found some barbitone at the post-mortem. It was established that death was due to coronary disease, but the coroner found that his condition had been aggravated by worry and emotion.

I still have a soft spot for Ralph Deakin. The Official History acknowledges that he was a very good foreign news editor, and he wrote well. He should have been promoted to foreign editor. Dawson of course wanted to control the news reported from Nazi Germany, and in any case must have known that Deakin spoke good German and knew the country better than any other man in the office. I heard later that when Dawson's efforts to placate Hitler had come to nothing Deakin was not promoted because he had tried to defend Ebbutt, the Berlin correspondent, who had complained that his copy was being censored. That was hearsay, and probably Barrington-Ward decided that a foreign editor was not necessary during the war and the years of newsprint rationing. At least it was a rational explanation.

When I knew Deakin his dignity appeared not to have been bruised. He had an unlined, plumpish face of good colouring and impressive self-composure. Some people thought him pompous, but he carried himself well and I noticed that doormen and cab drivers saluted him. Most days he lunched at the Reform club, where he entertained correspondents on leave or between assignments. The lunches never varied: dry sherry in the rotunda, a carafe of the club claret with the meal and coffee, port and a cigar upstairs. I have not forgotten the lunch he gave me in 1948.

Little of consequence was said during the meal and later, when his cigar was drawing well, he seemed reluctant to talk about my new assignment. He talked knowledgeably about the Middle East, but had little to say about nascent Israel. The paper had always been sympathetic to the Zionist cause, but was pained by the shrill untruths of its American propagandists who portrayed the British troops in Palestine as Gestapo thugs and gloried in the terrorism of the Stern Gang and the *Irgun Zvai Leumi*. The end of the mandate was a defeat for British foreign policy and the beginning of the end of British power and influence in the Middle East. That apart, there was a great deal to talk about; I did not want editorial guidance, anything but that, but I wanted some idea of what was expected of me. Deakin, I assumed, would want to brief me. He was also my immediate boss, and would presumably be held responsible if I made a mess of the assignment. I was confident enough, probably too confident; I had done well in India, but was no stranger to the country and the main story was basically simple; the great political decisions had been made, and I only had to report the consequences. Israel would be very different.

We finished the port, and after he had collected his bowler and umbrella stood silently on the steps of the club waiting for a cab. One eventually responded to Deakin's peremptory wave of his umbrella, and as it came to a halt he said, 'Be decent to those chaps, Heren, be decent.' It was the only guidance I was to receive during my many years as a foreign correspondent, and he did not tell me which chaps I should be decent to. I assumed that he meant the Israelis, who the Arabs were threatening to push into the sea, and I was told later that he felt deeply for them. Some of his Jewish friends in Germany had disappeared in the holocaust, and perhaps he remembered the articles on Dachau which Dawson or Barrington-Ward had refused to publish. Whatever the reason, Deakin's oblique, almost shy remark summed up his attitude to the foreign correspondents. Most of the time we were just little coloured pins stuck in a map of the world to mark our disposition. He had little time to think of us personally; his attitude further strengthened our editorial independence, already guaranteed by tradition and the shame of Dawson's self-confessed efforts to keep out of the paper anything that might offend Nazi susceptibilities. It was comforting to know that Deakin was in the office.

On my first foreign assignment I told myself on the plane going out that it was the greatest story since the birth of Jesus Christ. A slight exaggeration, although the withdrawal of the British from India was a great historic event. I had no such hyperbole when I flew out to Haifa a year later. The holocaust had persuaded me that the Jews should have a state of their own, but for me it was just another little war to be covered. Despite Churchill's assertion that he would not preside over the dissolution of the British empire, it seemed that I was destined to report its passing. As an anti-imperialist I had few regrets about India, and none about Palestine. It was a mandated territory which Britain had administered for only twenty-six years, most of them violent due to Arab opposition to the Balfour Declaration; this said that the British government viewed 'with favour the establishment in Palestine of a national home for the Jewish people'. It subsequently stated that this did not mean a Jewish state, but after the holocaust and the revolt of the Jews in Palestine the United Nations partitioned the country and Britain withdrew.

The first few weeks were intensely exciting, but lonely. All relations between Britain and Israel had been severed – my visa was issued by a Major Lee of the Jewish Agency in Bloomsbury – and the postal service had been stopped, which meant that Pat and I could not correspond. I was prepared to like the Israelis but they did not like me. They appeared to have a pathological hatred for Britain, and a deep distrust of all Britons. Ben Gurion, the first prime minister, at first refused to see me, and the few ministers who did delivered tirades against anti-Semitic Albion. Moshe Shertok, the foreign minister, regarded me as a paid agent of Ernest Bevin, the British foreign minister, who had opposed the foundation of Israel. I was annoyed. I had joined the army to fight Hitler, and had long been pro-Zionist. Moreover, I was interested in the socialist experiments of the earlier Jewish settlers, and admired the *kibbutzniks* after reading Arthur Koestler's *Thieves in the Night*. I was on the side of Israel in more ways than one, but was regarded as a kind of Nazi stormtrooper. A group of American Zionists staying at my hotel, who had flown in to see the promised land, were particularly nasty until I invited one of them to step outside for a bout of fisticuffs.

The freeze gradually thawed. Koestler, who was in Israel to

write another book and report for the *Manchester Guardian*, introduced me to some of his friends. Two or three officials of the government's press information office had been born in the East End, and we became mates. I suppose my reporting must have helped, especially after my sympathetic interview with Chaim Weizmann, the president. The meeting came about after the Israeli air force shot down four RAF fighters based on the Canal Zone in Egypt. Their intention was clearly not hostile and they were probably not over Israeli territory, but they were shot down without warning. Some members of the cabinet in Tel Aviv feared retaliation, and it was suggested by devious means that I should drive down to Rehoveth and interview Weizmann. He was a grand old man, highly respected in Britain, but very old and almost incoherent in his grief. Having not understood everything he said, I discussed the problem with the foreign ministry official who had accompanied me, and it was agreed that I should write what I thought the president wanted to say. It was an odd way of reporting a presidential interview in a period of crisis, but there was no alternative. My story led the paper, and might have done some good. It certainly improved my relations with the Israeli government.

Before relations were established, I had of course recognized the historic significance of the little war I was trying to cover, and was more than willing to be 'decent to those chaps'. It was clear that they would not be swept into the sea, and that the ingathering of the exiles would be realized. The dream and the propaganda were becoming true. After all those hundreds of years in the diaspora they finally had a home of their own; not the nebulous national home of the Balfour Declaration but a country and a flag instantly recognized by the United States and the Soviet Union. Israel was still a divided country, however; the armed forces were mainly the private armies, the *Haganah* and *Palmach*, of political parties in the government. The men of the *Irgun Zvai Leumi*, whose terrorists had blown up the King David Hotel and murdered British soldiers, refused to be integrated and separately manned part of the line in divided Jerusalem under their own commanders. It was potentially divisive, especially when the *Irgun* tried to import arms in the tank landing ship *Altalena*. Ben Gurion recognized the dangers, and the army attacked the ship and killed twenty-four *Irgun* men. These dissidents were of course very news-worthy, and I got to know some of the leaders. Menachem Begin, the leader of the *Irgun* who many years later became prime minis-ter, treated me with great courtesy when he emerged from the underground, and said that we must be friends. I was surprised, but he was newsworthy and in any case I was then ambivalent about terrorism. The allies and resistance groups had used it extensively in the second world war, but there was more to it than that. I was always on the side of the underdog, which helped in Israel and elsewhere.

I also became friendly with two members of the Stern gang, Goldfoot and Nimeri were engaging men despite the gang's repu-tation for cold-blooded assassination. They were at first left strictly alone by the government, for whom Goldfoot had great contempt. I must admit that they made me uneasy, but their light-hearted approach to life was almost alien in Israel and again they were potentially newsworthy. One Friday in Jerusalem after most of the foreign correspondents had driven down to Tel Aviv for the weekend, they invited four of us who had stayed behind to lunch. We drove to Abu Ghosh, an Arab village, drank too much of the wine made by the French Catholic priests of the old crusader church, and returned to Jerusalem for a siesta. After all, nothing ever happened on sabbath. I was dozing on my bed, wondering why Goldfoot and Nimeri had given us such a good lunch, when the Associated Press man dashed into my room shouting, 'They've shot Bernadotte.'

Count Bernadotte, the United Nations' conciliator, was shot at the Mandelbaum gate, the crossing point for UN personnel between Arab and Israeli Jerusalem. It was an easy story to cover despite the immense political significance of the assassination. It was basically a police story. Who shot whom, when, where, why? Getting the story on the wire was more difficult. The censor refused to pass it. We hired a cab and drove to Tel Aviv where the censor had also been instructed not to pass any reports of the assassination. After fighting off the mob of correspondents, half crazy because they sensed something dreadful had happened but knew not what, we drove on to Haifa which had been overlooked by the government and got our stories away. It was well after midnight when the last message was transmitted; we had missed the first editions but knew that we would lead the final editions and were content.

The Stern gang, including Goldfoot, was rounded up the next day and sent to the old prison in Jaffa. They quickly organized an audacious escape, but Goldfoot chose to stay. The main prison gate was wide open when I arrived, and Goldfoot was taking his ease sitting in the exercise yard. It was another good story, and when I left Goldfoot asked me to bring him a carton of American cigarettes. I obliged the following day.

The gang was a savage organization, and the argument that it was an inevitable product of the holocaust was questionable and hardly defensible. Ben-Gurion was obviously relieved to get rid of it, and Goldfoot was quietly returned to his native South Africa.

Just before I finished my tour in the Middle East, Deakin wrote saying that a Mr Goldfoot of Johannesburg had sent his best regards. Later in London he asked me if I wanted Goldfoot's address. He seemed interested in this admirer of mine. In those days we were anonymous and rarely received fan letters, but I did not respond. He and the other editors must have realized that foreign correspondents were required from time to time to mix with people they would not invite to their clubs. The world beyond Printing House Square could be nasty, but still had to be reported. All the same I suspected that Deakin knew who Goldfoot was, I had written enough about him and Nimeri; but was reluctant to tell him about the lunch at Abu Ghosh, the drinks we used to have in a café in Jerusalem's Zion Square, and the carton of American cigarettes. I thought that he would be shocked or disapproving if I did. Consorting with such people was unbecoming for a gentleman. Presumably he had chosen to believe that we worked through official sources, and I decided to leave him with his illusions.

6

Middle East Adventures

Israel's first war came to an end after Pat joined me, and we were nearly killed by what were probably the last shots fired in Jerusalem in that war. I was showing her the old city from the French hospice when it was suddenly sprayed with machine-gun bullets. We scrambled for shelter behind one of the columns of the colonnaded terrace, standing side by side because the column was only about a foot in diameter, and waited until the gunner got bored. I was impressed by Pat's calmness, and then remembered that her family had been bombed out of two homes during the blitz and she was alone in a train compartment when it was strafed by a German plane. She was the ideal wife for a foreign correspondent.

After the ceasefire an armistice agreement was negotiated in Rhodes under the chairmanship of Dr Ralph Bunche of the United Nations. The talks did not go well at first, the Egyptians refused to sit in the same room as the Israelis, but Bunche eventually got them together and the agreement was hammered out. The Egyptians flew in some goodies from Cairo to celebrate the occasion, and I can still remember the babble of conversation in English, French and Arabic as the two delegations and the few correspondents present toasted each other. Shertok, the Israeli foreign minister, afterwards said that peace negotiations would follow, and I was more than half convinced that Egypt had accepted the consequences of military defeat.

This was before Colonel Nasser seized power, but their invasion of the Negev was half-hearted. It was difficult to believe that the operation was anything more than a propaganda exercise to placate Arab nationalists because it was halted by the defenders of two *kibbutzim*. They were built more like military strongpoints than communal farms. I visited one of them, Negba, during a break in the fighting. The children and some of the women spent most of the time underground when the drab utilitarian buildings were destroyed during the first attack. The destruction looked pathetic, but huddled behind coils of barbed wire Negba proved more effective than the concrete forts of the Maginot Line. The defenders were literally fighting for their home, held together by inner discipline and motivated by a belief bordering on fanaticism. That said, a battalion of well-trained troops, led by good officers and supported by a few tanks, could have overwhelmed them within a few hours – even less with close-support aircraft. The Egyptian army was not well-trained, but it had many battalions available and armour and aircraft.

Looked at objectively, Israel's first war was won largely because of the lack of enthusiasm of its enemies. Their indecision and cross purposes were evident at an early meeting of the Arab League called before the partition of Palestine. King Abdullah of Jordan planned to seize the Arab part and then come to terms with the Jews. The Syrians were determined to thwart Abdullah by seizing as much as they could of northern Palestine, and Egypt, Iraq and Lebanon were cool to armed intervention. Almost until the last week before the end of the mandate, it was not certain that Palestine would be invaded. The league demanded an invasion plan only after the *Haganah* had taken Haifa and Tiberias, but the objective was not military victory. It was convinced that a show of force would persuade the major powers to intervene.

The army which fought well was Jordan's Arab Legion. With only 4500 men, but led by British officers, it seized the old city of Jerusalem, cut the Tel Aviv–Jerusalem road at Latrun and later occupied the port of Aqaba before it could be reached by an advancing Israeli column.

To recall this is not to denigrate the Israeli forces. They fought well, many magnificently, under their youthful commander, Yigael Yadin. He was a seasoned *Haganah* soldier who had fought against Arab guerrillas before partition and independence. Yadin was also an archeologist who knew the terrain better than the Arabs after years of scientific field work. At the beginning he had about 21,000 men under his command compared with the combined Arab force of about 27,500. These were not bad odds for a defending army even if the Arabs had been good troops, but in the early days he was desperately short of aircraft, tanks, armoured troop carriers and artillery. This was quickly reversed when supplies were brought in during truces organized by the UN. The Israeli forces became the best equipped army I had seen until that time, and foreign volunteers and hurriedly trained conscripts also reversed the numerical odds.

This convinced me that Israel would survive and that peace was possible after the Egyptian–Israeli armistice. It seemed inevitable given Israeli strength and determination and the apparent lack of Arab enthusiasm for the cause trumpeted by the Mufti of Jerusalem, the spiritual and nationalist leader in Palestine. I thought that Egypt, Lebanon and Syria would not attend a peace conference, but would accept the new *status quo*. Iraq was too far distant to worry about, and an understanding had long existed between Jordan and the Jewish Agency, the quasi-government of the Jewish community during the mandate. Golda Meir twice met King Abdullah before the war began, and at their first meeting she assured the king that there were no objections to Jordan annexing the Arab sector in the event of partition. When they met again in Amman a week before the birth of Israel was proclaimed – the doughty lady was disguised as an Arab peasant woman – Abdullah hoped that relations would not be severed despite the inevitable hostilities. Britain was also agreeable, and warned Jordan not to invade the Jewish sectors of the UN plan. When the two countries decided to negotiate an armistice both had reason to be more or less content. Jordan had achieved most of its objectives, including the old city of Jerusalem; Israel held 8000 square miles or a fifth more than had been allotted under the UN plan.

My cautious optimism was widely shared in Israel although religious groups regretted the loss of the old city of Jerusalem. Life in the new city was transformed; the shops had some goods to sell, the price of beer was no longer outrageous and water flowed through the taps again. I can still remember my first shower in the Salvia Hotel where foreign correspondents stayed throughout the siege because it was well supplied with food and drink by the smuggling branch of the Stern Gang. Earlier water had been strictly rationed, and there was none for baths. I went dirty until Jim Pringle, an Irish photographer working for the Associated Press, found an empty villa which like most old and substantial Arab houses had an underground tank instead of a basement. It stood on an exposed slope well within the range of Arab fire, and we had to drive to it at top speed to avoid being shot. The risk was worthwhile; the tank, which was reached through a trapdoor, was about four feet deep and deliciously cool. We swam in the dark quietly for fear of attracting a patrol.

I knew that the armistice was being negotiated by Colonel Moshe Dayan who made eleven secret visits across the line, most of them to Abdullah's winter palace at Shunah, near the Dead Sea. He was a *sabra*, that is country born, and had grown up in Daganiah *kibbutz*. He joined the *Haganah* while still in his teens, and lost an eye fighting with the British against Vichy troops in Syria during the Second World War. We first met in the northern Negev when he led a commando column modelled on the British Long Range Desert Group in the western desert. It was much better equipped than the LRDG, and Dayan was a natural commando leader. He was also a modest man; I liked and admired him.

I got to know him better when as military governor of Jerusalem he was negotiating with Abdullah. He lived with his wife, Ruth, in a fine house once the residence of the British chief justice in the Terra Sancta neighbourhood in the new city, and Pat and I were frequently invited to Ruth's 'At Homes'. Dayan, the commando leader, didn't look at home at these functions, but Ruth loved them. She was a good-looking vivacious woman who looked as if she might have come from Golders Green or Finchley. She often reminisced with Pat about London, which she loved. Her father, Zvi Schwartz, was always smartly dressed and looked and sounded like a successful member of the London bar. They were in fact a Jerusalem family who had been educated in London, but we were accepted mainly because of Ruth's friendship with Pat. They also respected *The Times*, and I became well informed about the negotiations. My reporting was cautious and I made no reference to Dayan's secret visits for fear of making them more difficult. In any case, I knew that it would not get by the censor, and instead we made couple of trips to Cyprus, then still a British colony, where I wrote background notes for the leader writers in London. Deakin was most impressed; I did not tell him that Pat's friendship with Ruth Dayan was largely responsible. Dayan could be communicative when he liked people and was politically shrewd, but I doubt that I would have been so well informed if Ruth had not invited us to her 'At Homes'.

Life was very pleasant, it was a change not to fall asleep with tracer bullets lighting up the sky. Jerusalem had a special magic, and its people were less intense and anti-British than the inhabitants of Tel Aviv. Nevertheless I was growing bored; there was not enough to report and it was frustrating not be able to visit the Arab countries. I mentioned this to Dayan one day, and he arranged for us to visit the old city. It was only for the day, but we drank pink gins with the British consul-general, ate a splendid lunch in the courtyard of an Arab restaurant, visited the holy places and returned with a dead lamb over my shoulder. This made me popular with my colleagues; food rationing in Israel was more severe than in wartime Britain. It was very decent of Dayan. No other foreign correspondent had been allowed to cross through the Mandelbaum gate except at Christmas when the UN arranged press coverage of the annual pilgrimage to Bethlehem. The division of the city was complete except for one telephone line to the consulate-general. Extraordinary in the circumstances, but nobody on either side was prepared to explain why.

I wanted to make extended visits and again Dayan agreed. I was grateful, as was Deakin. I just wanted a change of scene, but the foreign news editor wanted news from the northern Arab states which were rarely visited by our Middle East correspondent, Cyril Quilliam or rather Brigadier C.O. Quilliam. Barrington-Ward, who preferred experts to journalists, had appointed him soon after the second world war; and Quilliam undoubtedly was an expert. He had served most of his thirty years of soldiering in the Middle East on special duties, the euphemism for intelligence, and was head of the political intelligence department when he retired. He spoke Arabic and Turkish as well as good French which at that time was the preferred second language in Egypt, Lebanon and Syria. He knew everybody and apparently everything in the Arab world, but was no journalist. He preferred to write long background reports which were welcomed by the leader writers, but rarely shared his knowledge with the readers. He was also reluctant to travel from his elegant home in Zamalik, and Deakin welcomed my offer to travel far and wide throughout the Middle East with of course the exception of Egypt. I could travel through the country and frequently did, but accepted that it was Quilliam's territory.

I first met Quilliam in Beirut where the UN conciliation commission had arranged a meeting of Arab leaders to decide what was to happen to the Palestinian Arab refugees. As I recall, he stayed with the ambassador and I at a small French hotel recommended to me by Glubb Pasha, the British commander of the Arab Legion. The first evening we dined together at a very good restaurant with the boss of Tapline, the Trans-Arabian oil pipeline. He was a short and pugnacious American with stomach ulcers, who left soon after eating some kind of milk dish. We dined sumptuously, and to my surprise drank vodka between the courses although the wine was excellent. I was cautious; he was the older man, it was his territory and, I thought, probably resented my presence. He in turn was an admirable host, and regarded me as the expert journalist. I was to report the meeting, and he – here he paused – would renew acquaintance with the assembled Arab leaders. Sipping his final cognac, he offered to help whenever he could.

At first glance, Quilliam looked very much the staff officer in mufti. He was tall and slim, with a well-cut suit draped from sloping shoulders and the obligatory silk handkerchief in his left sleeve. His shoes were polished, but no more than his manners. I could imagine him reporting to General Paget, the CIC Middle East, who had recommended him to Barrington-Ward, after making the rounds of Cairo's salons where politics were the main topic of conversation. He was said to have been the centre of a web of political intelligence stretching from Damascus to Casablanca, from Baghdad to Beirut. The UN meeting had attracted political leaders from all over the region, and he was completely at home in their company. I was impressed. If he was typical of the disappearing breed of empire builders, they must have been more interesting than I had supposed.

After that first dinner Quilliam said that it was too early for bed and suggested a nightcap at the Kit Kat, a nightclub on the sea front. It was crowded with well-to-do Lebanese and other Levantines who looked vaguely sinister in black silk suits and heavy gold jewellery. Quilliam exchanged affable greetings in French, Arabic and Turkish with a number of them. Later I asked who they were, and he said traders in every known commodity, from arms to drugs. Lebanon was Egypt's main supplier of hashish, he explained, and the market for arms was immensely profitable. He added that Beirut was also expanding as an espionage centre. The French, the former colonial power, were well dug in, the Russians were increasing their 'representation' and the Americans, who were still new to the game, were showing interest.

When we were eventually seated, he chatted up the hostesses who had followed the waiter who brought the champagne. He ordered another bottle and more glasses and asked if I was interested in any of the girls; no leers or innuendo, but with the attentiveness of a good host. I was not, and they drifted away when the champagne was finished. He then ordered a couple of brandies, and half listened to a French girl singing a Piaf song.

Quilliam, as I quickly discovered, was also intrigued by me. He had been hired in Cairo, and I was the first *Times* foreign correspondent he had met. I was also the first man he had met from Israel, and he quickly forgot the singer as we discussed my experiences. He was of course an Arabist, but not an anti-Zionist. Palestine had been one of his major concerns for many years, and he clearly knew most of the Israeli leaders. However, he was worried about Britain's position in the Middle East. He was convinced that it was vulnerable; not because of rising Arab nationalism, with which he was in sympathy, but because Britain was seen to have let down the Arabs. He also believed that Israel was determined to get Britain out of the region. I answered his questions honestly but with caution. For reasons I did not understand, the Israelis had given me permission to cross the line and I did not want to betray their trust. Not that I had military secrets to divulge, but I wanted to play fair if only because I wanted to cross the line again.

That first visit to Beirut was an eye-opener. The Israelis were determined not to permit Palestinian refugees to return to their villages, which was the main reason why peace negotiations with Jordan did not get very far, and I had assumed that sooner or later they would be resettled in Arab countries. It had seemed the obvious solution in Israel, but the Arab politicians I met in Beirut said that the refugees would stay in the camps until they could go back to their homes. There would be no resettlement or negotiations with Israel. They were unanimous in their declarations of intent as they sat in the foyer of the St George Hotel fuddling their beads. It was an appalling prospect.

I was doubly appalled when I visited my first refugee camp a few days later. It was near Jericho, and Glubb Pasha and I drove down from Amman in a Rolls-Royce – another first. He wore a red and khaki forage cap squarely on the top of his head, and with his blue eyes and almost non-existent chin looked like an elderly curate playing soldiers. He was an uncomplicated man, simple in the best sense of the word, who shared an affinity with Arabs among whom he had spent his adult life. He was unsentimental about them, knowing their strengths and weaknesses. I gathered after spending several hours in his company that he was as fatalistic as the refugees we met. Perhaps that was a refined kind of propaganda, but I doubted it when we moved slowly between the primitive huts stopping frequently to talk with small groups. His translation was peremptory, and I remembered that he had more sympathy for the beduin than town dwellers and villagers. I was surprised by their physical neatness and cleanliness, and saddened by their hopelessness. There was no anger, only a numbness. Some of them seemed unable to comprehend that Britain no longer governed Palestine, and presumably mistaking me for a colonial district officer pleaded for help. I remembered those refugees in the Punjab, kneeling in the dust and touching my shoes. I cursed my fate; I seemed destined to report the nasty residue of a departing empire, and as in India there was nothing I could do beyond that. The Palestinians were more unfortunate. At least in India and Pakistan some of the refugees were settled on land abandoned by other refugees, but there was nowhere for the Palestinians to go. The Israelis, for cruel but understandable reasons, did not want them, and the Arabs were determined to use them as bargaining counters. Most of them were doomed to spend years in camps.

During another trip to Cyprus I wrote again to Deakin giving him details of conversations with Israeli ministers and officials and King Abdullah which I had been unable to report even indirectly because of censorship. I said that secret Israeli–Jordanian talks would fail, that while Israel had offered to compensate the refugees they intended to deduct the cost of the war from any agreed sum. In theory, the refugees could finish up owing Israel a great deal of money. I also warned that Britain should not guarantee the existing boundary between the two countries because Israel would advance to the Jordan river within a few years. It took a little longer, I was in the United States when Israel seized the West Bank, but the relative accuracy of my forecast gave me no pleasure.

By courtesy of the Israelis, I spent a great deal of time in Jordan, Syria, Lebanon, Iraq and Sudan. I also wandered farther afield to Ethiopia and Eritrea, then a former Italian colony administered by Britain. I enjoyed it immensely, as did Pat who frequently travelled with me. It was a time, as Evelyn Waugh once said, when the going was good. Tourists were rare, and the Europeans and Americans we met were largely diplomats, oil men, archeologists, scholars and the occasional spook, as intelligence men were known among the cognoscenti. Apart from Beirut and Damascus, good hotels were few but some had charm. I remember a delightful one in Aleppo, small with a shaded terrace and run by a French-trained Syrian family. Aleppo was also said to have the best belly dancers in the Middle East. The Grand hotel in Khartoum had a splendid view of the Nile, but Scotch was rationed and groundnut soup was served every day. In Amman we stayed with an Arab Legion colonel who had been in my regiment during the war. His old Arab house was wonderfully cool in summer and like an icebox in winter. The only warm place was the bathroom where water was heated in a wood-burning stove fed from the outside.

We first travelled with passports stamped with Israeli visas. A Lebanese consul burst into tears when he saw them but nevertheless issued us with visas. When driving into Syria from Jordan it was customary for the driver to take the passports into the frontier post where they were stamped in return for a bribe of five Syrian pounds. On one occasion our cab driver, a very intelligent Armenian whom we always tried to hire, returned grinning from the post saying that he had to double the bribe because of the Israeli visas. Otherwise we travelled without hindrance, but Glubb Pasha eventually suggested that we should have second passports, presumably because he did not want attention drawn to our frequent crossings. The next time we went through the Mandelbaum gate the Jordanian immigration official, a woman, handed us two new passports issued by the British consulate-general. We added our signatures and sallied forth.

It was just as well when I flew into Damascus from Beirut to cover a *coup d'état*. The story was easy to cover because of the cooperation of the new regime which wanted to demonstrate its devotion to democracy. The next day was spent interviewing the new president, and only then did I remember that *The Times* had a local correspondent in the city, a Colonel Stirling who had fought with T.E. Lawrence in the desert and had led an adventurous life, including organizing the Albanian gendarmerie for King Zog. I called on him in his lovely old Arab house just outside the city walls, and found him reading *The Times*. He was a military looking man of great presence, and because of my years in the army I instinctively stood to attention. He gazed at me with distaste, as so many other colonels had done in the past, and pointed imperiously at my story about the coup which led the paper. We were anonymous in those days, and the byline was 'From Our Special Correspondent'. Was I the author? I nodded, and he said that everybody in Damascus would think that he wrote it. Most embarrassing, he added.

It was a strange thing to say, but I thought no more of it and after lunch we drove up to Aleppo to sound out opinion on the coup. We came slowly back via Latakia, Hams and Homs, and arrived back in Damascus after being away for nearly a week. The next day was full of surprises. Hearing a babble of voices outside while I was shaving, I opened the bathroom window and saw that five or six men were being hanged in the square. Another demonstration of the new regime's devotion to democracy, I said. We went thoughtfully down to breakfast, and glancing through the local French-language papers found excited accounts of the Syrian visit of Britain's master spy in the Middle East. He was identified as *The Times* correspondent who had been visiting Aleppo and other towns to rig the forthcoming elections. No

117

wonder the concierge had eyed me with unusual respect when he handed me the papers.

We thought it was very funny, but in Damascus Colonel Stirling was known as *The Times* correspondent. That evening, three men went to his house and told the servant that they had messages from the Gezira, a desert area, for the colonel. They were shown upstairs, where one of them shot the colonel at almost point blank range. Stirling was wounded five times, but survived. The assassins escaped into the souks of the city, and no more was heard of them. There was a great fuss. King Zog, who lived in Portugal after being deposed, sent his bodyguards to look after Mrs Stirling while he was in hospital. I had to report the assassination attempt, but this time had no cooperation. The British legation did not want anything to do with me, and I had the impression that the minister believed I really was an MI6 man and resented my presence in his territory. I was told to report to the *Serai*, the government offices, where my passport was demanded and scrutinized by two officers of the security service. I wondered if they had had anything to do with the public hangings, and thanked my lucky star that I had taken Glubb's advice and had a passport without an Israeli visa. They asked when I was planning to leave the country, and seemed relieved when told that I had ordered a car for the morrow. We drove to Amman and then to Jerusalem, and the Salvia seemed like home. We had a second martini to celebrate.

Our forays into Arabia were invariably newsworthy, and the office seemed grateful. My salary was raised to £900 a year and the herograms arrived fairly frequently. I also felt that I was being indulged. Not all my journeys were made in search of hard news; occasionally I just wanted to see places I had read about, such as Petra, and if Deakin complained it rarely read like a rebuke. For instance, in Addis Ababa I received a letter from him thanking me for my messages from Eritrea. He also referred to my suggestion that I should visit Aden on my way back to Israel:

As to Aden, it cannot be said that people here have so little to read about in the paper that they wait impatiently for news from southern Arabia, but I leave the length of your Aden stay to your discretion.

Equally typical of *The Times* of that period was the response to 'my discovery' of the Dead Sea Scrolls. Pat and I were having lunch in Jerusalem one Friday and an Israeli acquaintance came to the table to help finish the wine. He asked if I had heard of the scrolls, which he said were of immense antiquity and historical importance. They were found just before the siege in a cave above the Dead Sea by beduin, who sold them to Dr Sukenik of the Hebrew University and the Archbishop Samuel, Metropolitan of the Syrian Orthodox Church, in the old city. Sukenik had worked on them throughout the siege, and was preparing to publish his findings.

I called on Sukenik that afternoon. He spoke Hebrew, German and imperfect English, and we conversed in a mixture of German and English. It was difficult because I knew nothing about the subject under discussion, but slowly and painfully I was persuaded that the scrolls might be the find of the century. Recalling that nothing was supposed to happen during the sabbath, I filed a tentative 500-word story and a service message asking if they were interested. Within the hour the answer came marked urgent. The scrolls were indeed the find of the century, and I was to drop everything until I had the complete story. I returned to Sukenik, and topped up the story for the night. The next morning I got in touch with the Assyrian bishop at St James', who was handling the archbishop's share of the scrolls. The Mandelbaum Gate was closed because of the sabbath. I had to interview him by telephone, and was exhausted after more than three hours of questions and answers, but filed everything I had over the weekend. I was also given a photograph of a fragment of scroll by Sukenik, and to its everlasting shame the paper published it upside down. I cursed – could nobody read Amharic in PHS? – but it was my greatest scoop although the story was more than 2000 years old.

During my two years in the Middle East I learned a great deal about *The Times*, including the heavy burden of its past. Barrington-Ward had decided on a new beginning, but it was not easy. For instance, Brigadier Quilliam, Colonel Stirling and Brigadier Sanford, our Addis Ababa stringer, were survivors of its earlier imperial policy. They were empire men, members of an extraordinary network which had once encompassed the world. They were not spies in the accepted sense, but they had believed in and were still willing to promote or defend Britain's imperial role. I was to meet them in other parts of the world, including countries such as Thailand which had never been part of the empire. There was an honorary consul in Chiang Mai although British interests as normally understood were almost non-existent. He was a former member of the old China consular service, and was in Chiang Mai to watch movements between China, Burma and Laos. I suspect that he would willingly have become a stringer if asked.

They seemed to be thick on the ground in the Middle East. No doubt such men were useful for earlier editors, especially Geoffrey Dawson who attached more importance to the empire than to European security, but they bothered me. We no longer needed them, and I felt that they could damage the paper because their priorities were no longer ours. I said as much to Deakin in a letter from Beirut after the attempt on Stirling's life. It had never been properly explained, and as far as I knew the legation in Damascus did not try to investigate. I probably triggered it inadvertently but the gunmen, or the people they were working for, must have had some reason to want to kill him. I thought that Stirling knew more than he cared to admit, and went on:

> It might be part of a rather stupid, unnecessary and certainly dangerous unofficial struggle being waged between certain Frenchmen and Englishmen in these parts. There are too many would-be successors to Lawrence; too much unnecessary bitterness between the two groups of nationals ...

Deakin did not need much convincing. He was a professional journalist, and did not want the paper involved in such machinations. There had been enough of that in the past, as he told me later when I was passing through London. Flora Shaw, the first woman correspondent to be employed by the paper, and its first colonial editor, was deeply involved in the Jameson raid into the Transvaal in 1896. It was part of a larger plan, but the chief conspirators had different objectives. Those in Johannesburg wanted to change the Transvaal government but remain in the Boer republic. Cecil Rhodes dreamed of a federal union in southern Africa dominated by the British. Joseph Chamberlain, the colonial secretary, was at least kept informed. Shaw admired and supported Rhodes, and was at the centre of the conspiracy, acting as a link between the conspirators and goading them on. It was hardly in the best traditions of the paper, but being a good journalist she insisted that the raid must not take place on a Saturday. She did not want *The Times* scooped by the Sunday papers.

The raid was a fiasco – Jameson's men had hangovers after drinking too much champagne the night before – but Shaw escaped censure at the official enquiry. She was a formidable woman, and gave a spirited performance when she testified. Dawson told Morison, the paper's historian, many years later that Chamberlain also helped. As assistant private secretary to the colonial secretary in 1901, Dawson learned what had happened behind the scenes. 'There was a great deal of discussion at the time about the "damping down" of the commission of enquiry,' he wrote. Chamberlain was primarily concerned in saving his own skin, but *The Times* was saved from public disgrace.

This is not to suggest that Quilliam played some kind of double role. He was appointed because he knew the Middle East better than any journalist. He was also an honourable man, but after a lifetime of intelligence work his approach was not that of the professional foreign correspondent. He retired to Canada soon after I left the Middle East, the last of the gentleman amateurs who had served the paper during its imperial period. One of them, James David Bourchier, a southern Irishman, old Etonian and naturally a classical scholar, became a Bulgarian national hero. Obviously a born *Times* man, it was probably agreed at the time, although he was born stone deaf; apparently that was not regarded as in insuperable handicap. The Official History gleefully notes that King Ferdinand of Bulgaria shouted selected state secrets into Bourchier's tympanum. It goes on:

Bourchier's deafness gradually became a feature of Balkan political life, an obstacle to get over, not a reason for shunning him. A diplomat was wont to declare that whenever a great noise was heard in the Balkans it was either Bourchier telling a great secret to a prime minister, or a prime minister telling a great secret to Bourchier.

Bourchier's original interest in the Balkans derived from his classical scholarship. Again quoting the history, he was equally familiar with ancient Greece and medieval Byzantium, and resentful of the blight which five centuries of Turkish rule had brought upon the lands between the Euxine and the Aegean. He sympathized warmly with the struggles of the Balkan peoples, especially of the Bulgars and Macedonian Greeks, for complete freedom from Ottoman overlordship. He became the confidant of Balkan kings and nationalist leaders, but unlike Quilliam he was not appointed Balkan correspondent because of his expertise. He just drifted into the job when consulting an aurist in Vienna where he met *The Times* correspondent, Brinsley Richards, a fellow Etonian. Merely on the strength of the old school tie, Richards sent him on a trial mission to Bulgaria and Rumania. Bourchier lived hard, often having to sleep in the mountains in a bug-and-mosquito-proof sleeping bag which he had designed. One of his many scoops was the Bulgarian massacres, which caused a diplomatic crisis throughout Europe, and thereafter he abandoned the sleeping bag for more diplomatic accoutrements.

Bourchier helped to organize the Balkan alliance against Turkey, and actually conducted negotiations between Bulgaria and Greece. For a time he successfully combined the roles of *Times* correspondent and founding father of independent Bulgaria, but it could not last. He was invariably late with his copy, and he over-filed. One message from Crete infuriated the manager who informed him that:

> An average copy of *The Times* contains about 160,000 words, and if you send us 1400 words on Crete you are proposing to take up 1/115th of our space for that insignificant island, whose entire population is only 1/136th of even the British Isles and 1/540th of the British Empire.... These mathematical calculations will, I know, be insuperably difficult to your Cambridge mind, but the net result may be intelligible – we really must have shorter telegrams.

On another occasion, when Bourchier sent an over-long and glowing report from Greece, he was again rebuked by the manager who wrote, 'I am tempted to say that if you cannot be laconic you can at least avoid being Ionic.'

Bourchier's love of Bulgaria eventually affected his reporting, which could not be countenanced. Apart from the ethics of journalism, the Balkan wars were a major European upheaval involving Germany, Russia, France and Britain, and led, if only indirectly, to the first world war. He was replaced, and thereafter nothing more was heard from Bulgaria's national hero.

His memory was, however, nurtured by the romantic in Printing House Square. A full-length portrait of him in Bulgarian national dress had a place of honour in the boardroom, and when deputy editor I was obliged from time to time to retell his story for distinguished guests who came to lunch or dinner. Despite the austere image the paper presented to the world, it was in fact permeated by this curious romanticism. Dawson ignored the European correspondents during the appeasement period, but the great foreign correspondents were remembered as good regiments remember their heroes. Christopher Lumby was remembered for driving with Italian resistance fighters 200 miles to report the murder of Mussolini and his mistress; James Morris for reporting the ascent of Everest in time for the coronation, and many others were also remembered. Their portraits did not hang in the boardroom, but they were part of the living history of the paper. It was probable that Deakin indulged me in the Middle East because he was romantically inclined. No doubt his colleagues in London failed to see the romantic behind the composed face and slight pomposities, but in his own way he brought me and other young correspondents along, to use his phrase, before he was finally embittered.

My wanderings continued into 1950 when the price of newsprint was increased and economies had to be made. Travel was curtailed to the irreducible minimum. It was doubly painful for me; apart from my wanderlust, my effectiveness as a correspondent was also reduced. Unlike most of my colleagues, I was not stationed in a capital which generated a more or less constant flow of news. Israel remained fascinating, but at that time did not warrant a staff correspondent. I wrote as much to Deakin, who told me to be patient. Louis Hinrichs, the New York correspondent, was due to retire and would be replaced by another correspondent who I would replace. Deakin was reticent as always, but said enough to suggest that I would soon be returning to India. I welcomed the prospect, but the best-laid plans could go awry on *The Times* for the most improbable reasons. In this instance, the paper could not bring itself to ask Hinrichs to retire although he had just celebrated his seventieth birthday. He was still in the New York office, writing a weekly column on Wall Street, when I was transferred to the United States ten years later.

I thought I could see why when we got to know each other. Hinrichs was a very good journalist, but equally important he was an old-fashioned New England gentleman, which meant that he was more civilized than most English gentlemen. It was difficult to explain why. Somebody said that I had read too much Henry James, but well-educated New Englanders of his generation had most of the attributes once associated with gentlemanliness. Hinrichs was tall and elegant, with a presence all the more impressive because of his courtesy and modesty. The son of well-to-do parents, he attended private schools and Harvard, did a grand tour of the Far East after graduation, and then settled in New York. His interests were artistic, but he played the stock market and lost his money in the crash which followed the San Francisco earthquake. It did not shake his equanimity. He heard the news while lunching in one of the better restaurants near Wall Street but finished his cigar and brandy in his usual leisurely manner. During the afternoon, and in good time for the cocktail hour at the Harvard club, he got a job as a financial journalist on one of the New York papers, and joined *The Times* in 1916. According to Claud Cockburn, the black friars were afraid of Hinrichs:

The Times, in fact, liked its correspondents to be familiar with history, archeology, the classics, and the higher reaches of diplomatic society in whichever capital they happened to be established, but it was bothered by people who knew too much about money and economics and even tended to regard these subjects as of greater importance than the personal relationship existing between a cabinet minister, member of political party A, and a politician, member of political party B. The idea that they had a correspondent who really understood Wall Street and positively regarded Wall Street and its problems as essential in the affairs of the world, was to *The Times* awe-inspiring. Hinrichs, in fact, was to them a man from Mars.

The fear or awe was still apparent in 1950 when it was decided that Hinrichs would have to accept the custom and practice of the paper and retire. It was five years overdue, but neither the editor nor foreign news editor was willing to make the first move. The proprietor, who was about to make one of his periodic trips to the United States, was prevailed upon to break the news. Alas, for all his wealth Astor was a shy man. He lost his nerve, and Hinrichs remained as chief correspondent in New York for two more years and thereafter continued to write his weekly Wall Street column until he died. The Official History, which does not touch on the background, merely says that Hinrichs went on writing until he was 87, 'achieving the firmest of his ambitions, which was never to stop being a working journalist'.

Amen to that, but in 1950 I was left high and dry in the Middle East with only half a job. Pat has also gone home to have our first baby; it was unsettling, but at least I had time to take stock. One evening I dined with a senior Israeli official who I knew well and asked him why I had been allowed to make to many visits to the Arab countries. He was an Oxford man with a sense of humour, and lighting yet another locally made Nelson cigarette – British influence had not been totally eradicated – said that it was a long story. He went on to say something like this.

It appeared that Moshe Dayan's decision to let me cross the line in Jerusalem had surprised a number of people in the government, but somebody remembered my sympathetic handling of the interview with the president after the RAF planes had been shot down. My subsequent cautious reporting of the secret negotiations between Dayan and King Abdullah suggested that I could be both trusted and useful. Propaganda was an essential weapon in Israel's armoury, but there were more than enough friendly committed correspondents in Tel Aviv. Most of the American correspondents could be trusted to report favourably, which was important for fund raising, but a more rounded view of Israel and the Middle East was no less important for Israel's friends abroad. I had worried them from time to time; the Stirling affair, my coverage of Aqaba and my friends in the Arab Legion were obvious examples. Some suspicion about my true role in the Middle East had been aroused, but was dissipated when it became clear that I was only interested in news.

I was fascinated by his explanation; I knew that there had to be an ulterior motive for Israeli cooperation, but inevitably asked: 'Why me?' Come, come, he said, or words to that effect. 'It ought to be obvious. You are the correspondent of *The Times*.'

I must have been simple-minded; it had not occurred to me that some Israelis were suspicious of my visits to the Arab Legion, perhaps because it was almost home from home after my fairly recent service in the army. Many of its officers were seconded from the regular British army or were former officers on contract to the legion. They were not mercenaries. A few could not stomach British postwar austerity and had joined for adventure and a tax-free income. For others the desert exerted the powerful attraction it had had for many Englishmen since Doughty wrote *Arabia Deserta*. The regulars on secondment sought experience and responsibility above their rank which could be useful when they returned to their regiments. Those I met were not politically motivated. They showed a polite interest in Israel, but for most of them it was an impersonal adversary who they were paid to fight or not fight according to orders from Glubb Pasha or presumably London. Only once did I see one of them angered. A visiting American correspondent joined me and my host at a bar in an Amman hotel; he worked for a newspaper which was uncritically pro-Israel, and baited my companion inferring that he was an anti-Semite. Rocky, as he was known to his friends, was so provoked that the whisky glass in his clenched hand splintered. Blood and whisky dripped to the floor, and the American's face paled. He obviously expected a fight, but instead Rocky wiped his hand on the wall to shed some of the glass splinters, and said: 'You were saying, Mr ...'

As far as I could see they were typical British officers who enjoyed playing soldiers, obeyed orders and never discussed politics or women in the mess. They could not have been more different from their Israeli opposite numbers. I can remember having lunch in Jerusalem with one of Dayan's battalion commanders. He was a first-class soldier and looked it, but over the inevitable schnitzel talked like the philosophy don he hoped to become after the war. He was also an amateur archeologist, as I was fast becoming, and he questioned me closely about Jordan's department of antiquities. He was relieved to hear that it was in capable British hands.

Later that day I crossed into Jordan, and spent the first night at the legion's field headquarters in Ramallah. I was frozen after the night ride in an open jeep, and ran to the blacked-out building as soon as the vehicle stopped. As I crossed the threshold a hand came from behind the door proffering a large whisky. Down it quickly, urged the unseen benefactor. Champers sharp at seven. It was very good champagne, much better than the dinner which followed. Duty-free liquor was obviously one of the advantages of service with the legion. I was stoically prepared for an evening of drink and jollity until I was introduced to Laish Pasha, the legion's field commander. He looked the usual red-faced brigadier, which made the subsequent conversation doubly surprising.

He asked me if I was planning to emigrate; Britain was finished and could offer few opportunities for bright young men. I should go to America. He did not attack the Labour government or regret the passing of empire. Both were accepted as inevitable, but he argued that Britain was incapable of adjusting to her new circumstances. It would continue to decline because the politicians, the civil and military services and press would not be able to shake off imperial attitudes. We were still behaving as if we were a great power although we had to get out of Greece and were pushed out of Palestine. We should pull out of the big power game.

Laish gestured to the group standing by the fireplace, who began to sing the round song about the harlot of Jerusalem. They certainly did not think that, like the legions during the decline and fall of the Roman Empire, the time had come to pull back the British legions from the glacis of a crumbling empire. They probably looked forward to tours of duty in Malaya and Hong Kong, the Canal Zone and the West Indies, and Africa and Germany until retirement. I went thoughtfully to bed, thinking that Laish, a relatively obscure officer serving in a small foreign army, was the first Briton I had met who perceived the realities of the postwar world. It was to be a long time before I met another. The diplomats still assumed big-power status for Britain. Some took pride in what was seen as our graceful withdrawal from empire, but could not see, or would not admit, the consequences. They were not alone. Much later, in Washington in 1964, Harold Wilson was to insist that we were still a world power, and was not amused when I said that we should stop kidding ourselves. That was in the distant future. In Ramallah that night I quickly fell asleep, and was awakened by an orderly with a silver tankard of black velvet. I had expected tea, but even a declining empire had its moments.

Like Cyprus, where Pat and I used to spend an occasional long weekend to get away from the Israelis and Arabs, the legion was a useful antidote to the utter earnestness of Israel.

As for the Aqaba story, I was surprised that it had raised Israeli doubts as to my integrity. I could see why the Stirling affair had suggested that I was also an intelligence agent, but not Aqaba. I was in Tel Aviv when I heard that the Israelis were planning to seize the port at the head of the Gulf of Aqaba. It could provide direct access to the southern hemisphere denied to Israel by the closing of the Suez canal to its ships, and was therefore a military prize of great importance. The information available was hazy, it came to me by way of the mysterious process of osmosis which can precede newsworthy events, but I knew that foreign correspondents would not be allowed to accompany the expedition. I therefore took a cab to Jerusalem, crossed through the Mandelbaum gate and cadged a ride to Amman. Glubb already knew of Israel's intentions, presumably from British headquarters in the Canal Zone where troops were already embarking to secure the port. The danger was that the Israeli forces, moving along internal lines of communication, might arrive first and legion reinforcements were on the way. I was told to be at the railway station by midnight if I wanted to join them.

It sounded very promising, and I looked forward to travelling on the railway which T.E. Lawrence had repeatedly attacked during the first world war. He and the Arab tribes had been so successful that the line went only as far as Ras en Naqb on the Naqb Ashtar escarpment, but it still gave the legion an advantage over the Israelis travelling on desert tracks.

There was one problem; I had checked into the Philadelphia Hotel and was sharing a room – not uncommon in those days – with Colin Reid of the *Daily Telegraph*, who was on a swing from his Beirut base. He was a friend from the India days, but that did not warrant my sharing a good story with him. I faced the remainder of the evening with trepidation. We dined together at the Amman club, and Colin suggested a late movie. I declined, and we went to the hotel bar for a nightcap where Colin reminisced about India. The clock above the bar ticked on, and I became restive. I refused a third whisky, and Colin admitted that it was getting late. He spent a long time in the bathroom, and I took off my shirt and shoes and got into bed. He bade me goodnight at about eleven, and soon began to snore. Cautiously I got up and dressed, packed my musette bag and crept out of the room. A legion officer was waiting impatiently at the station, and without further ado we were soon hurtling south while dear Colin snored on at the Filthydelphia, as the hotel was known to correspondents before it was rebuilt.

We travelled in a rail car powered by a petrol engine. It was fast but unheated; and I gratefully accepted a red-and-white legion headdress and wound it about my face against the desert cold. At Ras en Naqb we transferred to an army truck and continued south without lights. Some miles from Aqaba we spotted on our right the Israeli column, moving with blazing headlights. Its commander presumably thought that he had no opposition, or was in a hurry. The legion officer anticipated a fight, and ordered the men in the back of the truck to blacken their faces. He shared a tin of boot polish with me, and I smeared the stuff on my face wondering what would happen if there was a fight and I was captured by the Israelis.

Fortunately we were moving faster along a well-travelled track, and reached Aqaba as dawn was breaking. It looked peaceful enough despite the hurried preparations for its defence, and we drove to the little fort by the sea and drank hot tea laced with rum. I was starting on my second mug when a wireless operator came in and announced that the British had arrived. We went down to the beach, and they were already coming ashore from tank landing craft. I approached the command group, and introduced myself to the brigadier as Louis Heren of *The Times*. He looked at me suspiciously, and no wonder. I was wearing the legion headdress and an old American army field jacket, and my face was still blackened. I produced my press pass, but alas it was the wrong one, the Israeli and not the Jordanian pass. His orderly quickly unslung his rifle and the others closed in. I seemed forever destined to be mistaken for a spy, but fortunately a legion officer identified me and all was forgiven. I filed my story, and finally relaxed after receipt of the final take was acknowledged by the telegraph office in Amman. I was dirty, tired and hungry, and spying a British frigate anchored offshore cadged a ride. She was the *Magpie*, and the number one was friendly. He lent me shorts and a shirt after I had showered, and after breakfast we sat aft sipping pink gins and watched the arrival of the Israeli column at a beach which is now the port of Elath. I never did find out whether it would have seized Aqaba if the British had not arrived first, but it was a good story. I was also told afterwards that the number one was Lieutenant Philip Mountbatten.

There were other forays. At the suggestion of Glubb, I spent five or six days with a Beduin tribe grazing its camels near the Saudi Arabian frontier. It sounded romantic, the old sheikh had fought with Lawrence and we were to accompany the Desert Patrol, which keeps the peace in the frontier area, but it actually snowed one night and teetotal Beduin were not ideal companions for long winter evenings.

Attended by a legion officer wearing the sheepskin-lined scarlet cloak of the patrol, I flew south in a de Havilland Rapide and landed on the desert where a jeep was waiting. We drove for miles across grazing grounds where the grass was so thin that it could not be seen except at ground level. This explained why the black tents of the tribe were scattered over a vast area, and we reached the sheikh's tent after dark and just as snow was falling. We both needed a large whisky, but knew that only coffee and tea would be offered in the *majlis* tent, a kind of sitting room for male members of the sheikh's family. They sat cross-legged round a small fire of camel thorn, and after a ceremonious welcome a bare-foot boy served coffee from two hook-spouted pots.

The Bedu were small men with soft women's hands – only the women, who we never saw, worked – and their eyes were alive with curiosity. No wonder. In that empty desert they must have exhausted the possibilities of conversation long ago, and we were fresh faces from the outside world. The conversation was not enthralling although something might have been lost in translation. Many of the tribe's young men were in the legion but there was no reference to the recent war. They just made small talk, which went on and on until they withdrew for the night. Thankfully I had a slow snort of whisky, and wrapped in one of those marvellous scarlet cloaks fell asleep by the fire.

The remaining evenings were a repetition of the first, except one night we had a feast of mutton, rice and unleavened bread. I swallowed one of the sheep's eyeballs as desert courtesy apparently required. The greasy food kept out the cold, but I was uneasily aware of unseen guests at the feast. Only the tribal elders participated, and outside the tent a fairly constant whispering indicated that a group of lesser mortals had gathered. At first I thought that they had been attracted by the strangers in their midst, but when the remains of the feast were taken away their voices rose to shouts and through the tent opening I saw some bare-foot youngsters scrabbling for bits of meat.

The days were much better when we accompanied the Desert Patrol on their camels. I was invited to ride one, but the swaying movement of the so-called ship of the desert made me slightly sick and the wooden saddle felt too precarious. Thereafter I tagged behind in the jeep feeling rather foolish, but enjoying the immensity of the desert and the coldly brilliant sky above. The patrol was originally organized by Glubb to police the tribes migrating across the frontier in search of grazing; it fathered the legion but still performed essential duties. The frontier area would have been less peaceful without it, and of course it kept alive the myth that the Beduin were the noble savages of the Arab world; a fighting people more concerned about dignity and honour than the crass materialism of the settled areas.

Presumably this was why Glubb, the English romantic, had organized the excursion, but the few days I spent in the desert did not convince me. Perhaps myth is too derogatory; even allowing for Lawrence's romancing in *Seven Pillars* they did fight magnificently under his leadership. I could not but admire their physical toughness, but they played little or no part in the flowering of Arab culture which contributed so much to world civilization before collapsing into religious obscurantism. Nor could I see the point of living in the desert herding a few camels, and my last night in the desert left me wondering how they survived.

After leaving the tribe we drove to a legion fort where the officer who had been my guide and interpreter was to remain. He explained that the Bedu preferred to travel by night, and after dinner I was to be driven to Ma'an where a plane would collect me. I was assured that I would enjoy the drive; it would be cold but the immensity of the desert could best be appreciated at night. I suppose that was one way of putting it. The moonlight was very thin, and we soon lost our way. We then followed the accepted desert practice of driving in ever-increasing circles until we found the track, which I was told later was first made by Lawrence's armoured cars. The driver paused for a moment, and then turned right. I looked up at the sky, located the north star and realized that we were driving in the wrong direction. At the speed we were travelling we would soon fall into the Wadi as Sirhan across the Saudi frontier.

I was in a quandary. How could I, a cockney, tell the driver, a true son of the desert, that he was driving in the wrong direction; but I was also cold and tired, and after taking another look at the north star above our port beam, I told the driver to stop. He probably thought I wanted a pee, and stopped willingly enough. He was a sergeant, and spoke a little English, and when I told him to turn round he became rebellious. I was apologetic, but pointed to the north star and said that Ma'an had to be behind us. He was not persuaded, and eventually, and ashamedly, I had to play the role of the colonial master. Turn the bloody thing round, I said in a hard voice. He shot me a look of distilled hatred, but obeyed. We did not speak for some hours, and when dawn broke I was beginning to wonder if I had mistaken the north star. Then we breasted a low rise, and there was the town. He dropped me at the Ma'an hotel, and drove off with a muttered *salaam aleikum*, and I went into the hotel and ordered a large cold beer, a hot bath and breakfast in that order.

The worst was yet to come. The DH Rapide arrived on time, and after another beer with the pilot we took off and headed for Amman. The English pilot was amiably chatty and laughed at my account of the night's journey. He explained that the Beduin normally followed the grazing and took their bearings from landmarks as he was following the railway. As he said that the rails disappeared as did the clear sky above. We had flown into a sandstorm, or *khamsin*. Not to worry, he said, I have the compass bearing. We'll soon be out of this. We were not, and after a while he lost altitude to look for a landmark. Only the desert floor emerged, and we zoomed up to about 500 feet. We did this again and again, and the third time the altimeter registered zero and there was still nothing to be seen. We dropped a few more feet with the altimeter needle swinging against the stop, and I noticed that the pilot was sweating. Not to worry, he repeated again without conviction, and again put the nose of the plane down. I began to say 'Hail Marys', a nervous habit of mine when perturbed, and then suddenly we were flying in clear if overcast air. Christ, he said, we're over the Dead Sea and below sea level.

He laughed, again unconvincingly, and passed a flask to me. Have a swig while I find out where we are.

The whisky tasted like nectar as we followed the Jordanian shore and gradually gained height. The air became murky again as we reached sea level, and the whisky was no longer delectable. Then the plane swerved to the right, and as we completed the 90 degree turn I spotted the Jericho–Amman road on my left. This we followed, twisting and turning with the road as it wound up to the Amman plateau. It was exciting, I suppose; the sandstorm became thicker as we gained altitude which meant that we had to fly as close to the ground as possible. When we reached the plateau the *khamsin* was almost as dense as an old London fog, but the pilot was over home ground. Nevertheless, when the airport was sighted he flew in for the landing without asking permission. We grinned at each other in relief, and he reached for the flask and drained it. That was rather hairy, he said.

I supposed that it was, but not nearly as hairy as a flight aboard a UN plane with the American photographer, Bob Capa, a British international civil servant and 2000 gallons of industrial alcohol in four-gallon, non-returnable cans. We were bound for Gaza, but had to fly by way of Ramallah which had a short airfield at the foot of a rock-strewn hill. The young American pilot, wearing a red jockey cap and a cigar, had previously flown freight to Berlin during the blockade, and apparently thought that he was landing the DC3 at Tempelhof. Capa and I instinctively knew that he could not stop in time, and as the plane ploughed up the rocky hill, losing its under-carriage and propellers, we opened the door and did forward rolls to safety – Capa with his cameras clutched to his belly and me with my typewriter. Miraculously the plane and its load of highly inflammable alcohol did not catch fire and rather shamefacedly we sauntered back. The first to emerge from the wreckage was the pilot with the cigar still clenched between his teeth, and then the civil servant. He brushed industrial alcohol from his moustache, muttered, 'Bloody bad show', and stalked off in the general direction of Jerusalem.

The crash was reported on Israeli radio, and when I got back to the hotel in Tel Aviv Pat was sitting on the verandah wet-eyed, and reading the *Palestine Post* upside down. The maid, an Israeli of German origin, was cleaning the room and rather inhibited our fond reunion after my return from the dead. Never at a loss, Pat asked the maid to fetch me a dry martini, and the girl, with whom I normally conversed in German because she had no English, hurried away and brought back three martinis. It was a suitable celebration.

7

More Wars

My Middle East tour came to an abrupt end when our first baby died at birth. I had planned to be home for the event, but another *coup d'état* in Damascus delayed my departure, and I was having a farewell drink with friends when the telegram arrived. This made it doubly worse, but I got back to London before Pat left the hospital.

A few days later Ian Morrison, our war correspondent in Korea, was killed in the early weeks of the war when his jeep went up on a mine. No less appalling, an old friend, Colonel Unni Nayar of the Indian army, was also killed. I had known Nayar during the war and my recent stint in India, and we had been very close. He and his wife were passing through London when I was married, and he wanted to be best man. The priest protested because he was a Hindu, but the colonel could not be denied. He stood at the altar in full regimentals as a kind of honorary best man, and got the priest drunk at the wedding breakfast.

We heard the news from the BBC, and neither of us said very much. Then Pat broke into my reverie, and speaking matter-of-factly supposed that I wanted to replace Morrison. I only protested half-heartedly. In retrospect, this seems surprising, even callous on my part; but we had grown up during the war and were accustomed to sudden departures and long absences. I was also a foreign correspondent, and Pat understood and accepted the consequences. The next day I received a hand-written letter from the editor. It read:

My Dear Heren,

The tragic death of Ian Morrison leaves us in need of a Far East correspondent. We also need, urgently, a war correspondent in Korea. Would you be disposed to take either of these posts?

Yours sincerely
W.F. Casey.

I thought about that letter some weeks later as I sipped whisky from an American canteen cup in a Korean schoolhouse which had become a temporary press camp. I was tired, dirty and fed up. It was my third war since the big one, we – that is the UN forces – were still retreating and communications were almost non-existent. Typical, I thought. Too damned nice to make it easy by ordering me to Korea.

The paper's decision-making process, if that is the appropriate term, was even curiouser. I had phoned Casey, and without reference to the letter was invited to lunch the next day. I was a few minutes late, and he was already seated in his Rolls chatting with the driver, Nobby Clark. The seat next to the editor was piled high with books to be returned to the London Library, and I sat in the front. As we were pulling out of Printing House Square, Casey said that they had been talking about Dawson's last night as editor, and asked if I wanted to hear about it. Nobby, always a garrulous man presumably because of the long hours spent waiting for the editor, obliged.

It seemed that Dawson came out of the back door into the square at about nine. For once he was not bound for some dinner, and though the air raid warning had sounded he told Nobby to drive round a bit. This was not unusual, he often wanted to see the bomb damage, and Nobby turned towards the docks. Not much was happening despite the ack-ack fire, and knowing that Mrs Dawson was in the country Nobby asked him if he would like to come home and have a cup of tea with the missus. He nodded, and the old lady brewed up a pot just as the all clear went. None of them moved; the editor just sat there in his old cloak, sipping tea and talking about how different life would be after the war. Nobby took him home about midnight, and when he got out of the car he shook hands and asked Nobby to thank his missus for a pleasant evening. 'He was a nice gentleman,' added Nobby as we arrived at the Garrick.

Long afterwards when I remembered Nobby's tale, I was struck by its poignancy. Dawson must have realized at that moment that without the editorship he had become an ordinary citizen. He had his Yorkshire estate and his clubs, but he would never again be in a position to help shape or influence national policy. He was one of the men who had deposed a popular if inadequate king, for which I gave him credit; he had also closed his eyes to the rise of Hitler and had ignored or muzzled his correspondents in Europe, and I wondered if he saw the connection between that and the devastated streets of London. Probably not. Then I tried to visualize him in Nobby's flat, sipping tea. I had known Nobby from my messenger days when he used to sit in the com-missionaires' lodge while the great man was upstairs. He was a short and slight cockney with an alert face. He could look def-erential when necessary, but was as classless as Dawson. For different reasons, of course: Dawson had the classlessness of a man sure of himself and his place in society and in Nobby's East End of London there was nobody to look down or up to. I was certain that Mrs Clark was not a bit put out by the arrival of such a distinguished pillar of the establishment.

At the time I did not know what to make of the story. I could see no connection between Dawson's last night as editor and my immediate future, and over drinks Casey continued to talk about the old days. I guessed that he could not bring himself to ask about Korea, and soon after we were seated in the coffee room I told him that I was raring to go. He smiled with delight or relief, and said that we must celebrate. We did, with a very good claret. How else could one ask a man to go to war again?

William Howard Russell was paid £600 a year when he covered the Indian mutiny in 1857. When I was assigned to cover the Korean war in 1950 my salary was raised to £1000, a fraction of Russell's untaxed and inflation-proof gold sovereigns. That was not the only difference, according to his own account of his arrival at the headquarters of Sir Colin Campbell outside Lucknow.

I made out Sir David Baird, senior aide-de-camp to the com-mander-in-chief, and sent in my card. The flap of the little tent was raised immediately, and I made my bow to Sir Colin. He was frank and cordial. After a few remarks about the Crimea, his excellency said, 'Now, Mr Russell, I'll be candid with you. We shall make a compact. You shall know everything that is going on. You shall see all my reports, and get every information that I have myself, on condition that you do not mention it in camp, or let it be known in any way, except in your letters [reports] to England.'

Russell was of course a household name. Many of the senior officers in India had known him in the Crimea, where as more junior officers they had been grateful to him for the honesty of his reporting. No less important, he was the only correspondent with the troops in India. At any one time in Korea there were at least three hundred and the competition was intense. The *Express* had six correspondents and the *Telegraph* three. I was alone. Nor was there any hope of having a cosy relationship with the commander-in-chief. General Douglas MacArthur had his headquarters in Tokyo, and was almost as unapproachable as the emperor of Japan.

The war was fought under the blue-and-white flag of the United Nations, and troops of twelve nations served under MacArthur, but it was largely an American war. Most of the troops were American, as was the logistical support. This had its drawbacks; for instance, a ban on hard liquor imposed by some puritanical lobby in Washington made campaigning unnecessarily hard, but the Americans remained true to their constitutional guarantee of press freedom. Correspondents were free to travel anywhere, unaccompanied by press officers, and in the early months without censorship. They could go into action with the troops, and American divisional commanders willingly discussed their battle plans. General Hobart Gay, the commanding general of the 1st Cavalry Division (the horses had been sent to the knackers' yard long before) was especially helpful. On more than one occasion he invited me into his caravan and briefed me over the scotch I had brought from Japan. The British brigades kept correspondents at a distance, and as a consequence we spent most of our time with the Americans. A pity; much of the British effort was hardly reported until the Gloucesters were overrun.

Working alone meant that I got more into the paper, and the editor and foreign news editor were generous with their hero-grams. I was also authorized to draw on the company's blocked yen account. (Japan had not recovered from the Second World War, and even the relatively small amount of money earned from syndication could not be exported.) This was useful, but not in Korea where correspondents had to pay for their meals in army messes with US dollars. We could have starved as far as the British embassy in Tokyo was concerned, but the paper made strong representations to the Treasury and I was allowed a sizeable dollar allowance. Neither my yen nor dollar expenses had to be accounted for; the paper also kept an avuncular eye on Pat in London, and passed messages between us when I was at the front. To that extent its customary parsimony and aloofness were in abeyance for the duration.

That said, Korea was a very nasty war. The initial retreat was almost a rout, and we were nearly pushed into the sea. American troops had become soft during the occupation of Japan, and knew more about massage parlours than discipline and battle drill. Most of them were terrified of the 'gooks' and 'slopeheads', as they called the enemy, and in those early days broke ranks even before shots were fired. It was most disconcerting for the lone correspondent moving towards the front and watching them stream by. It was known as 'bugging out', a term the troops used without shame.

The Inchon landing turned the tide of battle – the British troops and US marines also helped – but the battle for Seoul, the South Korean capital, was very trying for correspondents. There were no telephones or telex, and every night we had to fly back to Japan – a four-hour flight – to file our stories. The C119 transports, known as flying-boxcars, were empty flying out and I would squat on the floor to type my story. At Ashiya, an air force base in Japan, I would eat a steak dinner in the officers' club after filing, buy some scotch, and then line up to fly back to Korea. The planes were generally overloaded with ammunition or petrol. Only one correspondent was put aboard each plane, and one night two planes crashed on takeoff and burst into flames. This did not halt the operation, and planes continued to depart every four minutes. My name was called, and still stunned by the crashes I walked like a zombie into the night. The crew chief, a young sergeant who looked as scared as I felt, reached down for my typewriter and musette bag and I stumbled up the ladder. The plane was filled with 50-gallon drums of aviation spirit, and I managed to say four or five 'Hail Marys' before the pilot pulled her off the ground. The wing became yellowy-pink as we banked over the funeral pyre of the photographer killed in the first crash. I sipped scotch from the bottle and dozed until we landed at Kimpo as dawn broke. I ate breakfast at the air force mess, and hitch-hiked back to the front to begin another day's work.

It was an exhausting routine and lasted for about a week until Seoul was recaptured. The enemy fled across the parallel dividing the two Koreas, and assuming that the war was over I returned to Tokyo. The idea was to write a few more stories to tie up loose ends, and then return to London. To my dismay rumour had it that although the UN forces had achieved their objective we were to advance into North Korea and reunite the peninsula under Syngman Rhee, the South Korean president. I did manage to interview MacArthur before going back, and despite myself was impressed. He was tall with a good soldier's face, and was dressed informally in an officer's shirt and slacks. He was a living myth, and knew it. We discussed the Korean campaign, the Pacific, the future of Japan and world strategy, but not the rumoured advance into North Korea. The interview was informative, and MacArthur spoke with benign authority and a sense of mission. He was determined to impose a *Pax Americana* in the Pacific basin, not only for the greater good of the United States and himself but he also believed that it would be good for the natives.

I withdrew from the presence, feeling like one of those early English adventurers kowtowing as they backed out of the divan of the Great Moghul in Delhi, to discover that some of his authority had rubbed off on me. His entourage treated me with respect, and I took quick advantage of my transitory importance and asked for a briefing on North Korea. An intelligence colonel told me that the invasion would be a walkover. The North Korean army was badly battered and demoralized, and the civilian population longed to be liberated. I was willing to believe that it could not survive a sustained United Nations attack, but was worried about China which shared a frontier with North Korea along the

Yalu river. The communist victory was only one year old and Sardar Panikkar, the Indian ambassador in Peking, had warned that the Chinese would fight if the UN forces advanced to its frontier. I knew the Sardar, and respected his judgement. It also seemed obvious to me that a victorious revolutionary army would instinctively respond to what its commanders must regard as a counter-revolutionary move by the arch-capitalist enemy. The colonel shrugged off my apprehension with an indulgent smile: China had not recovered from the revolution, and sections of the country were opposed to communist rule. The army was badly equipped, and much of it was pinned down by Chiang Kai-shek's KMT forces on Taiwan which were ready to return to the mainland. The communists had only a few thousand troops on the frontier, and were incapable of bringing up reinforcements unseen. He patted me on the shoulder, and said that I would be home for Christmas, a promise repeated by MacArthur when he ordered the troops to advance.

I was not convinced, but reluctantly returned to Korea. On D Day we drove into North Korea unopposed in an eerie silence, but the advance was not a pushover. I almost got killed in one short, sharp fight, but the enemy was incapable of stopping the drive to Pyongyang, the capital. The US 1st Cavalry Division was in the lead, and morale was high. One of its regiments, Gary Owen's Own, had been wiped out with Custer at the Little Big Horn river, and in the curious way with soldiers this made them feel superior. I had a drink with General Gay the night before the attack on the capital. He promised the use of a telephone for correspondents, but said that I would have to go in with the leading battalion if I wanted to be certain of making the paper.

The final approach march was made after dark, and with head-lights blazing. Never could an army have been so confident, and it was wonderfully exhilarating. I was driving the jeep which with three other correspondents we had bought from a friendly but thieving transportation sergeant for $400, and we belted along with the leading battalion. At one point we were waved over to let the general pass. He waved the shotgun he always carried in the field, and I shouted good luck as if we were out on a farmers' shoot. With little or no opposition we crossed the river and took the city.

Gay was as good as his word. A telephone was made available, and we drew lots for who would file first. I was the seventh or eighth, and the waiting was relieved by vodka and caviar looted from the abandoned Soviet legation. My call eventually came through on a very bad line. I could hardly hear the copytaker in Tokyo and dictated 1200 words more or less blind. It made the paper, but I did not know that at the time. There was nothing to do except drown my anxiety, and I emptied a vodka bottle into my canteen cup and smeared about two ounces of caviar on an army biscuit. Ralph Izzard of the *Mail* was not so fortunate. He got through to a colleague, Ward Price, at Tokyo's Maranuchi hotel where Price was celebrating the final victory. He invited Izzard to join him, and Ralph patiently explained that he was in Pyongyang, P-y-o-n-g-y-a-n-g, and would Price take the story. I saw him blanch, and asked what was wrong. Stuttering more than usual, he said that Price told him the war was over and not to be so tedious. He had hung up. The last story of the war, he whispered, and the blighter hung up.

It was not the last story, alas. Troops in pursuit of North Koreans fleeing northwards captured some Chinese prisoners, which wiped the smile from our collective face. At 1st Cavalry Division headquarters intelligence reports were scarce, and there was no contact with X Corps which was advancing up the east coast. An officer tried to make a joke of it, and announced with mock solemnity that the 8th Army had sent out patrols but had failed to make contact with X Corps. The map showed the danger of our situation. In his haste to end the war quickly MacArthur had sent columns up each coastal belt, and in between was a vast expanse of uncovered territory. The flanks of both columns were completely exposed. What to do, somebody asked, if the Chinese came down the middle?

The question was quickly answered. The Chinese did come down the middle, and we withdrew. There was no alternative, but the mysterious chemistry which governs the collective spirit of men in times of acute danger turned the retreat into another rout. With the other part-owners of the jeep, I drove back to the press camp and found it deserted. We drove out to the airfield, where an agitated air force captain said that the planes preparing to take off would be the last out of Pyongyang. We had no idea how far the Chinese had advanced. There was the possibility that our retreat had already been cut off, and we clambered aboard a DC4. I had two bottles of vodka in my bag and a can of caviar in my field jacket pocket, but I could have wept with vexation as we took off. There by the runway was our abandoned $400 jeep, and in the back, plain to see, were the remaining cases of vodka and caviar.

We landed at a temporary airfield near the parallel for no apparent reason, and I walked over to the road where traffic was streaming south and stood in the classic pose of the hitch-hiker. A command car eventually stopped, a colonel of 1st Cavalry Division said jump in and I obeyed with alacrity. There was no conversation until we stopped to refuel as night fell. A sergeant issued C-rations, and we stood eating the cold food from the cans with plastic spoons. As I recall, mine was chicken and rice, and I was longing for some British army bully beef when the colonel said that it was time to move on down the pike. I dozed off, one of the things I was good at.

It was dawn when I awakened, and the convoy was pulling off the road on to the narrow shoulder. The road was raised above the paddy fields, and to the left was a low line of hills. I felt horribly exposed, and said as much to the colonel. He said, not to worry; he had just talked to division, and the latest air reconnaissance reports confirmed that the enemy was miles behind. The division was re-forming, and we would move into defensive positions later that day. Reassured, I took the neat little packet of toilet paper from a C-ration case and scrambled down into the paddy for my morning exercise, another thing I was good at even on a diet of cold C-rations and vodka. I was crouching and wishing I had a newspaper to read when heavy machine-gun fire sprayed across the road from the other side. I heard shouts, scuffling and the starting of engines. Grit was scattered as the vehicles jerked off down the road, and there was I alone in the paddy literally with my trousers down.

The firing stopped, and there was silence except for the distant sound of the departing convoy. I zipped up my trousers and was about to scramble back on to the road when I realized my dilemma. If I stood on the road I would be a sitting duck for the machine-gunner, if he was still there, and if I showed myself when

143

a vehicle approached I might be mistaken for one of the enemy and shot. I sat on the bank and smoked a couple of cigarettes while occasional vehicles thundered by above. There was no shooting, and when the sound of approaching vehicles was still distant I scrambled quickly on to the road and waved my arms energetically. The jeep at the head of a small convoy slowed down, and a Thompson submachine-gun was aimed at me. I was bearded, but in uniform and obviously not Korean or Chinese, and I thankfully rejoined the US army.

Later I made my way to divisional headquarters where a press camp had already been set up with customary American efficiency. A lieutenant welcomed me like a lost brother, and produced my typewriter and bag. He added that the guy who left them said that they had lost me in the retreat. It was hardly a fair report of what had happened, and I ate my supper morosely. The situation was still fluid, to use the military cliché, and brooding over my recent experience I remembered the observation of an old soldier: only disciplined troops survive in a retreat. I thought of joining one of the British brigades, which were good but hardly communicative, and decided upon the US marines and made my way over to the east coast.

It was a bad error of judgement on my part. Winter was approaching, and the wind was coming out of Manchuria with early flurries of snow. The American parka and winter underwear were first class, but nothing could keep out that cold. The war was also going badly. The Chinese had withdrawn after their initial attack, and the marines were ordered forward again. They had recovered much of the lost ground when the Chinese responded in even greater force. On the map at least we were trapped, and the only alternative to surrender was a fighting withdrawal. I had joined not another retreat to safety or a stabilized defensive line, but a desperate rearguard action.

The marines fought with the doggedness of disciplined fighting men, and each phase of the withdrawal was planned. The disengaging troops marched in battle order on both sides of the road while their armour, guns and transport moved slowly southwards on the hardtop. Oddly enough, I felt secure. I was with a body of men held together by discipline and *esprit de corps*. We were in the shit together, and nothing could be more sustaining. Many of the trucks were filled with marine dead, and frozen arms and legs made grotesque silhouettes against the grey sky. Frozen stiffs, I told myself, knowing that I would not use the phrase if and when I had the opportunity to write about the withdrawal. Even in this desperate situation the marines did not leave their dead behind. The withdrawal began to resemble a mobile charnel house, or so it seemed in subsequent nightmares. At Wonsan, the bodies were stacked like cordwood waiting to be taken off by allied ships. It was macabre, like a Henry Moore sketch, but reassuring for the troops; final proof that they would not be left behind, alive, wounded or dead. So I thought at the time, and still do. Who would want to be left behind as manure for some foreign fields?

I was thinking like a marine, but of course I was only a war correspondent, and a useless one because there was no way of sharing my experience with the readers. I was dead tired, and so cold that I could only think that the beach was the end of the war – at least for me. I cannot remember making an objective decision. Perhaps I was also bugging out as did those frightened young soldiers so long ago. It was only about four months but seemed a lifetime. I told myself that I had done more than my bit for the bloody paper, and got on a boat and was ferried out to a waiting British ship. An officer led me to a shower and lent me clean clothes. I ate some dinner, and then drank scotches until sleep came. The trip to Yokohama was short, but long enough for me to make up my mind. Within forty-eight hours I was on a plane flying home, and only when we stopped over in Hong Kong for the night did I remember to send a telegram to the paper saying that I was on my way.

I ought not have left Korea without permission, but nothing was said when I reappeared at Printing House Square. Indeed Casey was obviously pleased to see me again. Eighteen war correspondents had been killed in the early months of the war, from the initial retreat to the Chinese invasion, a casualty rate proportionally higher than that of the armed forces, and the editor had been worried about my safety. He had sent me a telegram insisting that I should return to Japan to rest, not knowing that after their flying experiences during the battle for Seoul most correspondents were terrified of flying again in those overloaded and overworked planes. Over a pot of tea in his room before the afternoon conference, Casey said that I was a worthy successor to Morrison, who I was to replace in Southeast Asia, and it would have been tragic if I had also been killed. The world was in crisis, and the paper needed every good man it could get.

That may have been a bit of Irish blarney, but the world was certainly in crisis. Korea was only one front of what appeared to be an international communist offensive. Revisionist historians subsequently claimed that this was western, especially American propaganda, but much of the Euro-Asian landmass was under communist domination after Mao's victory in China, and there were genuine fears that the remainder could be overrun or subverted. Soviet imperialism in eastern Europe, the Greek civil war, the Berlin blockade, the guerrilla wars in Indo-China, Malaya and the Philippines, and the Korean war suggested a coordinated plan of expansion. The United States had demobilized much of its armed forces, western Europe had not yet recovered from the devastation of the war and West Germany was still disarmed. There was little to stop a Soviet invasion of western Europe except the atomic bomb, and the United States no longer had the monopoly. The immediate task was seen to contain communism – the strategy devised by George Kennan in an article signed X in *Foreign Affairs* quarterly – until the west re-armed. The theory was that it would then be able to resume negotiations with the Soviet Union. The outlook was dour. I had begun my career as a foreign correspondent covering the dissolution of empire, and for the foreseeable future I could be covering what the communists were to describe as wars of liberation.

That was a personal and limited view of the future, but it was much more complicated for the paper. Earlier Barrington-Ward had been determined not to publish anything that could frustrate a continuing alliance with the Russians. This was the period when the paper was known as the 'Threepenny Pravda', and those who disagreed with him said that having appeased Hitler before the war he was equally determined to appease Stalin. The charge was unfair, but it did seem that Barrington-Ward had got it wrong again. It must have been personally painful for him, and it was a blow to the paper's self-esteem. McDonald, who was responsible for the paper's foreign policy under Casey, had to come to terms with the new reality of Soviet imperialism. This was certainly painful; McDonald spoke Russian, and liked the country and its people. Not the communist regime of course, but the eternal Russia and its literature. He had travelled widely in the Soviet Union; he had his own reasons for seeking détente, and knew that diplomacy was impossible while Stalin lived. The cold war was also a double blow. Containment and re-armament had led to an increase in Britain's overseas commitments which meant that the hope of restructuring British society must wait.

During these few weeks in London I occasionally sat in the conferences McDonald had with his leader writers. These daily meetings were one of the internal reforms introduced after the departure of Dawson and Barrington-Ward, and were a return to the collegial tradition of the paper. Even a junior leader writer could contribute to the formulation of policy. That at least was the theory. I was not in the office often enough to discover if this was the case, but the meetings helped me to understand better the enormity of the change which had occurred. Britain was formally committed to the defence of western Europe, and for the first time in history a large peacetime army was permanently stationed on continental soil. We had troops fighting in Korea and Malaya, and naval fleets in the Far East and the Mediterranean. The programme to make Britain a nuclear power was well under way, and the V bombers were being designed. That was not all; the extension of the Anglo-American alliance and defence arrangements with European allies, together with the birth of many new nations, led to further overseas commitments. This was illustrated by one of the leader writers who noted that the diplomatic service had grown from less than 500 overseas posts before the war to several thousands. Mini-Whitehalls were established in the embassy in Washington and in Singapore under a commissioner general for southeast Asia.

A similar expansion, albeit more modest, of the paper's foreign news service was also under way, and it was accompanied by changes in priorities. Before the war foreign correspondents had been mainly stationed in the European capitals for the simple reason that Europe was seen to be the centre of the civilized world. The other continents were made up of colonial dependencies and countries that played little or no part in international affairs. Paris was the most senior post, and Washington an outstation. All this had changed. Washington was the centre of the western world, and the paper's most senior post. Datelines in the foreign news columns had become more exotic; Paris, Brussels and Rome frequently giving way to Delhi, Tel Aviv, Singapore and Hong Kong. Before the war, every correspondent was expected to be fluent in French, the language of diplomacy, but subsequently there was a demand for Russian- and Chinese-speakers, to mention the two obvious languages. It was still assumed that correspondents had good French, but it was no longer a requirement. The Americans had made English the international language.

The special relationship with the United States had replaced the entente with France as the cornerstone of British foreign policy, but Britain was very much the junior partner. The foreign news pages were still headed 'Imperial and Foreign', but the old dominions had grown up and looked to Washington for their security. Relations remained intimate and cordial, but Britain no longer spoke for the Commonwealth.

These developments necessarily influenced the attitude of the British press, and especially *The Times*. For more than a hundred years the paper had reflected the interests of the greatest empire in the history of the world. It had developed the world's finest foreign news service because a vast empire could not be governed or defended without prompt and accurate news; arguably the growth of the empire depended to some extent upon the paper. Certainly the reputation it established for omniscience depended as much upon early dispatches from faraway places as upon the ability of its editors to treat with successive British governments on equal terms. Long before the invention of the telegraph, an overland route was developed to hasten messages from the Far East. Before the Suez canal was dug, when ships arrived at Suez messages were raced across the isthmus, forwarded by sea to Marseille, and then galloped through France to the Channel ports. The pony express of the American West paled in comparison. In 1840 dispatches sent from China on 13 July, from Singapore on 13 August and Bombay on 1 October reached Printing House Square at three o'clock on the morning of 11 November and filled eight columns of that day's issue.

This had been the true strength of *The Times*, and it enabled editors and leader writers to formulate policies and opinions that were required reading in most capitals as well as Whitehall and Westminster. In 1950 the sun was setting on the empire, perhaps accelerated by the enlightened policy of the paper; but Britain still had considerable influence, as did the paper. Foreign ministers knew that the paper was often better informed than their embassies. Its foreign correspondents still enjoyed enviable access to the seats of power. The old story of the butler announcing the arrival of the press and the gentleman from *The Times* may have been apocryphal but was an indication of the respect the paper still enjoyed. I wondered how long it would continue; one has to accept that the respect a newspaper commands internationally depends largely upon the country in which it is published. My own experience had convinced me of that; and in the Middle East I had had to share my most-favoured status with the correspondent of *The New York Times*.

What would happen to the prestige of the paper was anybody's guess. It was of course secondary to the larger problem of adapting to internal change in Britain; our economic survival as a newspaper depended upon that, but the loss or diminution of international prestige was at least part of that problem. One thing we had to sell was our reputation as a great newspaper respected throughout the world, if not so widely read at home.

I discussed it one evening with Oliver Woods over dinner. He was one of the rising men on the paper, about eight years my senior, who had begun to concentrate on colonial affairs. He once said that he was writing himself out of a job, which meant that he expected the empire to disappear in the foreseeable future. He seemed to understand the probable consequences better than the other senior men, but that may have been because I was closer to him. We got on well together, perhaps because we enjoyed the good things of life. We were serious journalists, but never too earnest. We welcomed the end of empire, although he was less impatient. That evening he poured a bumper round of port when I asked what effect the loss of prestige would have upon our older colleagues. Woods thought that it was easier for us to face the uncertain future with equanimity than for the older men accustomed to being mentors of a great imperial power. Indeed, it would not be easy for most of our readers. The most intelligent people could be resistant to change. One thing was certain, he added rather sombrely; we would not get any leadership from Casey. He ordered more coffee from one of the club servants, and asked when I was leaving for Singapore.

I arrived in Singapore on New Year's Day 1951, and almost got killed in a race riot. I had checked into the old Cecil Hotel, and feeling restless after the long flight from London – about two and a half days with an overnight stop in Karachi – walked down to the Padang to watch. I was careless, probably because of my recent wars; a riot seemed tame in comparison, and a colourful riot story was a good way of informing London that Hawkeye Heren had arrived and was already on the job. Alas, I had forgotten that Joseph Conrad had got it right, that southeast Asia could be a savage region despite the charm of its peoples. The savagery that day erupted over the legal efforts of a Eurasian couple to regain custody of their daughter, who had been cared for by a Malay Muslim family when they were interned during the Japanese occupation. Malay mobs ranged all over the city, killing eighteen and injuring 173 Europeans. I might have been added to the total except that a friendly voice called from the Cricket Club, and I reached the safety of its deep verandah before the mob got me.

Singapore was then very colonial. The governor sat in splendour in what is now known as the Istana. Official members of the legislative council who were members of the Malayan Civil Service wore white uniforms and solar topees with plumes in the council chamber. The Tanglin and Cricket clubs were for whites only, and the tuans and memsahibs, tended by servants, lived in spacious bungalows standing in large gardens with tennis and badminton courts. Even modest households had a cook, a number one boy, a mali or gardener, and a driver. The British dressed for dinner, and the conversation was mainly about tin and rubber prices or sport. Somerset Maugham, who had passed that way many decades before, would have recognized it immediately.

It no doubt sounds awful, and it could certainly be stuffy and pompous. I often had a fit of the giggles – on reflection I seemed to have giggled my way round the world – especially after being invited to the Istana for dinner. The ladies had retired to powder their noses and the men had smoked their cigars when a major domo appeared and struck the floor with his staff of office. He then led us, two by two, with the governor and the guest of honour in the van, to an enormous lavatory under the main staircase. There, each man in his stall relieved himself and then waited for the governor to finish before zipping up. The uniform for such occasions was a white bumfreezer jacket, black tie, cummerbund and trousers. Medals were also worn although I had not bothered to collect mine after the war.

Between giggles my youthful liberalism was offended until I realized that the British did not enjoy much of an unfair advantage. Nothing prevented the Chinese and Indians from making money – the Malays seemed destined to be drivers, gardeners or policemen – and many of them did well. The rich Chinese merchants were far richer than the British tuans who, for all their airs, were mostly hired hands of London-based companies. The obvious example was Aw Boon Haw, the Tiger Balm king. He gave an annual reception for the leaders of the British community in a bungalow especially built to house his jade collection, and I soon realized that the Chinese were more racially superior than we high-nosed, red-haired barbarians. While I refused to join the Tanglin club because it would not have Asian members, I could not become a member of the Chinese swimming club. Except for the resentful Malay minority, the various communities nevertheless lived more or less peacefully alongside each other and prospered. Arguably there were worse ways of running a colony – not a country in the usual sense but an entrepôt manned by outsiders attracted by the opportunity to make money. They had no shared history or sense of nationhood. They were divided as much by the pursuit of the dollar as by language, race and religion. They were immigrants or sons of immigrants on the make. Most of them were not interested in politics.

There was an independence movement; it appealed to the English-speaking middle classes, but not to the first-generation Chinese immigrants who were officially regarded as aliens. They had long been penetrated by the Malayan communist party, which was mainly Chinese, and most of the party members were fighting the British in the Malayan jungle. Some cadres were well established in the trade unions and Chinese schools, but were inactive because the party's town committee had been arrested the year before. As a consequence life in Singapore was peaceful and pleasant, especially after Pat's arrival when we found a bungalow on the outskirts of Kampong Loyang, a Malay fishing village near Changi. It was large and well furnished, and the garden, which had a tennis as well as a badminton court, swept down to a private bathing beach. A staff of five went with the bungalow; the number one boy, a cook, a gardener, a driver and his wife who cleaned and did the laundry. Pat was taken aback by such affluence, and said, let us enjoy it while we may but remember that we will have to return to reality one day.

It was good advice, but the unreality was more than affluence. Singapore was in the eye of a political hurricane which was sweeping away the last vestiges of colonialism. While the Union Jack and the French tricolour still flew over vast areas, the struggle for political independence had already been won in Indonesia and was well under way in Indo-China and Malaya. Not that the white expatriates in Singapore appeared to be aware of it. The Korean war had led to a rubber and tin boom, and in turn to undreamed riches for the business community. The colony was unashamedly organized for their benefit. They were conceded a special status denied to them in India, where before independence they were dismissed by officials of the Indian Civil Service as box wallahs. They were well represented in London where the banks, shipping lines and rubber and tin companies had their head offices. Their boards, upon which retired members of the Malayan Civil Service invariably sat, were powerful pressure groups, and in 1946 their support of the Malay sultan's opposition helped to persuade the British government to drop the proposed Malayan Union. This was to have comprised Malaya, Singapore and the Borneo territories, ended racial discrimination in politics and citizenship and reduced the authority of the Malay sultans.

They actually did this when Britain was preparing to quit India. Like the white settlers in Rhodesia later, they believed that they could maintain a way of life enjoyed by the British upper-middle classes before the First World War despite the political hurricane. The colonial administration, which eventually had to answer to Westminster, prevented them from taking racial prejudice and commercial advantage too far, but they were oblivious of the fundamental change brought about by the defeat of Britain by Japan in 1942 and the subsequent occupation. They could not perceive that Asians no longer regarded them as supermen. Instead, they returned after the war assuming that nothing had changed, except the rubber and tin prices. Their wealth made many of them more insufferable, which was one reason why we chose to live in Kampong Loyang. It meant that we could live as far from them as we could without falling into the South China sea.

In any case, Singapore was only a base. My parish included Indo-China, Indonesia, and Thailand as well as Malaya and odd places such as Sarawak and British North Borneo. Thailand then had a *coup d'état* at regular intervals, but Indo-China and Malaya were the main stories and, with or without Pat, I spent a good deal of time in them. The war against the Vietminh in Indo-China was more serious, and was being lost before I left Korea. Defeat was delayed by General Jean de Lattre de Tassigny, a great soldier in the romantic Gallic tradition. He just might have reversed what was recorded as the tide of history if he had not died of cancer. I admired him, and was grateful for his help. Correspondents were not allowed to roam freely in Indo-China as they were in Korea, and at our first meeting he invited me to accompany him on a tour of Vietnam, Laos and Cambodia. He said that he had already invited Graham Jenkins of Reuters. 'I have invited you because you are *The Times*, I have invited Graham because I love him.'

Jenkins was a dour Australian and a very good journalist. We got on well together, and we both learned a great deal about the war under the tutelage of de Lattre. He was an intellectually honest man, but even without his help it was clear that the Vietminh were a formidable enemy. The general had too few troops, and large areas of the country were policed by private armies belonging to curious sects such as the Bao Daists. Their loyalty was suspect, but they helped to fill up blank spaces on de Lattre's map. Worse, the political situation was more dangerous than in Malaya. Unlike Britain, which in theory had always assumed the eventual independence of its colonial territories and in practice had gone part of the way in preparing its subject peoples to assume power, the French had done little or nothing. A modern war of national liberation supported by the new communist regime in China was being resisted in the name of three puppets – the rulers of the three associated states – who looked as if they should be performing in *The King and I*. It was not de Lattre's idea. Indeed, on our first foray with him into the field we met the three rulers, and I suspected that he wanted us to know that the political arrangements under which he had to fight the war were hopeless. The three so-called associated states were invented in 1949 by the politicians in Paris. Malcolm MacDonald, the British commissioner general for southeast Asia, chose to see the elevation of Bao Dai to head of state of Vietnam as a great act of statesmanship, but it was a cruel farce. Bao Dai was interested mainly in girls and tiger shooting, and would have preferred to live in the south of France except that there were no tigers along the corniche. It was one of the many mistakes which made the war the longest in modern history, from 1946 when the Vietminh first took to the jungle until thirty years later when the American ambassador was evacuated by helicopter.

The last time I saw de Lattre was at a splendid reception at the palace in Saigon. He was supposed to be returning to Paris for talks with the government, which seemed to be a strange reason for such an occasion. He was in great form, and his face broke into a smile when it was my turn to wish him a safe journey. The conversation went something like this: 'Louis, do you remember when we first met, and I said that you could accompany me because you were *The Times*, but that I had invited Graham Jenkins because I loved him?' I nodded, and he said, 'I have learned to love you too. We must travel together again when I return.' He kissed me on both cheeks, and flew home to France to die.

No love was lost between me and the British authorities in Malaya. I got on well enough with district officers and company and battalion commanders in the army, but my assumption that the war could only be won by offering early political independence to Malayans angered their superiors. I recognized that it would not be easy; power could not be transferred while the war continued in the jungle, and communal differences were a problem. The Malays resented the economic dominance of the Chinese, who comprised about two-fifths of the population. The loyalty of the Chinese was also suspect. Most of them had strong family links with the old country, and some still expected to go home to die. The success of the Chinese revolution in 1949 had revived racial pride, and the communist cadres believed that they could extend the revolution throughout southeast Asia. Yet it was difficult to believe that the numerous entrepreneurs wanted to live under a communist regime. Because of their family links, they probably knew more about the terrible communist excesses committed immediately after the revolution than British intelligence or the CIA. Thousands of Shanghai businessmen had fled to Hong Kong, and the flow of ordinary Chinese across the colony's frontier was already in full flood. Moreover, Malay political leaders and Chinese businessmen had come together to work for independence. It was an uneasy alliance, but the Chinese accepted, willingly or otherwise, that in an independent Malaya they would have to yield political leadership to the Malays. I was convinced that an independent Malaya would be safe from communism.

The army strategy to defeat the communist guerrillas was intelligent. Unlike the Americans in Vietnam later, no attempt was made to defoliate the jungle and few bombs were dropped. Basically it was a police action; the guerrillas were separated from most sources of supply, and acting on information army patrols sought out the guerrilla camps. Inevitably it was a protracted operation, and stronger action was called for when Sir Henry Gurney, the high commissioner, was ambushed and killed. In fact, the war had already been won, but nobody outside the jungle knew that the victory flags could be hung out until an enemy document was captured early in 1952. It was a directive from the politburo of the Malayan communist party which in effect conceded defeat. It admitted that violence had not won popular support, and the state and district committees were ordered to end hostilities. The guerrillas were to come out of the jungle, most of them withdrew into Thailand, and more attention was to be given to political organization in towns and villages.

The directive was not published, but General Sir Rob Lockhart, the deputy director of operations, showed me a translation. The war was to drag on because the communists did not have radio transmitters, and the directive had to be delivered by messengers. This took months, but the number of terrorist incidents declined dramatically, from about 6100 in 1951 to 1100 two years later. I wrote my little scoop after promising not to reveal the source, and to my surprise it caused widespread official anger. The search for the leak was as extensive as anything attempted by President Nixon's plumbers many years later. It mattered not that my report was correct. The new high commissioner, General Sir Gerald Templer, was furious, presumably because it could diminish the claim he hoped to make that he had defeated the guerrillas. As a matter of fact, it did not – somebody called him the Lion of Malaya, and the label stuck – but from then on I was one of the enemy.

The British, or rather some of them, can be very nasty when thwarted. Their attitude genuinely puzzled me, and a senior official, who remained a close friend, described it as the 'antipathy of a military and civil service oligarchy against the few who refuse to conform'. He was an Irishman who naturally had a detached view of the British, but for me it was further proof of the corrupting influence of colonialism. There were few internal checks and balances under the emergency regulations, and London was thousands of miles away. Moreover, the Tories had recently been returned to power, and independence for Malaya was not high on their list of priorities. The rubber and tin boom had made the country Britain's largest dollar earner, and the business community suddenly had greater influence in London. Templer was also tougher, or more brutal, than his predecessor. He accepted the conventional wisdom that the struggle in Malaya was for the hearts and minds of the people – a cliché popular with the Americans in Vietnam later – but ordered the mass punishment of villages when they failed to cooperate. He had the countryman's sympathy for peasants – he belonged to an Ulster landowning and military family – but disliked politicians despite the role they would have to play in any settlement. His contempt for the press was unconcealed.

A member of the Malayan war council, another Irishman, told me that I had been accused of being a communist and that Templer was determined to have me removed from Malaya. I sighed wearily into my martini. Was I to go through life eternally damned as a commie and a spy, I asked rhetorically. The Irishman laughed, but said it was no joke. He was right. Whatever the high commissioner intended to do, I felt that I was dangerously exposed. Casey had recently retired, and Sir William Haley had been appointed editor. He did not know me, and not having a byline I must have been a shadowy figure. According to the paper's official history, Iverach McDonald and Gerald Norman, the new foreign news editor, vouched for me. Haley wrote me a friendly note, and asked me to explain the situation as I saw it. I did as requested, and he quickly thanked me for a good letter. His instinct to defend one of his men in the field against a most serious charge was apparently reinforced.

It was not the end of the affair for Templer. He was an ambitious regular soldier who from no fault of his own was denied the opportunity of proving himself as one of the great captains of the Second World War. He made a joke of it, claiming that he was wounded more than once but never by enemy action. The first time he was hit when watching a demonstration of close aerial support; a plane firing live ammunition came too close to the reviewing stand and he spent the next few months in hospital. The second was when he was wounded by a grand piano in Italy. The piano, apparently looted, was in the back of a lorry which Templer's staff car was trying to pass. As usual he was impatient, and his driver repeatedly sounded his horn until the lorry pulled over onto the verge and blew up on a mine. The piano landed on the unfortunate general, and put him out of the war. He was often in pain, but that did not entirely explain his irascibility. Absolute obedience was demanded, and disobedience was instantly punished. Malaya was his last chance of glory, and he was determined to seize it.

This must have prompted the decision to mount a large military operation in the jungle to capture a reported communist headquarters despite the fact that his predecessor had forced the politburo of the Malayan communist party to admit defeat by eschewing such military extravagances. Unbeknown to Templer, I covered the operation, which was a failure. I thought nothing more of it; it was just another second-rate story I was required to file, but not for Templer.

Soon afterwards I went up to Kuala Lumpur, the Malayan capital, to cover a meeting of the legislative council. Templer, dressed in the tropical garb of a full general, presided and was attended by two ADCs. The session was uninteresting, but fortunately legislative business was never allowed to interfere with the luncheon engagements of the official members and it was over by gin time. I was talking with some Malay politicians in the lobby when Templer approached with his ADCs. He held his sword in one hand and with the other was waving an airmail edition of *The Times*. He was working himself into a paddy as he approached, and was almost speechless with fury when he arrived. The Malayans, accustomed to the ill tempers of *tuans* over the decades, drew back. Still waving the paper, and with his face contorted, Templer shouted, 'What do you know about war? You, you ...' I realized that he was referring to my report of his unsuccessful operation. I was also aware of the Malayans watching me, but I was fed up with his behaviour and assaults on my professional integrity. I snarled back, 'At least I have been in fucking battle.' I regretted the words as I mouthed them. They were unfair, but he had asked for it. I thought he was going to strike me, but after a moment which seemed an eternity he stalked away followed by his gaping ADCs. At least the smirks had been wiped off their faces.

Meanwhile, Haley had not forgotten Templer's accusations. I do not know exactly what happened, but that friendly Irishman on the war council told me that there had been an exchange of solicitors' letters. He ought to have known because he was the attorney general. Soon afterwards I was invited to King's House, the high commissioner's residence, where Templer apologized to me. He did it with ill grace, kicking his desk in anger, but I did not care. The important thing was that the new and unknown editor in London had supported me in the best possible way. Templer could kick his desk to pieces, but I would remain the southeast Asian correspondent until he chose to post me elsewhere.

I still cannot understand why Templer carried on so. My story of the Malayan communists' admission of defeat was soon forgotten. He was eventually given full credit for ending the war – unfairly for his predecessor was mainly responsible – and went home to serve as the Chief of the Defence Staff. Whatever the reason, it rankled for years, for nearly 20 years to be precise.

In 1971, after I had returned to London, Pat and I were invited to dinner by the Malaysian high commissioner. We were late as usual because of Pat. As I was fond of saying, she was only punctual when producing babies, but hosts were willing to believe that it was the exigencies of journalism. We arrived on the heels of the guest of honour, Sir Alec Douglas Home, the foreign secretary, and his wife. We knew each other, and went in together. I naturally receded into the background as our host approached, but Templer, who had arrived earlier, saw me. He glared with the old intense anger, and I half expected him to throw his gin and tonic at me.

I am told that before we went in to dinner his wife, who looked nice and competent, suggested to him that it really was time to forget old grudges. True or false, he managed to make conversation over the dinner table, and I went home relieved to know that if the army ever staged a *coup d'état* I would not be immediately arrested as a danger to law and order.

Little was known about Haley in Printing House Square when I enquired from Singapore. There was widespread regret that Tyerman had been passed over once again. He had offered his resignation, and had then agreed to stay until Haley was firmly in the chair. (In fact, they got on together extremely well, and Tyerman remained for some years before accepting the editorship of *The Economist*.) That was reassuring, as on reflection was Haley's decision to leave the director general's office of the BBC to join the paper. It indicated that he had a proper sense of values, but the gossip from Broadcasting House was not encouraging. He was said to be a typical Manchester nonconformist who did not drink or smoke. The men who had served their apprenticeship on the old *Manchester Guardian* groaned. They remembered C.P. Scott whose basic diet was bread, cheese and apples washed down with water. It was also reported that Haley was an aloof and unsmiling man who eschewed personal friendships and preferred to preside over a rigid staff structure. J.B. Priestley had labelled him 'the man with two glass eyes'.

I discovered much of this to be true when I was ordered to return to London in 1953, several months after the troubles with Templer, and offered the Rome job. This was seen as promotion, a move into the bottom half of the first league. I was duly grateful, but unenthusiastic. I was still reluctant to take a collar-and-tie job. I would have to submit one day if I was to reach the summit of my ambition, chief correspondent in Washington, but for the time being preferred to cover the expanding frontiers of the new world created by decolonization. It was not the brave new world anti-imperialists such as myself had hoped for. Yesterday's colonial subjects, including those who had attended the London School of Economics or had eaten their dinners at one of the inns of court, could be more oppressive than their erstwhile white masters. I suppose that I knew from the beginning the lot of ordinary Africans and Asians would not necessarily be improved, but they were changing the world, and if I was to realize my own ambition a knowledge of the new countries would be useful. The paper's great foreign correspondents of the past, such as Morrison and Russell, had made their reputations in faraway places.

That, if you like, was the respectable reason for wanting to stay east of Suez, but there were others. I enjoyed the unbuttoned life, and was still young enough to want to see the other side of the hill. I did not want to go to an office whether or not there was work to be done. I wanted to be able to go hunting until the next great story broke or developed, and the vultures I had first met in India would come winging in to offer competition and good company. Nevertheless, I discussed the offer with Pat, and she suggested that we ought to give Rome a try. It was a pleasant city and not so busy as Paris or Bonn. Perhaps I could be the backstop for the Middle East where there was sure to be plenty of action. I was persuaded, and we took passage for the London river on the *Glenorchie*, a fast freighter which could carry twelve passengers.

I was invited to lunch by Haley soon after we landed, and he was impatiently waiting by the commissionaires' box when I arrived at Printing House Square. He dismissed my apologies politely enough, but hurried me down the stairs to the Rolls. Nobby Clark, the driver, welcomed me with a discreet smile, but unlike in Casey's time we rode to the Athenaeum in almost complete silence. Haley's club was another reminder of the extent of the change, and unlike Casey at the Garrick we went straight into the dining room and ordered the food. A wine waiter hovered, and Haley eventually supposed that I wanted a drink. I ordered a large pink gin and a half carafe of claret to follow, and he drank water.

It was a poor start but with the inconsequentials of food and drink out of the way he relaxed a little. The conversation was general but civilized, and I had the opportunity to take stock of him. He was undoubtedly an impressive man; he held himself well even when seated, his skin was clear as were his eyes. They were not glasslike, but the gaze was steady, almost unblinking, and exuded confidence. His clothes were ordinary, and I noticed that he wore a nylon shirt through which could be seen a string vest, but he was at home among the club's archbishops and vice chancellors. Nobody could have guessed that he'd once worked for the paper as a telephonist.

Lunch was quickly over, and we went upstairs to the library for coffee. No port of course, but sitting on an isolated sofa at one end of the long room I began to talk about working in Rome. Haley soon cut me short, saying that he had changed his mind. I could not possibly represent *The Times* in Rome because of my religion. He apologized; had he known at the time he would not have offered me the job. I protested that I knew more jokes about the pope than any C. of E., and was more than ready for the second reformation, but to no avail. The special correspondent who covered the first Vatican Council in 1869 was secretly converted to Rome by Jesuits with disastrous consequences for his journalistic objectivity. He was withdrawn in disgrace, and in its wisdom the paper had decided that the Rome correspondent must always be a non-Catholic.

It seemed absurd, but Haley was adamant. He then softened a little, and asked me to go back to Delhi. India under Nehru was becoming a political force, and he wanted an experienced man to cover it. I had no objection, I was fond of the country and knew that Pat was interested. Some of the best shooting in the world was freely available in northern India. I lit another cigarette, which he clearly detested, and asked when he wanted me to go.

8

It is *a Moral Issue*

The Times has been blessed with two great and some very good editors, which helps to explain why it has survived for more than 200 years. It's had its ups and downs, but it was no accident that in the years of ascendancy the editors were superior men. That might seem obvious, but very few other newspapers have prospered or approached greatness only because of their editors. C.P. Scott of the old *Manchester Guardian* was proprietor as well as editor. During its years of ascendancy, the proprietor of the *Daily Telegraph*, Lord Hartwell, was the man in charge. Similarly with Lord Beaverbrook and the *Daily Express*. In the United States, the Ochs and Sulzberger families guided the fortunes and editorial policy of the *New York Times*. Joseph Pulitzer owned and made famous the *St Louis Post-Dispatch* and the *New York World*, if only briefly, as did James Gordon Bennett with the *New York Herald*. Alone among the English-speaking world's great newspapers, *The Times* was the creation of its editors, hired men who could be dismissed at will by the proprietors.

A few qualifications are necessary. John Walter appointed Thomas Barnes as editor of *The Times* and left him to make it a great newspaper, but in the background his shrewdness made it all possible. John Delane, who succeeded Barnes, at first needed a guiding hand because of this extreme youth. Lord Northcliffe rescued the paper in the early part of this century and then almost ruined it, but it would have died of senility if he had not become proprietor. The arrangement between John Jacob Astor, the next chief proprietor, and Geoffrey Dawson formalized the supremacy of the editor, and it was unfortunate that Dawson was a deeply flawed man. Robin Barrington-Ward, for all his good intentions, was only marginally better. He pointed the paper in the right direction, and then it stood still under the amiable but quietist editorship of William Casey. Throughout those years Astor remained very much in the background, never intruding but exercising his right to appoint the editor. When he appointed Sir William Haley in 1952, the paper was reasonably secure, but Fleet Street with the rest of the world was changing rapidly. *The Times* had to adjust and find a new and larger readership. Much depended upon Haley, and all we knew of the man was that he'd had a remarkable career. That at least was reassuring.

Haley was not typical of the old black friars. He was a grammar-school boy, born in Jersey, and his father was a Yorkshireman who had married a local girl. He read Sir Philip Gibbs' *The Street of Adventure*, a book about Fleet Street, while serving as a very youthful wireless operator in a merchant ship during the last weeks of the first world war, and applied for a job on *The Times* as soon as he returned from his first and only voyage. His good French and shorthand won him a job as a foreign telephonist, and he was moved to Brussels after persuading the manager that the transmission of copy from the various European offices could be more efficiently handled and at less cost by a communications centre in the Belgian capital. Haley probably 'milked' their messages for the weekly newsletter he was soon writing for the *Manchester Evening News*, which he joined as a subeditor in 1922. Thereafter his progress was extraordinary: managing editor of the *News* and director of the parent company, Manchester Guardian and Evening News Ltd; director of the Press Association and Reuters, which he successfully reorganized; editor-in-chief of the BBC and then director general at the age of 43.

Haley was in many ways a very good director general of the BBC in the immediate post-war years. Apart from his administrative talent, he was widely read and had a well-stocked mind. He was an admirer of Lord Reith, the first director general, and shared his high-minded principles. He believed that the corporation had a cultural mission, while accepting the legitimate demand of the majority of listeners for light entertainment. Haley reorganized sound broadcasting, introducing the Home, Light and Third programmes to provide what he described as a cultural spectrum. He was especially proud of the Third. He also presided over the reorganization of the news programmes; demanding an accurate, impartial and dispassionate flow of news, but rejecting the idea that one function of the BBC was to become just another source of news. It had to bear in mind 'the permanent demands of the human spirit'. Similarly with television which was still in is formative stage. He fought and lost the struggle to maintain the BBC's monopoly, and before leaving Broadcasting House told the staff to 'fight against the lowering of standards ... television must remain civilized and adult'. The official history (*The BBC: the first 50 years*) also said, when passing judgement on Haley, that he was reserved rather than assertive in formal dealings but was nevertheless capable of going his own way whatever the government or governors might say. He was unflinching, with a touch of ruthlessness, in his moral judgements, and determined at all costs to give listeners 'the best in the world'.

The same history said that Haley, always realistic, knew when he resigned to go to *The Times* that the BBC was to lose its monopoly. That must have been a bitter blow for a man accustomed to winning, but probably not the only reason for his resignation. Like Reith, Haley always wanted to be stretched, and he told me later that he enjoyed new challenges. I well remember the occasion. We were sitting on the terrace of a restaurant overlooking the Rhine near Bonn, and he indicated that I was a stick-in-the-mud. I ought to have left the paper for a few years to seek new experiences. A strange remark to a foreign correspondent who had had more experiences than most people, but that is neither here nor there. I was convinced that he returned to edit *The Times* because he saw it as the best job in journalism. It might also have given him great satisfaction to recall that he had begun as a telephonist earning £2.50 a week.

Despite the gossip from the BBC and the sympathy for Tyerman, Haley was cautiously welcomed. We wanted a strong and talented editor and were raring to go, but Haley seemed reluctant to take charge. He hovered in the background listening and observing, and remarked that he was prepared to wait two years before changing the paper. But his first two senior appointments were approved. Iverach McDonald was made foreign editor, the first since 1928. A.P. Ryan, who Haley had known at the BBC, was appointed an assistant editor with rather vague duties. He helped to broaden the scope of the paper, and was eventually appointed literary editor. I occasionally wondered why Ryan got on so well with Haley; he was witty and amusing, and spent a great deal of time at the London Library and the Garrick. Arguably they were second homes for a literary editor, but Haley would not have been so indulgent with others. Arthur Crook, who began as a messenger and eventually became editor of the TLS, recalled that they always had a bottle of champagne when making up the books page. Haley surprised them one day and was not amused, but their friendship survived.

Haley also told Morison that he did not want an *eminence grise*, and that his views on editorial matters would not be welcomed. It was a cruel blow for the old typographer, but, alas, his special relationship with the chief proprietor and manager remained.

The editorial staff soon learned what they were in for. Only Tyerman, who acted as deputy editor, and the three assistant editors – Maurice Green was promoted to home editor in 1953 – were granted the right of access to Haley's room. His main means of communication with others was by memo dictated from his home in Blackheath before being driven to the office. His praise could be stimulating and his rebukes crushing. In any event, it was a cold-blooded and disconcerting way of communicating with loyal subordinates. At least one news editor was seen to break into a cold sweat when he saw one of the memos on his desk. Here are a few examples:

'Could you spend more money on covering live news and less on dead conferences?'

'Why, on the story giving election results in Manitoba, did we put a headline "Liberals Return to Power in Ontario"?'

'It is extraordinary that after so many years of prodding, it is still not understood that the *main purpose* of *The Times* is to be a *newspaper* – that means that it should go to press with all the news it considers important or interesting.'

'Why was every bit of colour cut from the Berlin correspondent's report of the Reuter funeral?'

Haley read every word in the paper – apart from advertisements about 150,000. The unsigned memos, typed by his secretary, Enid Knowles, and distributed before most of the recipients arrived in the morning, ranged from leading articles and lead stories to gardening notes and the fashion page. The assistant editors did not escape censure, especially when the paper was badly scooped.

In the early months Haley did not hold editorial conferences, which made his isolation from most of the staff total, and he remained distant when they were resumed. The news editors, leader writers and others sat in rows of chairs like so many school children, and Haley presided from behind his desk. There were no greetings as they filed in, and silent and expressionless Haley watched the clock until everybody was seated. Grown men averted their gaze as they scurried in a minute or less late. No smoking was allowed, jackets had to be worn, and little or nothing was said apart from the reading of news schedules. One experience of mine, when I was on leave, perhaps illustrates the dreary solemnity of those twice-daily occasions. A new recruit, a scared young man, read out the foreign news schedule and stumbled over some Chinese names. His pronunciation was brusquely corrected by a leader writer, which was unnecessarily hurtful and I spoke to him in Chinese. He stuttered that he did not speak the language and Haley, who was impatiently waiting to continue, said that he had not been informed that I was a Chinese speaker. I admitted that I was not, despite a year of study in Singapore, and had wished the leader writer a happy new year in Cantonese – the only Chinese I knew. Silly, no doubt, but there was a roar of laughter. Haley sat silently until it had lamely subsided, and then nodded to the foreign news man to proceed. Later, much later, I discovered that Haley had enjoyed my put down but was not prepared to have his conference interrupted.

This aloofness was hard to live with. *The Times* had always been a friendly paper, and for all his failings the retirement of Casey was occasionally regretted. But not often; Haley was a superb journalist, who commanded respect, and was completely dedicated to the paper. Most nights he was down at the stone in the composing room overseeing the makeup of the last pages, and often stayed to prepare the second edition. The stonehands respected him, and the night editor knew that he had met his master. For all his aloofness he had no side, and was genuinely modest. He was a Barnes – without the gin and another man's wife – and not a Dawson. He proved to be a writing editor, and the Establishment received rough treatment from him as it had from Barnes.

Haley waited nearly nine months before writing his first leading article. Entitled 'And After?' it appeared the day after the coronation of Queen Elizabeth and set the tone of his editorship. The party, it said, was over and not a moment too soon. The British people had had a holiday from reality long enough, and had to earn a new place in the world by their own exertions and not merely by past example. Then followed the refrain, a constant in much of his serious writing. Christian values must be re-established, morals reasserted, conscientiousness revived, energy renewed and national unity restored.

'It *is* a Moral Issue' was probably his most famous leader, and it appeared in 1963 after the resignation of John Profumo, the secretary of state for war. Profumo had lied to parliament about sleeping with a prostitute, who also had a Soviet military attaché as a client. That they first met at Cliveden, once the redoubt of the Establishment, gave their affair a significance it did not deserve; in any case, the political consensus held that it was not so much a moral issue as a problem of parliamentary standards and national security. Haley spiritedly disagreed, and blamed successive Conservative governments for bringing the nation psychologically and spiritually to a low ebb:

> They declared they had the right road for Britain. They would set the people free. Change, they declared, was their ally. Nothing else, they seemed to think, mattered, compared with the assertion that the nation had never had it so good. Today they are faced with a flagging economy, an uncertain future, and the end of the illusion that Britain's greatness could be measured by the so-called independence of its so-called deterrent. All this may seem far from Mr Profumo, but his admissions could be the last straw ...

It was in fact very far from Profumo. He had done something he ought not to have done, to paraphrase the Anglican general confession, but some readers might have concluded that a little Christian charity was in order. The leader was also unfair to Harold Macmillan; the prime minister had indeed said that most people had never had it so good, but only to warn them that prosperity would vanish if wages, prices and inflation got out of hand. Haley did occasionally get carried away by his moral indignation, but other readers might well have been comforted by his refusal to base the paper's policy only on economic forces and political calculation. He never wavered, and in his farewell speech to the staff still insisted:

> What I am going to say now I have said before, but I believe it so deeply that I will go on saying it till I die. The truth is that there *is* a difference between right and wrong, and there *are* things that we should not be ready to compromise. There is no half-way house between honesty and dishonesty. There are things which are bad and false and ugly and no amount of argument or specious casuistry will make them good or true or beautiful. It is time for these things to be said and time for the press to say them.

Haley was a prolific writer, in July 1964 he wrote seven leaders in one week, and was often relaxed and amusing. He wrote on cricket, Colette, Dr Johnson, Klondike Kate and window boxes as well as industrial relations, politics, NATO and nuclear deterrence: 'It is the great deterrent to war. It is also becoming, perhaps, the great deterrent to peace.' He had an agile mind, and could change it between editions. His leader on the Tory leadership after Anthony Eden's resignation leant towards R.A. Butler in the first edition but not in the last. He had a great affection for the United States, and wrote on the death of the last civil war veteran as well as its politics and literature. When I was in Washington he asked me to write a leader – an unusual request for a foreign correspondent – on the centenary of the surrender at Appomattox, and afterwards told me that he had been greatly moved. He shared with me the sadness of that terrible war.

Haley's great passion was books. He was an omnivorous reader, and had a photographic memory. This led in 1955 to the introduction of a weekly column on books under the *nom de plume* Oliver Edwards. It was written by three or four men in the early months, but was taken over by Haley before the end of the year. It became an unusual column; not a critical review of books, but a conduit for his love of literature, especially of British, American, French and Russian novels. The Official History says that no account of the editing of *The Times* is complete if it deals only with William Haley and not Oliver Edwards; adding that he disclosed part of his inner life when trying to open a wider world of books, many of them little known and by forgotten authors, to readers. This presumably explained his sensitivity to criticism, most notably when a selection of the columns published in book form was savaged by reviewers. He also answered me with acerbity when I disagreed with one column which claimed that no English author had written well about men at sea. Conrad was a Pole and not English. In a second note I reminded him of Masefield's *Bird of Dawning* and the first chapter of H.M. Tomlinson's *Galleon's Reach*. He admitted the error by return of post, but the *nom de plume* was a misnomer. Oliver Edwards, according to Boswell, had confessed that he tried to be a philosopher, 'but, I don't know how, cheerfulness was always breaking in'. Haley was not a cheerful man.

Haley nevertheless proved to be a very good editor. Lord Beaverbrook said that he was turning *The Times* into a newspaper, which was true to the extent that Haley was more interested in news than was Barrington-Ward or Dawson. He was a journalist first and last, and perhaps because of his background did not see himself as a member of an inner elite, a minister without portfolio in whatever cabinet was ruling the country at the time. He resented the assumption that the paper reflected the views of the government, and a leader proclaimed:

> It is an entirely unofficial, non-party newspaper appealing to men and women of reason and good will of all kinds of opinion. It seeks to judge each issue that arises only by reference to the broad national good. It will not subordinate this judgment to the interests of one class or another.

To keep himself informed, Haley regularly met government ministers, but in their offices and not in their clubs. Apparently he was as unbending with prime ministers as with his staff, and never granted favours in the hope of receiving information in return. He once told an assistant editor that 'we do not need to go truckling to them. They will come running to us soon enough when they have something to say.'

Haley accepted that the paper must remain a journal of record, but wanted to make it interesting and entertaining for intelligent readers of all ages and classes. As more newsprint became available, the sports coverage was extended and the women's and arts pages were introduced. The latter flourished under John Lawrence, an amusing man who had been a clerk in the advertisement department before the war. A series of interviews with well-known dramatists, actors and singers was one of his innovations, and William Mann, the music critic, further enlivened the page when he wrote his famous piece on the Beatles' music. This pioneering study of pop music, with its reference to 'chains of pandiatonic clusters', was reprinted round the world and sent readers to their dictionaries. Mann, who was to write books on Bach, Mozart and Tippett, and a translation of Wagner's *Ring*, was also a jazz enthusiast. When he came later to Bonn for the first concert in the new Beethoven Halle another secret fan, Henry Pleasants, who was attached to the American embassy, asked to meet him, and I arranged a dinner at the American club.

I can still vividly remember that evening. It was a Sunday, and the club was half empty. Herr Rahn, the head waiter, liked Englishmen for some reason, and made a special effort. The food, wine and service were exemplary, but I doubt that my guests noticed as they enthused over the great bands and instrumentalists. The two men could not have been more different. Mann was an old Wykehamist and Pleasants, behind his diplomatic cover, was chief of the largest CIA station in western Europe. He was a civilized man, and enjoyed the company of foreign correspondents. Whatever his hired guns did in the back alleys of Berlin was none of my business: correction, it was but I knew that he would not talk about it. He was, however, willing to talk about the two Germanies, and knew more about their politics than most diplomats. That was one reason why I used to say that some of my best friends worked for the agency. Later that evening we went to his house in Pech, a small village above Bad Godesburg. His wife, Virginia, was a well-known harpsichordist, and the large living room was crowded with harpsichords and spinets; and I discovered that evening that Pleasants had been an equally well-known musicologist.

I afterwards told Haley that he was succeeding in making the paper interesting and entertaining for intelligent readers, and he even smiled a little when I told him about Pleasants. It certainly proved for me that we could be more adventurous in opening up the paper; even our most distinguished readers probably had unexpected tastes and hobbies.

Haley also introduced a number of regular news features to make the paper more informative. There were the guides – the guide to American primary elections, for instance – which provided background material when a big story broke or developed. Then came the man (or woman) in the news, a series of short biographies of persons when they became newsworthy. Many other features were developed under Haley, but in 1957 the company made its first loss since the war. The main reason was the poor state of the economy which led to fewer advertisements, but it was disturbing. For all Haley's efforts, some people in the industry were persuaded that *The Times* could not be profitable in the changing postwar world although the *Telegraph* was flourishing with a circulation of one million, and still rising. The *Guardian* was not then a threat, but was attracting proportionally more readers.

There were a number of reasons why *The Times* was less successful. It cost more than the *Telegraph*, and without a second printing plant in Manchester could not distribute the later editions, with their up-to-date news, in the north and Scotland. A front page devoted to classified advertisements was uninviting; the layout and typography of the inside pages were elegant and logical, but austere. A few more pictures would have helped, except that there would have been less space for news in what was still a very tight paper. Another important reason, despite Haley's efforts, was the indifferent home news coverage. It was still starved of space; news stories were missed or not followed up effectively because there were not enough reporters. The *Telegraph* had three times as many. Haley's rigid definition of news did not help. Stories developed under the imaginative guidance of Robert Dobson, who was appointed home news editor in 1953, were frequently rejected by Haley as unsuitable. He even ignored the arrival of Marilyn Monroe in London to make a film with Laurence Olivier. She was at the height of her fame, and our serious-minded readers must have been interested, but Haley was adamant. Miss Monroe was not *Times* material.

The reporters remained frustrated. Green, the home editor, had already warned Haley about their deteriorating morale. He wrote that the paper was losing its most promising young men because of the limited scope for advancement and the little recognition given to the practice and status of reporters. The really good ones were dissatisfied because they felt diminished by the considerably higher ranking given financially and in other ways to leader writers and specialists. The paper needed good men, well paid, to do big stories comparable to the big dispatches from Paris and Washington. The reporting staff was now unequal to the task because of the premature loss of the best men. He concluded by urging the paper to offer the best possibilities of advancement to attract promising youngsters.

Green's supplication has some effect. A minium salary of £1040 a year was introduced in 1957, but as is often the case the minimum became the maximum for most reporters. Rather like industrial workers, they were in effect paid the rate for the job regardless of merit. The highest salary on the home side was £1350 – as a foreign correspondent of middling rank I was then paid £1750 plus living allowances – and some of the best men got less than that. The minimum on the *Daily Express* for a reporter was £1750 plus generous expenses.

Low pay was not the main problem, at least not for ambitious young men coming down from university or emerging from the provincial press. They wanted to prove themselves and get on. They wanted recognition, and this was denied them. Apart from Haley's aloofness and his apparent inability to communicate except with a few intimate friends, the paper's anonymity rule was absolute. Every journalist joining *The Times* immediately became faceless. As a foreign correspondent my stories were bylined 'From Our Own Correspondent' except when I was on special assignment when they were labelled 'From Our Special Correspondent'. Reporters were generally doubly faceless in that their stories had no bylines. The nearest approach to a personal attribution was 'By Monitor' which headed Kyril Tidmarsh's articles on Soviet affairs, and of course 'By Oliver Edwards' which appeared over Haley's weekly column on books.

Anonymity had been the rule for all British newspapers until the popular press adopted American practices, and eventually all the serious papers fell into line except *The Times*. Northcliffe had

given Wickham Steed a byline as a favoured foreign correspondent, but the anonymity rule was reimposed after the great
if mad proprietor's death. It was upheld by Haley who still
believed that the idea of *The Times* as a corporate body, speaking
in its own right, gave the paper's views greater authority than any
individual writer could command. Many years after his retirement
he defended anonymity in an article published in *The American
Scholar*:

> It may be that the circumstances which could hold a band of
> people together, each satisfied with sharing in a common
> purpose without individual acknowledgements, no longer exist.
> I still have greater respect for a view, or a review, offered me
> by a paper than one presented by a person. Signed writing
> invites exhibitionism, though it may be unconscious.

Anonymity suited Haley. In many ways he was an anonymous
man, and rarely gave interviews or made public appearances. I
once urged him to write his autobiography, arguing that it was
his public duty to pass on his experiences, but he refused. Men with
long service with the paper willingly accepted or were resigned to
not being known as authors of their work. We accepted it along
with the poor pay as the price for working for *The Times*. We
may not have been known for our writing, but at least it was
published as written. Anonymity also had its uses; as a correspondent in the Middle East I moved freely between Israel and
Arab countries because my name did not appear over stories
disliked by the various authorities.

The new men were not inclined to be modest about their work.
Apart from normal vanity, they believed that their future prospects depended upon being known. They also resented the rule
that they could not write for other publications. It denied them a
useful secondary source of income, and reinforced the anonymity
rule. I also disliked having to sign a memorandum of agreement
whenever I changed posts. Paragraph 3 of the memorandum I
had to sign when I went to Washington in 1960 read:

> The Employee during the continuance of his engagement
> (a) will render his exclusive services as *The Times* Cor-

respondent in Washington to the Company and write solely and exclusively for the Company

(b) will devote the whole of his time and attention to his duties in relation to the business of the Company and use his best endeavours to promote the Company's interests

(c) will not without the express written permission of the Manager of the Company being first obtained

(i) write or contribute any article or matter for publication in any other newspaper or for publication in any magazine periodical book leaflet

(ii) write or contribute any script or matter for broadcasting or television or take part in any broadcast or televised performance

(iii) write any book play or film script for publication or public performance

(iv) engage or be concerned in any other business whatsoever

(v) render any services of a literary nature to any other person firm or company for reward.

Permission to do any of these things was rarely given, but some years later I was asked by the American publishers, Harper and Row, to write a book along the lines of Lord Bryce's classic, *The American Commonwealth*. I agreed without reference to London largely because I wanted very much to write such a book. Bryce wrote his in 1888, and despite some updating the United States had changed almost beyond recognition. I also needed the money to pay for my children's education, but there were other reasons. I resented being treated as an indentured servant, and was no longer convinced that *The Times* could regain its former greatness. I remained loyal, and refused a few lucrative job offers because it was still the best British paper for a foreign correspondent. But I also lectured and wrote the occasional magazine article.

The youngsters back in London needed the money more, but for some of them Haley's aloofness was the last straw. Haley had cast his shadow over Printing House Square, and it was no longer a friendly place. The new men also had a different life style, and did not join any of the sports clubs run by the Companionship. The senior men went to their clubs for lunch, and there was a minimum of social activity. A young man could feel lonely as well as frustrated, and junior leader writers and reporters drifted away. They included some of the best and brightest: Henry Fairlie, Peregrine Worsthorne, James (Jan) Morris, David Holden, Godfrey Hodgson, Tom Pocock, John White and John Ardagh. Most of them were unwilling to go; and Holden, who was subsequently murdered in Cairo, wrote to McDonald:

'Please believe me that I am terribly grateful for the opportunities *The Times* has given me, and that I really love the damned old thing – in a way, perhaps, that I shall never love another.'

The paper lost about half a generation of promising young men, many of whom made their mark elsewhere. Fairlie, probably the best polemical writer of his generation, emigrated to the United States; and Worsthorne eventually became the brilliant editor of the *Sunday Telegraph*. Some were poached by the *Sunday Times*, which under a different proprietor offered more pay, bylines and lots of space. They were followed later by Frank Giles, the chief Paris correspondent, and White became an international civil servant. The paper's troubles would have been over if they had stayed and been given bylines – and if Haley had not edited behind a purdah curtain. Apparently unaware of his forbidding isolation, he became alarmed and warned the manager, who was responsible for salaries, that the traditional prestige of working for *The Times* was no longer everything for a talented young man; money and prospects were also important. He added that the paper ought to be in a position to keep the men it wanted to keep.

The tone of Haley's warning indicated that he held the manager responsible, and he was half right. Francis Mathew was a disappointing manager. He had arrived at Printing House Square with firm ideas as to the future of the paper. He wanted *The Times* to remain a high-priced newspaper with a limited circulation, and was convinced that the purchasing power of well-to-do readers would attract sufficient advertising to ensure a comfortable profit. He said as much when I dined with him in 1948, and confirmed it in 1955 when I went to his office to seek a salary increase before going to West Germany. On the first occasion I was uneasy, and dismayed on the second. In between the *Telegraph* had gone from strength to strength, and advertisers sought by Mathew were obviously not deterred by its large circulation.

There was another factor. Mathew, presumably unwittingly, was dictating broad editorial policy in that the kind of newspaper he wanted was very different from what Haley was trying to create to attract intelligent readers of all classes and ages. He did not care if they could not afford to buy a Rolls or a second-hand Mini as long as they had an interest in the world about them. Nor did he care if they were not old Etonians or Oxbridge graduates. He was largely self-educated, and the Reithian spirit in him wanted to inform and educate those with a similar background, and broaden their horizons in every possible way. He wanted to make them good citizens. In broadcasting terms he wanted the paper to be read by people who listened to Radio Four as well as Radio Three. He had got rid of the sacred cows – that is, events that previously had to be reported though of little general interest – such as the Eton wall game. Apart from his aversion to Marilyn Monroe, he was doing everything he could to raise the circulation to 500,000. Mathew was determined to hold it below 300,000. Haley must have resented this subtle intrusion, especially when Mathew assumed that he had the same kind of independence from the board which tradition and the earlier exchange of letters between Dawson and Astor – the paper's constitution, as it became known – gave to the editor.

In the event, Mathew got his calculations wrong. The existing small circulation, due in part to newsprint rationing, did not attract sufficient advertising despite the purchasing power of the readership. Not enough advertisers were prepared to pay the high rates, proportionally much higher than the opposition's, set by Mathew. Nor had he foreseen that the print unions would hold Fleet Street to ransom; and that the proprietors of popular newspapers would be willing to pay to keep their presses running. One or two also wanted to squeeze out less profitable newspapers, and the *News Chronicle* was forced to close down although its circulation was in excess of one million.

Mathew had further compounded his errors of judgement before Haley became editor. In 1949 it became clear that the government would not abolish newsprint rationing in the foreseeable future. The country could not afford to import more, or so it was said, but official antipathy to newspapers was probably another reason. Most proprietors were happy to continue with small newspapers which were immensely profitable for them, but not for *The Times*. Advertising and not circulation was its main source of income. Moreover, the board believed that without more pages the paper could not provide all the information readers required. Mathew decided that mechanical paper was the only answer. It was not rationed, and Mathew said that this high quality paper guaranteed good reproduction which would attract advertisers. There were obvious disadvantages. It cost about 15 per cent more than newsprint, which explained why it had not been used in Fleet Street; but Mathew argued that the extra cost would be painlessly absorbed as more space became available for advertising. Mechanical paper was also in short supply, and the mill which made it wanted a long-term contract before expanding production. A 25-year contract was negotiated.

By 1956 larger issues were being printed, and much self-congratulation was heard on the managerial floor. But not for long; *The Times* was seen to have an unfair advantage over its competitors, and newsprint rationing was finally abolished. The real struggle for readers and advertisers began twelve years after the war, and *The Times* was in a bind. Its paper bill, a heavy item in newspaper production, was proportionally higher than its competitors', and it was saddled with a contract with about twenty years to run. Labour costs were still rising, and Mathew's prediction that advertisers would be attracted by the superior reproduction quality of mechanical paper had not been realized. The company was losing money, and Haley's plans to broaden further the scope of the paper were not implemented. Salaries remained low.

The postwar troubles of the paper were not its first; indeed, a similar misjudgement when the stamp tax was repealed a hundred years earlier led to its decline from being the country's largest-selling and most profitable newspaper to the near-bankrupt Victorian relic which Northcliffe rescued. The iniquitous tax was imposed to weaken and prevent the growth of newspapers, but over the years it became an unforeseen subsidy for *The Times*. The reason was that taxed newspapers were delivered free by the post office, and the paper had many more pages than its competitors and was often twice as heavy. Its enemies in parliament allied themselves with members opposed to the tax which was finally repealed in 1861. Newspapers had to arrange their own distribution, and the expectation was that the much higher costs incurred by *The Times* would clip the wings of its newshawks. Repeal also encouraged the launching of new papers, many of which sold for a penny. *The Times* reduced its price, but only to threepence. It was a disastrous mistake.

The proprietor, John Walter III, did not realize that repeal had brought about a revolution in newspaper publishing no less important and far reaching than the commercial and editorial independence achieved by his father. Sales of all newspapers were more than doubled within a few years. The age of the mass-production press was well under way; and with the invention of the linotype machine and the rotary press, and the introduction of universal education, circulations would eventually be counted in millions.

The misjudgement was not immediately apparent, and a century later Walter's decision was applauded by Woods and Bishop in their book:

> The paper became established as a high-quality product read by an educated elite. The social structure of Britain proved well able to provide a commercial basis for such a paper for some decades. If anything, the management of *The Times* had over-estimated the threat of the so-called popular press of the 1860s. The *Daily Telegraph* and its contemporaries were a threat to the circulation of the paper, but not to its profitability. (*The Story of* The Times, 1983)

The social structure did indeed provide a commercial basis for the paper for many years, but the circulation rose at a much slower rate. *The Times* really was the top people's paper, and their numbers increased every year as the industrial revolution created more wealth. Fortunes were being made from the railways, shipping, banking, insurance and overseas trade as well as manufacturing. New money became old money within a generation or two. The children were sent to public school and university, and some entered parliament and the expanding professions. The growth of empire was another source of wealth, power and rank.

It must have seemed that the possibilities for growth were infinite.

What Walter obviously did not understand was that new strata of the middle classes were being created as the growth of industry and commerce called for managers, engineers, accountants and other experts. The expanded class system which survived more or less intact until the first world war was coming into being. By addressing the paper to the top of the social pyramid, Walter denied it a share of the growing number of potential readers. That was not all. The *Telegraph* and other newspapers competing for this new readership discovered by trial and error that the new readers were developing interests other than politics and foreign news. They were bored by columns of parliamentary reports unrelieved by white space and display. The initiative came from across the Atlantic, and gradually the competition broadened their coverage and improved the layout of their pages. Walter refused to adjust, and in so doing ossified *The Times*.

The grandson of the founder was a Victorian of great moral rectitude, and had seriously considered taking holy orders in his youth. He was guided by moral as well as commercial considerations, and regarded the maintenance of the paper's character as a moral duty. He was responsible for its new and somewhat priggish self-esteem, which would have amused Barnes. A leading article declared that *The Times* was the most signal example of useful enterprise in the empire, and unblushingly referred to its unexampled devotion to the public interest and unsurpassed independence. 'We belong,' it said, 'to the public, we are proud to think that England is proud of *The Times*.' Woods and Bishop say in their book that the conception of the paper as an instrument of service towards the community and an object of dedication on the part of its staff derived from John Walter III. In later years it became crystallized in the mind of the nation, which thought of *The Times* as a national institution rather than a commercial undertaking.

A hundred years later Astor and some of the senior people on the paper still regarded it as a national institution, but history was not repeating itself. John Walter III had continued to preside over a profitable commercial undertaking, and not a loss-making paper. From 1849, the first year for which complete records have survived, to 1877, when Delane retired, the average circulation

rose from 32,195 to 62,193. Advertising revenue was doubled to
£234,518, and dividends were more than tripled to £79,600. The
actual bottom line was more impressive. The offices and printing
works belonged to the Walter family; and in 1877 they charged
£107,000 for printing the paper and £2,000 for rent. Other newspapers were more profitable; but the Walters were content, and
apparently did not notice the relative decline.

It was not reversed when exhaustion forced Delane to resign.
Walter had not thought of bringing a man forward as a successor,
and Thomas Chenery was appointed. He was 51, much older than
Barnes and Delane when they were appointed, but had done well
in the Crimean war. His work was overshadowed by William
Howard Russell, the star of the team sent to cover the war. The
Irishman was the prototype war correspondent, and had covered
the Indian mutiny, the beginning of the American civil war, and
the first Franco-Prussian war. He was a superb reporter, and his
eyewitness account of the charge of the light brigade at Balaclava
inspired Tennyson to write his poem. Chenery, who was the
anchor man in Constantinople, reported the terrible conditions
in the base hospital at Scutari, and his as well as Russell's dispatches led to Florence Nightingale's mission of mercy.

Chenery was writing leading articles from Oxford where he was
professor of Arabic when appointed editor. The foreign news
pages flourished under his editorship, but not the paper. Instead of
broadening its coverage, he published learned articles on Arabian
antiquities. Walter was impressed, but not the new middle classes.
Both circulation and advertising fell.

It was the beginning of an inexorable decline from greatness
and profitability, and the paper was almost bankrupted when it
published the forged Parnell letters in 1886. These purported to
prove that the Irish leader was involved in political assassination,
and they cost the paper more than £200,000. It still seems incredible that George Buckle, Chenery's successor, published them.
The only explanation is that he knew nothing about libel or
believed that the paper could do no wrong: he was in fact
appointed by Walter because his father, Canon Buckle, had been
connected with Newman and the Tractarian movement. The
world's first modern and independent newspaper, which set the
standards to which most journalists still aspire, was in a miserable

condition when rescued by Northcliffe in 1908. It had once sold twice as many copies as the combined circulation of the other Fleet Street newspapers, and was selling less than 40,000 copies a day when the circulation of the *Daily Mail* was in excess of one million. The circulation would have been less but for the foreign news pages which remained unsurpassed. It could have been very different if John Walter III had not regarded the paper as a national institution and chosen to restrict its appeal to a small elite readership. A hundred years later it seemed, despite Haley's efforts, that growth was once again being denied for much the same reasons.

9

Top People Read The Times

Despite the commercial mistakes and disappointments in London, I enjoyed life and my continuing education as a foreign correspondent. At least, that was how the paper saw it; first as an assistant to Britter in India and then in theory working under Quilliam in the Middle East. In fact, on both assignments I did pretty much what I wanted to do, which suited them. I always wanted to see what was on the other side of the hill, and they preferred the more staid life of the capital. I assumed at the time that their apparent reluctance to live rough was due to their age, but they were decent men willing to give a younger man the opportunity to prove himself. They also accepted the convention that all *Times* foreign correspondents were equal. While allowing that some were more equal than others, each of us, whatever our age and experience, corresponded directly with the editor. This is what separated us from the reporters at home; we were part of the corporate *Times*, that almost mystical concept which explained editorial anonymity. Our journalism was referred to as correspondence.

Having served my apprenticeship, I ascended a couple of steps within the hierarchy when I went to Korea and southeast Asia on my own. I also broadened my experience of the world, an essential part of my education, which was why I first thought that the return to India in 1953 was a setback. I knew India, and wanted to move on. However, I could see why Haley, after deciding that more attention should be given to the sub-continent, wanted me to return. I was well equipped for the assignment, being the only correspondent apart from Britter who had some experience of

India when it was still part of the British empire and had covered the bloodshed and turmoil of independence and partition. I had friends and acquaintances scattered throughout the sub-continent, and some of them had become editors, senior politicians or officials. It was just as well because India had changed out of all recognition; not the heat and dust or the poverty and squalor, but the spirit which invigorated New Delhi. Whatever could be said about British India, and much good had been done under the *raj*, the natural genius of the people had been smothered; then, six years after independence, it was flowering and promised the renewal long dreamed about. I discovered that there was still much to learn, and the experience stood me in good stead in later years.

India was the first colonial possession to be given independence after the war and it was the largest. Moreover, it was an ancient civilization and able to govern itself in part because of the officials and administrative structure left behind by Britain. India became the benchmark against which the progress of other former colonies was to be judged. It was a natural leader, if not always acknowledged, of what became known as the third world: first at the Bandung conference in 1955 and then in Belgrade in 1961 where the concept of non-alignment finally emerged. Jawaharlal Nehru tried to change the diplomatic map of the world as well as transform his own country. In both he was only partially successful, but it was essential for a foreign correspondent to understand what he tried to do.

Nehru was a patrician, fastidious and arrogant. Educated at Harrow and Cambridge, he was also a rational, modern man impatient with the intellectual cant of some of Gandhi's followers. He campaigned against British imperialism during the struggle for independence but retained the political, judicial and economic systems it had introduced. He was a parliamentarian with great faith in the Westminster form of government, and was convinced that India could only reduce poverty by rapid industrialization. His development plans depended upon foreign aid, which largely meant American aid, and he did not like Americans. He shared the contempt and resentment of upper-class Britons of his generation for the upstarts, and accepted their aid gracelessly. His antipathy was perhaps explained by the fact that India had recently got rid of one imperial power and did not want to become a client of another. John Foster Dulles, the American secretary of state, did not help; his assumption that those who were not with him were against him confirmed for Nehru his suspicion of American imperialism.

In turn, Nehru's assumption of moral superiority must have infuriated Dulles. He was no more or less moral than the average decent and well-disposed person, and his foreign policy was no proof of Indian moral superiority. He ought not to have accepted the accession of Kashmir from the Hindu maharajah, and having done so he refused to hold a referendum for its largely Muslim population. Kashmir soured relations with Pakistan, and although friendly relations with the neighbouring state should have been his first priority he refused to compromise over Kashmir. Relations worsened when Pakistan became an American ally, and eventually the two Commonwealth countries went to war.

My reporting of this and other aspects of his foreign policy and sporadic communal disturbances in India annoyed Nehru, and complaints arrived in Printing House Square. To be fair, officials in Delhi continued to be friendly and helpful. Two or three weeks before we were due to leave India – our son had contracted polio and we had to wait until he was declared fit to travel – one of them showed me a secret file containing official reports of Chinese military incursions through Himalayan passes into India. My guarded report of minor clashes with Indian border guards and exchanges of fire was angrily denied. I was accused of all known journalistic crimes plus enmity to India and a lifelong dedication to communism. It was of no importance that my source was an official file which I had read in the foreign ministry, and that it included reports from district commissioners and military commanders along the Himalayan frontier. The official who showed me the file had to deny its existence. Nehru was determined not to tangle with China. The Chinese did in fact invade India later, and in panic Nehru called for American and British help. Fortunately, the Chinese withdrew, but by that time Nehru was an exhausted man, overburdened with work, and possibly conscious at last that he was not necessarily infallible.

The paper ignored the complaints and charges of the Indian

government, and nothing was said about them when I visited London. Whatever Haley and McDonald, the foreign editor, thought remained a mystery until the fifth volume of the Official History, written by McDonald in retirement, was published. It says of me, '[he] showed a determination that became stronger in him to make his dispatches set the record straight about the deeds and misdeeds of men in authority, no matter how much he upset them ... a surprise awaited anyone who thought that moving him from a colonial territory to a brand-new independent country would dull his critical faculties. It was not long before his zeal for blunt truths forced him to criticize Pandit Nehru almost as severely as he had criticized the British authorities in Malaya.'

Obviously I was not the only correspondent to 'set the record straight', and in one way this passage says more about *The Times* than me. The so-called establishment newspaper respected lawful authority but the first priority was news. Prime ministers and presidents, ambassadors and high commissioners had the right to be heard but more weight was given to what the correspondent had written. This did not mean that the correspondent was free to pursue personal vendettas or report the news from his own political viewpoint. Nor was he expected to be a political eunuch, but he was required to discipline himself. He was an observer and not an active participant; he was assumed to be modest as well as honest. Otherwise there were no hard and fast rules, and as long as the correspondent produced the news and tried to scoop the opposition he could always depend upon the support of the editor and foreign editor.

It also seemed that Haley was doubly determined to defend correspondents who wrote 'blunt truths' because he wanted to prove that *The Times* was not a government organ. I was grateful but wondered if he realized that this wide-spread assumption was at least partly responsible for the complaints lodged by foreign governments. They did not appear to be much concerned about the reports of correspondents working for other newspapers, but they expected diplomatic discretion from *Times* men who they regarded as reconnaissance scouts for the more formal battalions of the foreign office. It could be annoying for British ambassadors when my stories were taken to reflect their reports to Whitehall. One of them complained to me after being called to the local foreign ministry and requested to explain one of my stories. He was a nice and intelligent man, and he smiled wanly when I suggested over a drink that independent reporting on my part would eventually establish that I was not one of his men.

That was one way of resolving the dilemma, and Haley had another. He posted me to Bonn as chief correspondent in West Germany. It was a promotion to the first division, Bonn was next to Washington and Paris in the established pecking order, and demonstrated that he had complete confidence in me. I was naturally gratified, if at first unenthusiastic although for the first time I had an assistant correspondent, a secretary and an office. Bonn appeared to be a sedentary job for a middle-aged man, and I was only thirty-six. It was of course an essential part of my education; Germany regularly dominated the news in the mid-1950s. German rearmament and Soviet threats to Berlin, to take two examples, were manifestations of the cold war and dangerously lowered the international temperature. At times the two Germanies were as exciting as Korea, Indo-China or Malaya.

I must admit to enjoying, at least in retrospect, such excitements as when Khrushchev broke up the summit conference in Paris and abruptly departed for Berlin. The expectation was that the impetuous Soviet leader could order another blockade, and war seemed imminent. I flew to Berlin, and that evening drove into the eastern sector with two or three other correspondents to cover a rally where Khrushchev was to speak. This was before the wall was erected, and although the status of foreign correspondents was ill-defined we had the right of access to the eastern sector as nationals of the occupying powers. That night we must have been alone in exercising that right. The Tiergarten looked deserted as we approached the flood-lit Brandenburger Tor, although we had been told that British troops were standing to near the Soviet war memorial, and I felt that I was a participant and not an observer of a great drama. I was also conscious of the theatricality of the occasion – the silence, the flood lights, the Russian sentries impassive before the memorial, and ahead two Vopos, the East German paramilitary police, emerging from the shadow of the Tor with their burp guns at the ready. No wonder English thriller writers were attracted to the city.

One of the Vopos asked where we were going, and I said it was none of his business. We were British and Americans, citizens of occupying powers who could go where we pleased. He jerked the muzzle of the gun forward, and then reluctantly retreated into the shadows to find a sergeant, a polite almost fatherly man who returned our passports with an apology. He asked if we were going to the Khrushchev meeting and gave us elaborate directions. Although the tension was almost tangible, he was the archetypal German again doing his duty. He then saluted and said, *auf Wiedersehen*, and we drove off into the ruins of East Berlin. Unter den Linden was deserted as was Alexanderplatz, and an English colleague wondered how many tens of thousands of allied and Soviet troops were standing by their tanks, artillery pieces and troop carriers on both sides of the dividing line. An American, who was a close friend of his ambassador, said that US air force B52 bombers were on red alert.

We were jostled by a crowd outside the hall until rescued by a Soviet diplomat who led us inside. The crowd was clapping and stamping to the persistent beat of a brass band, and I was reminded of those old newsreel shots of Hitler haranguing a similar crowd in that very hall. Only the political insignia and slogans had changed. A couple of demagogic speeches were delivered to enthuse the crowd, and then to a roll of drums Khrushchev appeared accompanied by Ulbricht. The East German leader's face was pale and drawn, and he did not look like a man who knew that his time had come. It was the first intimation that Khrushchev had had second thoughts. The Russian, enormously impressive despite his waddle and ridiculously wide trousers, acknowledged the cheers and forest of clenched fists, and looked like a patient man who had been wronged or misunderstood. The usual harsh words were said about Adenauer, the West German chancellor, but his speech made clear that his intentions had suddenly become wholly peaceful. The summit conference had failed because the Pentagon did not want to resolve the world's problems peacefully. Rage made the aggressors blind, and hot heads had to be allowed to cool off. He had postponed the summit to let the dust settle. There would be no separate peace treaty with East Germany before another attempt had been made to reach agreement with the west. He would do nothing to increase tension, but would strive for international relaxation, disarmament and the peaceful solution of controversial questions.

I could hardly believe my own ears. I was both disappointed by the anticlimax and relieved that the *Götterdammerung* had been postponed. Belatedly I realized that the anticlimax was the story, and we made our way to the exit again led by the Soviet diplomat who was suddenly jovial. I pondered my lead as we raced back to West Berlin, and we were not delayed at the checkpoint. The Vopos waved us through, and a West Berlin policeman shouted, '*Alles Gut?*' '*Alles gut*', we chorused as the driver drove towards the telephones. I dictated my story from the Reuter office, reporting the evening deadpan and quoting Khrushchev from notes I had scribbled in my notebook. The night editor came on the phone, thanked me for the story and said that I would lead the paper. He then asked what the evening had been like, and I said that it had been pretty hairy. He laughed, and sounded as relieved as I was. We had a few beers and Steinhagers somewhere – it was always difficult to sleep after an exciting story – and later I phoned Pat and said that I would fly back on the morning plane. She asked about Khrushchev, and I said that we would probably survive for a few more months.

That evening was not typical. Life in Bonn was pleasant despite its provincialism, and its smallness had advantages. The countryside was only a few minutes away by car, and the children enjoyed picnicking. I became a family man, and even helped Pat with the shopping. We discovered the pleasures of bourgeois life, more enjoyable in Germany and France perhaps because they were not denigrated by the snobbish. I developed a knowledge of wine; the paper published annual vintage reports – another of Haley's innovations – and I went on *Weinreisen* organized by the German wine producers. The Deutschmark was undervalued, and we could afford to rent a large house in Bad Godesberg. David Bruce, the American ambassador, enjoyed the company of journalists and arranged for us to buy whisky and cigarettes at diplomatic prices. We made some good friends, German as well as foreign correspondents. Life was indeed pleasant although we were perched on the eastern glacis of western defences. I thought occasionally of the Roman legions maintaining peace against the barbarians, and was grateful that most of the Hunnish tribes were now on our side.

I also travelled widely on both sides of the iron curtain; in East Germany foreign correspondents could only visit East Berlin and the Leipzig fair, but representing *The Times* I was occasionally given permission to make extensive tours of the country but always with a *Begleiter*, or accompanying official. The difference between the two Germanies was immense. The economic recovery of West Germany was only just beginning, but in comparison East Germany was still a devastated country. Driving from East Berlin to Rostock on the Baltic coast, about 150 miles, I saw less than a dozen private cars. More often than not the autobahn was deserted except for men removing grass between the sections of concrete. The towns and villages were battered and unpainted, the shop windows half-empty and the inhabitants poorly dressed. Perhaps it was my imagination, but the omnipresence of authority was palpable. It was rarely absent in West Germany, but in the East I really felt that Big Brother was watching.

This was evident in the behaviour of the people I met. I was long accustomed to being treated with suspicion, and not only in the Middle East. Foreign correspondents are unusual, even in a free and prosperous country such as the United States; but while I was regarded as an exotic creature in small Middle Western towns, in less free areas of the world I was frequently aware of suspicion. Not many people are paid to roam far and wide and ask questions; if I was not a spy I was an unknown best avoided. I thought that I was inured to this least attractive side of my job until I visited East Germany, my first communist country, and met my *Begleiter*, who I shall call Hans. He was obviously terrified.

Hans was new to the job; what was known as the delegation season was in full swing, and the professional guides were busy conducting groups of eastern Europeans and western fellow travellers round the People's Republic. The foreign ministry assumed that I wanted an English-speaking guide, and ordered Hans, a lecturer in English and American literature at the Humboldt university, to do his duty. I discovered later that he was an internal immigrant, that is he had retreated into himself to avoid Big Brother. The last thing he wanted was to travel with a foreigner who would be watched wherever he went.

Hans, who was about my age, was a nice and sensitive man and very much aware of the shabbiness he shared with the vast

189

majority of East Germans. He wore his best suit, and his change of clothing only half-filled a small bag. He confessed that he had never travelled in a private car. I had recently taken delivery of a new Mercedes. He was overwhelmed by its luxury, as he was by the hotels reserved for senior party officials, delegations and people such as myself. For the first time he had a bathroom to himself and as much butter as he wanted. The poor man had been a schoolboy when Hitler decided that he and other Germans would have guns, not butter, and then came the war and Russian occupation.

This taste of relative affluence overlaid his fear, and in the privacy of the car he could talk about the subject he loved. The only English-language books I had seen in the bookshop in Stalinallee were Dickens, Jack London and *Moll Flanders*; presumably the university had a larger selection, but he was starved of newer books and eagerly asked about them. The drive from Rostock and Stralsund on the Baltic coast, through Magdeburg, Meissen and Leipzig to Dresden near the Czech frontier, was for him a literary journey of discovery. We talked of little else until his reserve or protective mechanism finally gave way one day near Karlmarxstadt when he asked about life in West Germany. I answered as truthfully as I could, and added that I would be glad to help should he decide to cross over. It was then easy and comparatively safe. More than 3,600,000 East Germans fled to the west before the Berlin Wall was built in 1961, many of them on the underground railway which served all of Berlin's four occupied sectors. He shook his head; his old mother was still alive and he could not live without his personal library. He had 900 books.

About six months later, Hans phoned me in Bonn to announce his arrival in the west. He was staying with a relative in Wuppertal, but was anxious to move to Bonn. Did I know of a room or a flat, preferably a flat because of his books. All 900? I asked. *Natürlich*. He had brought them across on the U-Bahn. Not in one go of course, but about twenty at a time. What about the police? He said that he had always boarded the underground at the mainline station for Mecklenburg, where he had an aunt. If he was stopped and searched he said that he was paying her a visit. He made about fifty trips in four months, each time leaving the books with a family friend in West Berlin. He was a modern hero of sorts, or anti-hero, but in his own quiet way one of the indomitables. He was apolitical, and as a university lecturer was comparatively well paid. Life was no doubt colourless, but he had security and status. He found it difficult to explain why he, a mousey little man, had taken so many chances. I supposed that he just wanted to read the books denied to him in East Germany.

I filed a series of articles after that trip which was promptly published and praised presumably because I was one of the first foreign correspondents to have travelled more or less freely in East Germany. The constant flow of refugees was seen as proof of an oppressive regime epitomized by the savage Soviet response to the 1953 uprising in East Berlin. This was true, but nevertheless a crude caricature. I would have been among the first to flee if I had been an East German, but the vast majority remained. Many of course were too old or too young, or could not bring themselves to desert their families, but others were reasonably content. For instance, I spent a weekend at a little resort on the Baltic coast reserved for intellectuals. Its unspoilt beauty and quiet affluence reminded me of Cape Cod. These privileged ones drove West German cars and their clothes had obviously come from the west. The drinks cabinets were international. I could have been staying with Harvard friends on the Cape or Nantucket, except that the conversation was guarded. The intellectual freedom of America or Britain was entirely absent; they had paid a high price for their privileges but did not seem to mind.

Other groups seemed reasonably content; Ulbricht, the party boss, was providing elaborate sports facilities to train youngsters who later would become international stars. And of course millions were not prepared to flee or rebel as long as they were housed, fed and employed. It was ever so; in 1776 only about one-third of colonial Americans willingly rebelled against the British. Unless the Soviet Union withdrew from central Europe, Germany would remain divided. The demand of the West German chancellor, Dr Konrad Adenauer, for reunification would at best remain a pipe dream or, and this did not seem to have been considered by the old man, a *casus belli*. This was evident to diplomats but they had to remain silent; reunification headed the diplomatic agenda in part payment for West German rearmament, but I worked for an independent newspaper and my coverage infuriated the chancellor.

I had a sneaking admiration for Adenauer. He had cooperated with the western occupying powers, but retained his dignity. He had never been a sycophant; indeed, he was dismissed by the British when as *Oberbürgermeister* of Cologne he had refused to chop down trees in the city's parks to provide fuel in the desperately cold winter of 1947–8. He had been earlier dismissed by the Nazis, his record was clean, but he later refused to accept the concept of national guilt. As the first postwar chancellor, he had presided over the country's economic recovery, the so-called *Wirtschaftwunder*. He could not have done this without foreign aid, especially the Marshall Plan, but he treated the occupying powers as an equal, and had emerged triumphant from the struggle in part by enlisting the help of the foreign press. His use of the foreign press was masterful; he could not dictate to the correspondents of course, but by conducting much of his negotiations with the occupiers by press interview they vied with each other to keep him in the headlines. He was nearly always a good story.

This may have explained why, when sovereignty was achieved in 1955, so many tax allowances were provided for foreign correspondents. When a tax accountant completed my first return he said that the federal government owed me about fifty marks. It certainly helped to explain why he could be angry with me. One of my predecessors had been so cooperative that my more objective approach was seen as hostile.

One evening aboard his campaign train in the 1957 election he came back to a compartment where a group of us was sitting, ordered some good wine and passed on some interesting information. I thought that it might provide a good lead for my next story. That night the train was shunted on to a siding, and looking out of the window I saw a company of the frontier force erecting lights as a protective measure and then patrolling the area with dogs. It was a bizarre sight, and reminded me of films about German prisoner-of-war camps. The next day I reported what Adenauer had said and then described that scene, adding that Adenauer was like a governor passing through a restive province. I intended no connection between the two parts of the story, but

Adenauer saw it as a calculated affront.

He was also capable of going to extraordinary lengths to win the support of the *New York Times*, *Le Monde*, *The Times* and the *Neue Züricher Zeitung*, probably in that order. Switzerland was neutral, but the NZZ was important because it was the only foreign newspaper of repute he could read. We were invited, collectively and separately, to the Palais Schaumberg for a glass of wine or afternoon tea. The tea was always ruined by thick cream, but the conversation was often useful and enlightening. Behind that immobile American Indian face and iron will were doubts that rose and fell with the headlines. He was not convinced that the Americans would support him until reunification was achieved, and was worried about the backstairs influence of the British in Washington. He was not afraid of the Russians, but was apprehensive of Khrushchev's cunning. He had probably been told that we enjoyed meeting the Soviet leader when he came to East Berlin.

The meetings were nearly always jolly affairs; Khrushchev obviously enjoyed meeting foreign correspondents and the good-natured banter. He would ridicule western policies, invariably with a smile, and roar with laughter when one of us made a telling riposte. We had to be careful; he was known for his spasms of blind anger when his KGB bodyguards would unceremoniously remove the offender. On one occasion when he addressed a mass open-air meeting in East Berlin he attacked us as the jackals of the international yellow press, but we were nevertheless invited to a reception in the town hall the next evening. Before the reception I saw a necktie with yellow and black diagonal stripes in a shop window and bought half a dozen which we wore that evening. His eyes narrowed suspiciously when he saw us, and he roughly asked what we were wearing. By this time I was beginning to think that the joke had misfired, but said that it was the club tie of the international yellow press. There was a dreadful pause, but he finally roared with laughter and pressed on me another vodka.

Khrushchev's joists with journalists were widely known, and resented by some diplomats because he occasionally said something of considerable importance, which they believed should have been communicated to their foreign ministries more formally. I suspect some of them concluded that we were being shrewdly brainwashed. This was nonsense, but Khrushchev was cunning and a German chancellor caught between the two superpowers was naturally apprehensive. This became evident at one of Adenauer's tea parties after the Russian leader had proposed a confederation of the two Germanies. Each would retain its sovereignty and political and economic systems, but their separation would be ameliorated. Families could be reunited, and inter-zonal trade – to use the diplomatic lingo – could be improved. I could see why the idea should be received with caution, but not that it should be dismissed out of hand and said as much to the chancellor.

Adenauer answered obliquely. Recalling the time when he was briefly jailed by the Nazis, he said that he recognized one of the SS guards. He was the son of a good Catholic civil servant; he was not very bright, but Adenauer had helped to get him into the police force before the war. Adenauer went on: 'I asked him why he had joined the SS. "After a good Catholic upbringing, what can your poor mother think of you? You have disgraced your family and your church." He said, "*Herr Oberbürgermeister*, I am also a good German. I am doing my duty."' Adenauer paused for effect. We were all hanging on his words, and I was wondering what it had to do with the confederation proposal. He leaned forward from the little yellow love seat and sipped the tepid tea without a grimace. Then he flung back his arms dramatically and said, 'There you can't trust the Germans'.

I was astonished. It was monstrous of him to tell foreign correspondents that his own people could not be trusted, and I could not believe that he had such a low opinion of his countrymen. I assumed that he was prepared to do or say anything to further his political aims; I still do, but then, on reflection, I became half convinced that he did indeed distrust his own people. He had seen so much: two military defeats, the Weimar republic as well as Hitler, the Ribbentrop pact with the Soviet Union, the concentration camps and the postwar degradation and semi-starvation. He despised most of his cabinet colleagues, and had the Catholic's distrust of the Social Democrats. Not trusting anybody, he was determined to involve his country inextricably with the west, especially the United States and France. Britain rarely entered in his calculations, but I could only applaud his ultimate objective. I did not share his distrust of Social Democrats, who I admired in many ways, but was convinced that we would all sleep more easily if the West Germans remained friends and allies.

Adenauer nevertheless remained suspicious of me – the idea of perfidious Albion was then still widespread – and when I offended him again he called me a *Drahtzieher*, or wire puller, claiming that I was responsible for the dire state of Anglo-German relations. Haley was unmoved, but on one of his infrequent trips to Bonn we discussed Germany at some length. He knew that I was not prejudiced against Germans, but wanted to explore my view of them. He even agreed to have lunch, and we sat on the terrace of a restaurant overlooking the Rhine and talked. He was relaxed and unusually expansive. Perhaps it was the spring weather or the splendid view of the *Siebengebirge* opposite. Whatever the reason, when I dropped him off at the airport he was obviously satisfied. Certainly he continued to give prominence to my stories, and in 1960 promoted me to Washington as the chief correspondent in the United States. I had realized my ambition at the age of 41, one year later than I had hoped but I could hardly complain.

In Germany I was much closer to Printing House Square that I had ever been as a foreign correspondent. The telephone communications were excellent, we had annual leaves and often took short holidays in London in between. I got to know Haley better, and probably drew closer to him than most *Times* men except for the assistant editors. Not that we became close friends, but he relaxed when he and his wife dined with us at home in Bonn and the children – we then had three – came down uninvited to see the boss man. The usual reserve melted, and he played with them with genuine warmth. Nevertheless our relationship was formal; it was always Mr Heren and not Louis, and of course I addressed him as Sir William. I was probably never anything more for him than a competent fellow craftsman, but that was enough and occasionally, very occasionally, he took me into his confidence.

In turn, I discovered that Haley was an uncomplicated man, at least compared with other journalists or politicians of my acquaintance. He had no doubts, and to that extent reminded me of a simple Catholic priest whose belief in God is absolute. Haley's moral certainties gave him immense strength. He obviously enjoyed being the boss, and if he appeared to be authoritarian he was always fair and humane. He had no side, and was genuinely modest. The office Rolls was only used for official business; on one occasion when he and Lady Haley visited Astor in the south of France he insisted upon travelling to Heathrow by public transport.

The vast majority of the editorial staff, alas, did not know this man behind the alleged glass eyes. That was the tragedy of his editorship. Haley could have been a great editor, a worthy successor to Barnes and Delane, but a modern newspaper cannot be edited by memoranda. The best cannot be got from journalists by avoiding them. Why the interior man was never allowed to emerge was a mystery to the few who knew him, but I was eventually convinced that Haley's fatal flaw was shyness. There was no other explanation for the aloofness. It made him incapable of small talk and the easy geniality of Fleet Street. It could be ludicrous. When he visited Washington in the 1960s, he would come into the office with the self-effacing demeanour of somebody trying to sell magazine subscriptions. My American secretary could not believe at first that he was the boss man. He would hover on the threshold of my room until persuaded to sit down. I knew that he liked my American coverage – he once told Oliver Woods that my stories helped to sell the paper – but he had little to say during those brief visits. I would arrange for him to see the president and the secretary of state, and only then did the authoritative Haley which everybody knew emerge. I took him to the White House to meet President Kennedy in 1962, and I thought that the interview went well. Kennedy was obviously impressed, but afterwards when we were walking back to my office Haley said that I was right, Kennedy was not a great president. I was gratified, my conclusion that the 35th president was not necessarily God's gift to the human race was not widely shared; I assumed that we would discuss the interview over lunch, but the shyness returned and Haley retreated to his hotel.

Long after his retirement Haley came unannounced to our new offices in Gray's Inn Road to spend a few days in the archives. I was editing the paper at the time, and invited him to lunch in the boardroom to meet some of the men and women who had worked under him. They all stood to attention when he arrived, and at first conversation was not easy. It began to flow when he spoke of the sale of the company to Lord Thomson and our departure from Printing House Square, but as usual he revealed little of himself until he wrote to me later. The letter read:

> So long as I have any memory, the lunch you and your colleagues gave me will be among the greatest of its riches. I was deeply moved to be with you all again. To feel the tradition being carried on in the new circumstances and in new surroundings convinced me yet once again that, as I said, the right thing had been done.
>
> That was an ultimate happiness. More immediate ones were to be among you once more, to exchange memories and to enjoy your talk; and to be made to feel welcomed. I have never done much looking back. Too busy most of the time. But when the years return unbidden, or at someone else's bidding, when shared experiences can be re-shared, then the past gives new life to the present.
>
> My deepest thanks to you for thinking of and arranging the reunion, and to everyone who came to it. Good wishes to you all.

I found the letter deeply moving. It revealed the Haley we all knew, the strong-minded man convinced that he had done the right thing, and the unknown Haley, the warm-hearted man the others had rarely if ever glimpsed behind those steady, almost unblinking eyes. The pity of it was that when we had those good and worthwhile times together the interior man had never emerged. The future of the paper and some of those who worked for it might have been different if only he had overcome his shyness. I found a photocopy of his hand-written letter in the archives when I was refreshing my memory before writing this memoir. It was the only textual evidence I found of Haley's humanity, and I wondered why he had placed it there.

Shyness could not explain his failure to contest the determination of Mathew and Morison to confine the readership to a small elite. All the evidence confirmed that he could effectively use those glass eyes at board meetings; but whatever the reason, his own plan to attract more readers had been blocked by the manager and the self-appointed *custos custodium* of the paper's traditions. Astor was of course reluctant to make sweeping changes, but even this immensely wealthy man could not completely ignore the company's poor financial record. Matters came to a head after his two sons, Gavin and Hugh, joined the board in 1956. They had been warned by their financial advisers of the company's vulnerability, and suggested an independent enquiry. Astor agreed, and Cooper Brothers, the chartered accountants, were called in. Their report made grim reading, and Gavin Astor said that 'if a bomb had fallen on Printing House Square it could not have caused more disturbance'.

In effect it established that the managerial structure had hardly changed since the days of John Walter and his manager, Mowbray Morris. Too much power was concentrated in the hands of the manager who had no system of budgetary control. The principles of newspaper finance were unknown, and there was little comprehension of the relationship of the size of the newspaper, the cost of production and the proportion of advertising required to produce a profit. This and more amounted to an indictment against the manager, and the report's recommendations were equally damning. These also included editorial changes, many similar to those planned by Haley, and a circulation target of 600,000 within ten years.

A sub-committee under the chairmanship of Gavin Astor was formed to examine the report in detail and propose reforms, but a counter-attack was quickly launched. Morison claimed that the report assailed the traditions of the paper, and urged more freedom of action for the manager. Mathew agreed with Morison that the paper must remain the organ of the governing classes, and said that a larger circulation would compel a lowering of editorial standards. He warned against the dangers of a circulation war; assuming that new readers could only come from the *Daily Telegraph*, he said that there was a special market for *The Times* and another for the *Telegraph*. 'Neither impinges on the other, nor on the mass market as a whole. If either steps out of its defined market it will go under in the dog fight for circulations.'

This had the smell of defeat, and the sub-committee asked Haley for his views. That the man wholly responsible for the product which had to be promoted and sold was not a member of the committee was to say the least surprising; but once invited he spoke in no uncertain terms:

> The committee speaks of the 'continued existence of *The Times* as the greatest newspaper in the world'. I think in the privacy of this room we must ask ourselves whether the phrase represents a fact or whether we are merely making an empty noise. Can you be the greatest newspaper in the world when you are fourteen pages: with perhaps only six columns for home news and six for foreign news?

In 1958 all British newspapers were smaller than they have since become. *The Times* was larger than most, but Haley's intention soon became evident; he wanted to demolish Mathew's case for a small elitist readership. He agreed that the character of the paper must not be changed. It had to remain a journal of record, and continue to play a useful part in the running of the country, but that did not merely mean Westminster and Whitehall. It also comprised local government, banking, industry, the professions, science and 'all activities which go to make our national life'. It meant producing a balanced, interesting and entertaining paper for intelligent readers of all ages and classes. Change must not be too rapid, readers tended to dislike change, but the paper must cater for 'the new generation's new interests'. There must be more editorial space and more journalists who must be better paid.

Haley won the argument, or so it seemed. A few more journalists were hired and salaries were increased, if modestly, but then a blow was dealt which eventually proved fatal. The board decided to rebuild Printing House Square which meant that there would not be enough money to finance editorial expansion.

It must be said in defence of the board, which was split over the issue, that the decision was originally made in 1930, and the first phase, rebuilding the printing plant, was completed in 1939. The company emerged from the war with the most modern printing facilities in Fleet Street, which should have been enough. As Haley argued when plans to rebuild the editorial and commercial offices were discussed, journalists did not mind where they worked as long as there was space in the paper for their stories. Moreover, some of them already worked in the best possible conditions;

those book-lined rooms with open coal fires. Admittedly, others were less fortunate. The paper had long outgrown the imposing main building which fronted on Queen Victoria Street, and had taken over adjacent and inferior buildings. The complex sprawled from Water Lane in the west to St Andrew's Hill in the east and was an untidy mess.

I knew every inch of it when I was a messenger, and it was like an obstacle course because of the different floor levels. Moving eastwards, say, from the offices of the foreign newspapers which took the paper's news service, I would zigzag along a corridor between office partitions past the slummy reporters' room, up a short flight of stairs and across a bridge to the main building. The next section was tricky and confused visitors: down another flight of stairs and an abrupt right turn into the main stairwell before descending a few more stairs to the first editorial floor. Beyond the editor's room were more steps to the sporting department which was housed over a shop where copies of *Times* photographs were sold, and the corridor twisted by little offices hardly big enough for a table and chair. The door of one could not be fully opened when the occupant, a leader writer who always wore carpet slippers, was sitting at his table. The corridor was narrow and badly lit, and it was a relief to reach the last building. I sometimes hummed 'Excelsior' when I came to the photographic department and the offices of the art editor, Mr Bogaerde, the father of the film star, Dirk Bogarde.

Behind this row of buildings was the eponymous square, and on two sides were the original extensions of the main building. They had housed some of the printing departments before the new plant was built on St Andrew's Hill, and had since been partitioned into offices. The largest was the intelligence department or what lesser newspapers called the morgue. The reference books and filing cabinets filled with newspaper cuttings were presided over by John Maywood who smoked sixty cigarettes a day and was reputed to drink ten pints of Guinness in the same period. He still had a straight back and clear eyes and complexion when he retired at the age of 85. The ID, as it was called, had a large Victorian table where Peter Fleming, the explorer and writer of fourth leaders, occasionally wrote his pieces.

On the third side of the square stood the Private House, a

pleasing Georgian mansion where John Walter, the founder, once lived. It had a small walled garden with a plane tree, where I could sit when doing weekend duty. This was one of the chores for young reporters, and I did more than my share because we were paid £1.50 for doing nothing. After midday on Saturday the office was closed for twenty-four hours because in those days we did not have a Sunday paper. Apart from a commissionaire on the back door and a fireman the office was empty, but a reporter was considered necessary in case of a crisis. The Private House contained the board room, the editorial mess and the proprietor's office, and upstairs was a bedroom where I slept. There was also a pleasant sitting-cum-dining room, and on the sideboard stood an unlocked tantalus with a few measures of whisky in one of the decanters. Dinner was served by a footman from the proprietor's house in Carlton House Terrace; soup, a chop or steak, cheese and a half bottle of claret. Later the commissionaire would bring up the news agency tapes or any telegrams that might have been sent by foreign correspondents demanding cash advances before going on some trip. I would mark these urgent, and the commissionaire would later leave them in the accountants' office. I was also expected to warn one of the news editors if a big story broke in order that he could deploy reporters or a foreign correspondent. That was the sum of my duties, and the commissionaire, who ran the company's rowing club – it had a boathouse at Barnes – would generally help me to finish the whisky. He was an amusing if garrulous man, and we often chatted until midnight.

I once asked him about the bag of gold sovereigns which according to legend was kept at the back door in case of emergency. Apparently before the introduction of the telegraph a correspondent was ordered to cover a newsworthy event in central Europe but it was a bank holiday and no money was available. He had to postpone his departure, and the then manager decided that an official of the company's bank must sit at the back door every night with a bag of 200 sovereigns. This practice was said to have continued long after a banker's draft could have been telegraphed to await the correspondent's arrival at the point of crisis. Northcliffe noticed the clerk sitting there with his Gladstone bag and cancelled the arrangement. I asked if this was true, and the commissionaire said that it was before his time but he had been told about it by one of his predecessors.

When the commissionaire withdrew to his cubbyhole I would have a shower in the well-appointed bathroom and then retire to the double bed with its crisp linen sheets. This was complete luxury for me at the time, and another reason why I often volunteered for weekend duty. In the morning one of the editorial mess waitresses would awaken me with a cup of tea and then serve eggs and bacon with the Sunday newspapers in the other room. I was expected to read these and mark stories worth following up, although the news editors were performing the same chore in their homes. They would come into the office at about midday and I would formally hand over the marked agency tapes and newspapers. It was a pleasant way of earning an extra 25 shillings.

Opposite the Private House on the other side of the narrow street leading from the square to Water Lane stood the Lamb and Lark, a beer house popular among the printers. It was also said to be frequented by an ageing whore; I never saw anyone answering to that description, but the pub's lights were a cheerful addition to the Dickensian atmosphere of the square which I loved. I was not the only one, and was convinced that most members of staff did not want to exchange it for a modern office block. Haley argued that the editorial and commercial offices could be refurbished at a cost of £500,000, which would leave sufficient reserves to finance the paper's expansion. He and two or three dissenting board members were overruled, and demolition of buildings, which were just as much part of the paper's traditions as the memories of its great editors and correspondents, began in 1960. It was an unmitigated disaster.

First, the paper still had to be written and printed during the years of demolition and rebuilding, and working conditions were worse than during the blitz. I was fortunately abroad, but the Official History admits that the noise and dust were appalling. The staff were repeatedly moved from one set of rooms to another, and they worked to the accompaniment of pneumatic drills. They had to shout to be heard, and there were a few narrow escapes as the demolition gangs swung their iron balls against walls built to last. John Buist, the foreign news editor, was nearly killed when some masonry fell through the glass roof of his temporary office. This went on for two years, and the rebuilding took another two.

Secondly, the financial cost was much more than the estimated £1,970,864. Mathew had assured the board that this would be met from current revenue over the four-year period, but a substantial overdraft had to be arranged and assets were sold to pay the final bill of £4,614,000. An interest-free loan from the *Observer*, which was to be housed in the new complex, helped as did the contract to print it, but the results were disappointing. Someone had decided that the heart of a newspaper was its library, which was nonsense; it is the communications equipment and the subeditors, and these were sited some distance from the composing room. Prepared copy for the printers was carried not by pneumatic tube but by a magnetized, moving rubber band. At least, this was the plan, but to the dismay of everyone some of the copy disappeared along the way. Dismay is an understatement. I happened to be visiting the office that evening, and near panic was evident. The fault and the lost copy were not easy to trace; the moving band travelled through a number of offices, some of which were locked for the night. Eventually the searchers were rewarded, and their hysterical laughter was first heard with raised eyebrows. The moving band passed through the men's lavatories, and the different temperature caused much of the copy to fall into two or three cubicles. A leader written by the editor was found floating in a bowl.

This and other faults were rectified, but the allegedly purpose-built offices were not a success. The windows were large, the ventilation inadequate, and in summer it was like working in a hothouse. The editorial mess disappeared with the Private House, and the old staff restaurant was replaced with an industrial canteen. The distance between the editorial offices and the composing room weakened the ancient bond between journalist and printer. There was less toing-and-froing, which was resented by the older printers. They felt, one of them told me later, that they had been relegated. A colleague thought that the subsequent decline in the loyalty of the printers could be traced to the passing of the friendly even cosy atmosphere of the old Printing House Square. I was not persuaded, but an era was coming to an end.

It was heralded by the abrupt departure of Astor for the south of France because of the finance act of 1962. This imposed estate duty on all real property, including foreign holdings, owned by British citizens who died in the country. That meant that most of his American property, the bulk of his family's wealth, would have to be sold to pay death duties if he ended his days in Britain. It was a cruel blow for a man in his seventies; life in the family villa above the Mediterranean could not have been unpleasant, but he was parted from most of his lifelong interests.

In some ways John Jacob Astor was an ideal newspaper proprietor. He saw the ownership of the paper as a sacred trust and was a benign employer. If the pay was low in comparison with other Fleet Street newspapers, he was the first proprietor to introduce a pension scheme and provided recreational and other facilities envied elsewhere in the street. I later decided that his proprietorship, or stewardship as he no doubt saw it, was less than ideal but apart from the pay I had nothing to complain about. He had no side, and I was always royally entertained between assignments although my reporting could not have pleased such a conventionally minded man. Perhaps he did not read the paper closely; certainly when Adenauer was complaining about me he remarked how glad he was that I also admired the German chancellor. He may have been signalling something, but I did not enquire.

Gavin, the eldest son who had already become chairman, was similarly retiring. He served with the Life Guards during the war, and on his return was trained to succeed his father. He worked in a number of departments, ate in the staff restaurant and was genuinely friendly in his bluff red-faced way. We first met in Cyprus when Pat and I were briefly escaping from the Middle East and he and his wife were on vacation. Gavin and I got gently tight together. Later we were invited to stay at Hever castle, the family seat, during our home leaves from Washington. The wings of the castle had been converted into self-contained flats for his friends, and it was most pleasant to live like a lord for a couple of weeks. We were invited to dine in the castle, and he gave a tea party for the children. He complained of being hard up although the twenty-first birthday party for his eldest son, which was attended by the queen, must have cost thousands of pounds. I supposed at the time that everything was relative. He also complained about the paper's Rhodesian policy. Apparently he had told Haley that Rhodesians were splendid chaps, our kith and kin, and a few days later a leading article criticizing them was published. These were pointers for the future, which I duly noted.

Gavin was in fact rather strapped for a man with his responsibilities. He had taken over the company and the estate at Hever, two large and unremunerative assets, with no new capital or income. He had also bought the Walter family's shares for £250,000. The bulk of his personal fortune was locked up in the company, and the Astor fortune in the United States was beyond his reach. It was managed by a trust, and under American law his father could not renounce the income from it. Presumably John Jacob wanted to help, but not to the extent of giving the paper a new lease of life. That could cost millions, and he was fully aware that if he died within five years of leaving Britain death duties would have to be paid on the American fortune. No wonder Gavin was gloomy when we spoke at Hever, especially as there was little hope of making *The Times* profitable under the existing management. I could not understand why he did not pension off Mathew and start afresh. The Cooper Brothers' report had revealed his inadequacies, and apart from some editorial improvements its recommendations had been largely ignored. Apparently his father was not prepared to accept what amounted to a reorganization of the company.

Haley came to the rescue by suggesting the modernization of the paper – editorial layout, content and typography, staffing and other changes to attract more readers. In other words, the staid old format would have to go. Known as Operation Breakthrough, it was soon agreed that news must be published on the front page. Mathew was still reluctant to abandon his elitist readership, but finally acquiesced. Headlines were to be bigger, and new features such as a woman's page introduced. But no bylines; Haley was adamant about that.

At this stage Mathew died. Whether or not the stress and strain were responsible for his early death was not known – he was 57 – and Haley was appointed chief executive as well as editor. Obviously he could not edit the paper day by day, and Iverach McDonald was appointed managing editor. The first issue of the modernized paper, 32 pages instead of the usual 24, appeared on 4 May 1966, and the circulation rose from about 250,000 to nearly 300,000 after five months. It seemed that the breakthrough, which many of us had dreamed about for years, had been achieved at last.

We were wrong. Despite the circulation increase, there was some opposition to the changes, especially news on the front page. Even Noël Coward got into the act; apparently the personal columns and birth, marriage and death notices were part of the national heritage. The advertising campaign, with the slogan 'Top People Read *The Times*', was dismissed as vulgar by the chattering classes. They ignored the obvious, that it had been reasonably successful; but our reputation of being a national institution was a hindrance to expansion. Newspaper economics was admittedly a mystery for most people, but the only conclusion to be drawn was that the Astors were expected to support us as a national institution for the foreseeable future. Alas, Haley had estimated that Operation Breakthrough would cost about £3 million, and the company had exhausted its reserves. Interest on the bank loan for the new building was steadily mounting, Gavin Astor was still paying interest on the loan required to buy out the Walter family, and the increased costs of producing a larger and better paper could not be quickly covered by increased advertisement rates which inevitably lag behind rising circulation. Within a few months, and unbeknown to the staff, Haley was looking for a new proprietor. Gavin had had enough. As he said later:

> I have come to realize that to carry the entire financial risk as proprietor and no less than the full legal responsibility as chairman for the success or failure of the company, without also carrying executive power, is not a satisfactory situation.

To a large extent Gavin and his father had only themselves to blame. Dawson's appeasement policy demonstrated that the independence of the editor was not necessarily a great boon for the paper, and their reluctance to become involved in its management amounted to a dereliction of duty. Dawson and Mathew could have been dismissed without damage to the paper's independence. I came to this conclusion reluctantly; they were well-meaning men, but no editor or manager is infallible. Every organization requires a system of checks and balances.

There can be no hard and fast rules, but I have long been impressed by the way the Ochs and Sulzberger family has run the *New York Times* for four generations. It was modelled on *The Times*, but the family ensured that the paper was profitable. To its credit, much of the profits was ploughed back into the paper. The editors had considerable freedom, but accepted that the proprietor had the last word. They did not have to look constantly over their shoulders, but they knew the direction in which the family wanted to take the paper. To my knowledge, the proprietor only intervened once. A story about the CIA's preparations for the invasion of Cuba in 1961 was changed on grounds of national security. Whether or not it should have been published is arguable, but this single transgression was regretted. A speech by the managing director, Clifton Daniel, on the intervention was published verbatim across six columns. Some years later the proprietor, against legal advice, supported the editor when he decided to publish the Pentagon Papers, the documents establishing that the Vietnam war was badly run. He fought a government injunction against publication. The *New York Times* also follows the American practice of dividing editorial responsibility. Its chief editorial executive, the managing or executive editor, is primarily concerned with news, the *raison d'être* of a newspaper. Leading articles are the responsibility of a lesser executive, the editorial page editor. A Dawson could not have misled the paper's readers.

This is by the way, but the mystery remains why the Astors put up with Mathew. John Jacob resented his assumption that like the editor he was independent of the board, and did nothing. Gavin remembered how his early proposals for developing the business side were ignored or resisted. They included moving into television – which was also resisted by Haley who detested independent television – and book publishing. Mathew was even reluctant to print the *Observer* when the first approach was made; and of course he refused to reorganize the management structure along the lines proposed by the Cooper report. Stanley Morison's support for Mathew probably counted with the older Astor. As for Gavin, he was not a shrewd businessman, and had acquired other interests. He enjoyed being lord-lieutenant and *custos rotulorum* of Kent, and was a close friend of the royal family.

The company's difficulties had long been known within the newspaper industry, and in 1964 Lord Thomson, the proprietor of the *Sunday Times*, had made an offer. This was rejected out of hand, but two years later Haley investigated a possible merger with the *Guardian*, which was also in a bad way after moving to London. A merger would have produced a curious hybrid, and was resisted by Alastair Hetherington, the editor. He had a hard job, a member of the Scott family had lost heart although the sister paper, the *Manchester Evening News*, was profitable enough to keep the company solvent. Hetherington won, and by changing the paper's liberalism eventually made it profitable. A merger with the *Observer* was then considered, but it had few financial resources. The *Financial Times* showed interest, but it was prosperous and expanding and could have swallowed *The Times*. Discussions were resumed with Thomson, and in the autumn of 1966 it was agreed that a new company, Times Newspapers Ltd, would be formed to publish both titles. The proposal had to be referred to in the Monopolies Commission and the hearing took three months, in part because the takeover of a national institution by a cocky Canadian was unpopular.

When permission was granted Haley wrote to tell me that the new company would 'make the paper safe for all of us and our children'. The foreign news editor circulated all correspondents saying that Gavin Astor would be life president and Haley chairman of the board. Denis Hamilton, the editor of the *Sunday Times*, would be editor-in-chief and new editors for both papers would be announced in due course.

Judging from the tone of the circular, Printing House Square was in an uproar. Thomson was an unknown quantity, and some of the staff were understandably worried about their future. Sitting in Washington, I felt detached. I would not willingly leave the paper, but if the new company made a mess of it I was young enough and well placed to begin a new career. I felt at home in the United States, and knew a great many people. My first book, *The New American Commonwealth*, had won the first John F. Kennedy memorial award and had earned me a somewhat spurious reputation as a constitutional expert and scholarly commentator on American politics. I had been asked to write a second book, and while I would never be a second Alistair Cooke I believed that I could happily spend the rest of my life in the United States.

The *New Statesman* suggested that I would be the next editor, but I did not take it seriously. I had no experience of editing, and assumed that the job would go to McDonald. He had an impressive record as foreign correspondent, diplomatic correspondent and foreign editor, and had edited the paper when Haley was looking for a new proprietor. I was thankful that the paper had such a good man to take over until the foreign news editor telexed that the new editor was William Rees-Mogg. My secretary asked me who he was, and reverting to Cockney I said, 'Never 'eard of 'im, luv.'

10

A Licence to Lose Money

Strange as it must now seem, I knew nothing about William Rees-Mogg when he was appointed editor and very little about our new proprietor, Lord Thomson, when we first met in London in 1967 a few months after he had bought the paper. I had flown in from Washington to receive a press award for international reporting, and he said that he was tickled pink. I believed him; he was one of those generous North Americans who enjoy other men's successes as much as their own. It was also good for business. He talked of little else that morning in his office in Gray's Inn Road. It was on the top floor, and he had a private lift and a sergeant commissionaire to operate it and do other little services for him. He obviously enjoyed this attention, but otherwise was a genuinely modest man – apart from boasting about his business ventures.

He owned 69 newspapers and 138 magazines in various parts of the world when he bought *The Times*, as well as four television and six radio stations, three printing plants and sundry ancillary companies. He had also launched the world's most successful package-tour company, founded his own airline and was about to acquire sizeable holdings in North Sea oil. In other words, he was still expanding and this fed his natural ebullience; and, as I had been forewarned, he soon produced leather-bound folders containing the balance sheets of his companies. He produced them one at a time from below his desk, rather like a conjuror plucking eggs or playing cards from the air, and his eyes radiated sheer delight behind the pebble glasses. Despite the malicious stories told about him by some *Sunday Times* journalists, I warmed to him instantly. He was like a kindly uncle doing parlour tricks for a visiting nephew.

Thomson was a good raconteur, but without malice. Later,

much later, when we were travelling in China, he told innumerable stories, refreshing his memory with the aid of little coloured cards which he kept in his billfold. The cards listed the first lines, and the colours indicated the kind of company in which they could be safely told. The pink card referred to bawdy stories; not dirty ones, but the sort his Presbyterian upbringing decided were not fit for female company. He also showed me a photostat of a cheque, and asked me if I had seen anything like it. The cheque was made out to his son, Kenneth, and the amount was, I recall, for $315 million. I said that I had never seen anything like it, and asked him why he had been so generous. He said that Ken was growing up, and this was his stake. Mind you, he added, they were only Canadian dollars.

Thomson's simple delight in making money was refreshing, and at that first meeting he talked about his newspapers. Most of them were small, but they were all profitable. Much more profitable than *The Times*, he wryly added. I asked him why he had bought the paper; the smile became enigmatic, and no wonder. The old Times Publishing Company had lost £285,000 in the previous year, and that year the new company was expected to lose more than a million. The chilling news was imparted with solemnity, and he then reminded me of what he had said to the Monopolies Commission. He and his son were determined to keep the paper alive, and if necessary put the whole of their personal fortunes in Britain at its disposal for a period of twenty-one years. Moreover, he would have no say in running *The Times*. I had read the commission's report, and I was grateful, but why was he willing to pledge millions of pounds? Thomson replied that the paper must be saved; it was a great paper, and for him the jewel in the crown.

I was sure that was true, but there was more to it. He was in his sixtieth year when he arrived in Edinburgh in 1953 to buy the *Scotsman*. He was a millionaire, Kenneth was minding the shop in Toronto and busy adding more small newspapers to their string, and he had considered retiring to Florida where he had his eye on a small bank. Then his wife died, and he decided that grief would be best assuaged by hard work. The amusing second volume of his autobiography (*After I was Sixty*, 1975) tells of the adventures of this son of a Canadian barber in that reserved city, including the acquisition of Scottish Television. He described it as a licence to print money, in part because of the refusal of the stuffy Scots to join in such a venture with a brash Canadian. He was left with fourth-fifths of the shares, and he became very rich.

Six years after returning to his ancestral land wearing a blue suit, brown shoes and red socks, he brought the controlling interest in Kemsley Newspapers; thus becoming the proprietor of three British Sunday newspapers, including the *Sunday Times*, twelve provincial dailies, and several weeklies. He was on a lucky streak, and acquiring more newspapers became a habit. He bought them all over the world, and when in Moscow asked Khrushchev, the Soviet leader, if he wanted to sell *Pravda*. It was inevitable that he would buy *The Times*. Later he amused himself with North Sea oil, and made even more money, but *The Times* was his pride and joy.

Michael Foot once wrote that he loved Lord Beaverbrook, a surprising but honest admission for a socialist. I in turn became very fond of Lord Thomson. The two erstwhile Canadians were very different. Beaverbrook hungered for political power, surrounded himself with beautiful women and lived like a lord. He was also an inspired newspaperman, superior to the brilliant editors and writers, many of them socialists like Foot, who worked for him. Thomson had once run for the Canadian senate, but had little or no interest in politics. Unlike Beaverbrook, he did not own newspapers to make propaganda, and certainly did not interfere in *The Times*. Thomson loved being a lord, but despite the Rolls and country house his mode of life was more modest than that of many of his employees'. He occasionally stayed at the Savoy, admittedly, but ate in a caff frequented by porters in the old Covent Garden market. He did not smoke or drink, and his favourite dish was spaghetti and meat balls doused with tabasco. He often travelled by bus and underground, and always flew tourist.

Much of this was confirmed when we went to China in 1972. I was then foreign editor and had spent about six months negotiating with the embassy in London for a visa for David Bonavia, who I wanted to send to Peking as our first resident correspondent since the revolution. When Thomson heard about it, he suggested taking a large group of businessmen to drum up trade between the two countries. He said that we could fly in two 707s belonging to his airline. The embassy took fright, it was long before their new open-door policy was introduced, but the ambassador, a shrewd veteran of the Long March, agreed to issue ten visas. I was appalled; as an old foreign correspondent I was accustomed to travelling alone, and I had originally asked for only two visas, for Bonavia and myself. The prospect of travelling with Thomson, Ken, Denis Hamilton, the editor-in-chief of Times Newspapers, Frank Giles, the deputy editor of the *Sunday Times*, and a few others was not pleasing. Not that I had anything against any of them, but I had been a lone wolf for too long. From London to Shanghai was a long way, and I was doubly appalled to discover that we were to travel tourist.

Thomson sat across the aisle from me, and about twelve hours out of London remarked about my third dry martini. By the time we reached Rangoon, he chided me on smoking too many cigarettes; they were bad for my health and a waste of money. He ate little, and not having any balance sheets with him read cowboy stories throughout the night. Otherwise it was an agreeable journey in that he clearly believed that *Times* journalists knew everything, and I was happy to tell him what I knew about China. I had been there during and immediately after the war, and as Southeast Asian correspondent had taken a close interest in the country. I had also read FitzGerald and other experts, and had naturally boned up on recent events before beginning the trip. He interrupted occasionally with remarks such as 'Gee, you don't say' and 'Gosh, Lou, it must be great knowing so much'. I looked hard at him a couple times, thinking that he was having me on, but eventually decided that the old gent who owned *The Times* and many other newspapers was genuinely impressed.

We were treated as VIPs in China, and the first evening dined with the mayor of Shanghai who was then the third or fourth most powerful man in the Chinese communist party. The food was magnificent, but between courses Thomson whispered to me, 'When are they going to serve chop suey?' I said that they would not, that it was an American and not a Chinese dish. He looked incredulous but trusting, and asked about sweet-sour pork. I said that it was a homely dish and not considered fit for such a banquet;

it would be like serving steak and kidney pudding at Buckingham Palace. He looked disappointed, and thanked me for responding to the frequent toasts in mai tai, the Chinese vodka. 'But be careful, don't drink too much. It looks powerful stuff.' It was indeed powerful, but there was no way I could avoid the toasts or not drain the glass.

It was a strenuous trip. The itinerary I had suggested, which to my surprise was accepted, included provinces which westerners had not visited for many years. Long journeys by car and obsolescent aircraft were involved but Thomson, then in his seventies, kept up. His delight in seeing strange places and people was almost childlike; and wherever we went, in chilly Peking or sweltering Canton, he wore his homburg and dark, three-piece serge suit but with black shoes and discreet socks. He was treated with the greatest respect, and not only because of his age. He obviously enjoyed the attention, and I supposed that it was one reason why he acquired *The Times*. Such respect could not be bought, but was readily accorded to the proprietor of a newspaper universally known.

Similarly when we met Chou En-lai in Peking. The Chinese prime minister proved to be one of the most impressive men I had met, and I had looked forward to talking to him about the cultural revolution and his plans or hopes for national recovery. Chou first addressed himself to Thomson, which was to be expected, but to my dismay Thomson chose to play the role of a simple but brash Canadian. It was an act, as I had discovered, but, I admit to my shame, my toes curled tight with embarrassment when he led off the interview with a long lecture on the benign benefits of capitalism. It was as if he was addressing a Rotary lunch for small-town businessmen. I groaned inwardly, but then the tone and content changed and Chou listened intently. I knew that the Chinese were not always inscrutable, but I did not expect one of the greatest communist leaders in history to show such intense interest, especially in the suggestion that China should borrow from abroad instead of trying to pull itself up by its bootstraps. Thomson went on to explain the advantages of borrowing with considerable expertise. That did not surprise me, his knowledge of financial markets was a major reason for his success; but I marvelled at the two old men, so very different in every possible

214

way, hobnobbing together. Then after offering to buy the *People's Daily*, which Chou politely declined, Thomson looked over to me with his cheeky grin, and said, 'It's all yours, Lou.'

In one way Thomson understood China's economic predicament better than the journalists who accompanied him; but after that three-and-a-half hour interview, of which I had the lion's share, he reverted to being the innocent abroad gratefully dependent upon us. He was especially impressed by Bonavia when we arrived at the old Chiang Kai-shek residence in Canton which was used as a resthouse for VIPs. The manager spoke only Cantonese and the foreign ministry official who accompanied us was a Mandarin-speaker. It was an impasse, and the official was beginning to lose his temper when Bonavia intervened. Fluent in both Cantonese and Mandarin, he politely offered his services, and the sight of a Scotsman of Italian descent translating for two Chinese was a wonder to behold. Thomson was delighted, remarking that with such talent *The Times* had to be the world's greatest newspaper.

The trip finished in Hong Kong, and a few days later Thomson left for Bangkok to inspect one of his newspapers. He looked as spry as ever, and the day before his departure we had a long chat about the Thai capital. I had known McDonald, the American who founded the *Bangkok Post* after the war. He was a former member of the OSS, the forerunner of the CIA, and a civilized adventurer who preferred the easygoing life of Bangkok to the rat race awaiting him at home. Thomson invited me to accompany him, but I declined saying that I still had a few days work to do in Hong Kong talking to the governor and other officials who wanted to know what Chou had said about the future of Hong Kong. I had already reported that he had indicated that he was prepared to negotiate the eventual departure of the British from the colony, but not unnaturally they wanted to discuss my impressions as well as the interview. I hoped to learn something from them about the British attitude, and then I had to buy presents for the family. Thomson told me to buy a good one for my wife, and charge it to him.

I thanked him, adding that I expected to leave for London at the end of the week – and this time I intended to travel first class. Thomson's smile wavered, and he glared at me through the pebble glasses. It was a difficult moment, and then he said, 'Okay, but don't do it too often.'

If *The Times* was the jewel in the Thomson crown it had become a crown of thorns long before I finally returned to Printing House Square in 1970. The changeover had not gone smoothly; the realization that the Astor millions were not numberless was a shock, but the promises Thomson had made to the Monopolies Commission were reassuring. At one level of the editorial consciousness, it seemed certain that the paper would survive and even prosper. Thomson was rich and determined to make a go of it. His attitude was similar to Astor's when he bought the paper after Northcliffe's death, which was only to be expected. After all, *The Times* was unique. That was the general if unspoken view, which I did not accept. I had long refused to regard it as a national institution, and did not believe that we were doing Thomson a favour by accepting him as the man who would pay our bad debts. Nevertheless, in the collective view it was inconceivable that a national institution would be allowed to go under. We had had our troubles since the war, in part due to bad luck and poor management, but had tried to maintain the high standards required of a national institution. Haley had done a good job, and would have succeeded with a better management and sufficient capital. Thomson promised both.

Perhaps I had lived too long in the real world to see myself as part of a protected monument, but at another level of consciousness my colleagues were less happy. Some were offended by Thomson's brashness, or rather the brash front he liked to project, and remembered with regret the dignified demeanour of the older Astor. Those senior enough to have been invited to weekends at Hever castle or a cruise on the Astor yacht also had their regrets. I was also sorry that I probably would not stay at Hever again, but I suspected that much of this regret was corporate snobbery. Astor looked like a proprietor and not a radio salesman which Thomson was in his early days. Not that it mattered, but the general response to the senior appointments announced by Denis Hamilton, the new editor-in-chief, was far more serious. The few who had phoned me in Washington sounded furious. They had assumed, as I did, that Iverach McDonald would be appointed editor and that Oliver Woods would be his deputy. Instead, McDonald was made an associate editor, a non-executive post, and Woods was demoted to special assistant to the editor-in-chief. I thought that Woods had been shabbily treated, he deserved more than that; but Hamilton had the right to appoint his own men. He was responsible to Thomson and for the millions that were to be showered upon us. In any case, the belief of the old black friars that their abbots should come from within the order no longer held. The world and *The Times* were changing, but a bit too fast for some of my colleagues.

In fact, one of them admitted that William Rees-Mogg was suitable *Times* material, and wondered why he had not joined the paper direct from Oxford where he had been president of the union. The answer was that he was preparing himself for a political career when an article of his in *Isis* was read by Lord Drogheda, the managing director of the *Financial Times*. He was offered a job, and quickly moved up the ladder and was an assistant editor when he joined the *Sunday Times* in 1960. Promotion was equally rapid in Gray's Inn Road, from city editor to deputy editor within four years. It was inevitable that he would become editor of *The Times* when Thomson bought the paper.

Rees-Mogg was something of a paradox. Although only 39 when he took over, he looked and behaved as readers of other papers expected of the editor of *The Times*. Tall and well tailored, the double-breasted jacket hiding an incipient pot belly, he presented an image of a nineteenth-century gentleman; reserved, utterly conventional and slightly pompous. He was an intellectual in that he was genuinely and almost exclusively interested in ideas. He was useless with his hands, and could neither type, drive nor do much else. He dictated even his articles to his secretary. On one occasion when he returned unexpectedly from abroad and his driver was not available, I drove him to his house in Smith Square and was invited in for a drink. He fetched white wine for himself and whisky for me, which he assumed was my favourite tipple, but looked blank when I asked for ice. I had to get a tray of it from the refrigerator. He expected things to be done for him.

Unconsciously or otherwise, he saw himself as a member of the nation's elite born to rule, but his leading articles could shock as well as reassure his peers in parliament, the higher reaches of the civil service and the central office of the Tory party. He could be courageous, even foolhardy, but had a genuine journalistic flair and, at times, an impish humour. This was kept under control; the eyes behind the spectacles were more often gravely serious as became a man who knew his proper station. According to *Burke's Landed Gentry*, the Mogg family had been Somerset landowners since the thirteenth century, and later he was appointed high sheriff of the county. His mother was American, a former actress with a beautifully modulated down-east voice and a sense of humour. The trans-Atlantic parentage probably explained the paradox. Rees-Mogg inherited his Roman Catholicism from her, and his book, *An Humbler Heaven*, reflected the strength and simplicity of his faith.

I liked him. Although reserved, he responded when approached and welcomed new ideas. He reintroduced the old habit of using first names and was known to everybody as William. He was frequently silent, which suggested aloofness, but was invariably thinking about the next leading article. Like most journalists I think on a typewriter, but he could construct a thousand-word leader in his mind and dictate it in one sitting; and the writing was always taut and the argument logically presented. The sentences rarely had to be read twice. One senior leader writer said that he always wrote elegantly and persuasively even when the wrong conclusion was reached. That was said admiringly. In fact, Rees-Mogg, who regarded the leaders as the most important part of the paper, could be carried away by an audacious or contrary idea. The obvious example was his admiration for the discredited Richard Nixon. Long after the former American president had resigned, he decided that we should lead the front page with one of his speeches on foreign policy. I demurred and placed it below the fold – the lower half of the page – but he outraged American journalists by defending Nixon when speaking at the Washington National Press Club.

William was also capable of great dislikes. For instance, after he had left early one Friday evening for the country I read a proof of a leader he had written condemning Harold Wilson, the then prime minister. He began splendidly, but then getting into his stride he had written four or five paragraphs which might have delighted libel lawyers eager to make a killing. On reflection, I decided that they were not libellous, William was too good a journalist for that, but unnecessarily hurtful. Or so I thought. I was in a quandary; on *The Times* the editor's lieutenants can argue points of policy with him, but once he has made up his mind the leader becomes a kind of holy writ. There was no way of getting in touch with William before the paper went to press. I deleted four or five paragraphs but not the punch line which read: 'Better George Brown drunk than Harold Wilson sober.' It was too good a line, but I still felt that I had done what I ought not to have done. I need not have worried. On Monday morning, he arrived, his face enlivened by a boyish grin, and thanked me for saving him from himself again.

In some ways he was the ideal editor for *The Times*, and he shocked me one day by remarking that he intended to resign after ten years in the job. No doubt I was naïve or too devoted to the paper, but I could not imagine anybody voluntarily wanting to quit the best job in British journalism. I was no less shocked when I discovered that he still wanted to become a member of parliament – a bloody politician, I muttered to myself unbelievingly. He had stood twice as the Tory candidate for Chester-le-Street, the town in the Durham coalfield with an overwhelming Labour majority, and the shaming results had not stilled his political ambitions. Moreover, I could not imagine him on the stump haranguing coal miners or even commuters in the gin-and-Jaguar belt, but his ambitions were briefly revived when Edward Heath became prime minister in 1970. It was said that he expected a life peerage and a seat in the cabinet and was offered something a good deal less.

Whatever the truth, he remained at Printing House Square, and was a very good editor except that he went home in the early evening long before the first edition went to press. He had his defenders outside the office, where it was said that the editor of *The Times* could better spend his time reflecting on the events of the day in the comfort of his home than putting the paper to bed. Perhaps, but it was very un-*Times*-like, and conceded too much authority to the executive night editor. In the early years this was Michael Cudlipp, who had also been brought over from the *Sunday Times*. Cudlipp was a good journalist; he was also young and ambitious, and not unnaturally wanted to make his mark, and some of his methods were also seen as un-*Times*-like. In his book, (*Barefaced Cheek*, 1983), Michael Leapman, who was hired by Cudlipp from the *Sun* before Rupert Murdoch took it down market and who later became the paper's celebrated diarist, said that Cudlipp brought with him some of the bustle for its own sake that is a feature of popular journalism. He added that Cudlipp's habit of making radical changes to the paper in the small hours appalled the old guard, especially foreign correspondents who traditionally had not been obliged to keep on top of a breaking story until the last edition had gone.

This was not altogether true; on innumerable occasions I had continued filing until the very last moment. In Washington I would compose directly on to the teleprinter, and the words would appear in London as they were written. It was a matter of craftsmanship, and I enjoyed trying to beat the competition. I wrote in short takes, with plenty of space in between so the man in the communications room could tear them off and hurry them to the subeditors. He would sometimes warn me that I had only five minutes left, and after counting the minutes would say, 'Okay, squire, that's enough.' For some reason, we were always called squire.

Cudlipp had the annoying habit of demanding uncoverable stories. I was dining with the French ambassador when he called and asked for a story about a bridge which had collapsed in the Middle West. There was no way it could be covered from Washington, and a more experienced night editor would have used an agency report, as the *New York Times* and the *Washington Post* did. I must have been called a dozen times about an alleged Vietnam peace initiative dreamed up by the Agence France Presse man in Hanoi. I finally told the foreign news room in cablese to 'off bugger'.

To that extent, Cudlipp was another little cross foreign correspondents had to bear. More serious, and damaging to the paper, were the radical changes. I was not opposed to bigger headlines and more white space, though in those days the *Telegraph* flourished with a more modest layout. I strongly favoured shorter stories, most could be written in 250 words or less; but major stories required a great deal more. I was still in Washington when President Nixon announced a new foreign-policy doctrine, an obviously important story for *The Times* and most of its readers. Aware of the new style, I wrote a short story for the front page and a long explanatory account for an inside page. Only the short story was published, and the editor complained to me for not giving more. As I recalled, the subsequent leader contained information I had sent in the second and longer story.

My colleagues in London apparently suffered a great deal more, and for the first time in the paper's history senior journalists rebelled. They met in the White Swan, a pub in Farringdon Road and not one of the usual watering holes, and drafted a letter to the editor complaining about the new editorial style and direction. The thirty signatories were subsequently mocked by Fleet Street cynics, but they were not an old guard resisting the future. Most of them were good journalists, and some were promising young men who had made their mark on the paper and were destined to do well. They included the late Charles Douglas-Home, a future editor of the paper; Brian MacArthur, who later launched and edited *The Times Higher Education Supplement* and the *Today* newspaper; Hugh Stephenson, a former diplomat who became the paper's business news editor and then edited the *New Statesman*; and Geoffrey Smith, a leader writer who developed into a respected political columnist. The most senior was Edward Hodgkin, the foreign editor, a Middle East expert and the best writer on the paper. Their complaints were very real – I have mentioned some of them – and they concluded that the paper was losing its authority.

Cudlipp was not wholly to blame. The new strategy to win readers and advertising was devised by his seniors, who also wanted to develop a seven-day-a-week newspaper on the American model, apparently with the Sunday carrying the longer stories. Fortunately, that came to nothing; despite the similarity of titles they were two very different newspapers. Apart from that, I was reluctant to condemn them completely. After all, I had long believed that the paper could only regain its former greatness by attracting more readers and advertisers to expand the news service and secondary departments such as sport and general features. I was surprised, however, that Rees-Mogg had allowed the paper to be taken down market.

If his second title of editor-in-chief meant anything, Denis

Hamilton, the chief executive, must have been ultimately responsible for the new strategy. This was also surprising. Hamilton was a superb journalist, who had recreated the *Sunday Times* and made it the best-selling Sunday paper of its kind within a few years. This was an extraordinary achievement – under Kemsley ownership it had been a stodgy paper and had lagged behind the *Observer* – and his earlier career had been equally distinguished. A grammar-school boy who had begun on provincial newspapers, he had commanded a battalion of the Durham Light Infantry during the war and had won a DSO at Nijmegen. He returned to provincial reporting earning £8 a week, and had risen quickly to editorial director of Kemsley Newspapers when Thomson bought the company and appointed him editor of the *Sunday Times*. He increased the circulation by 100,000 by publishing the Montgomery memoirs, and it rose to more than 1,250,000 when he introduced the business news section and the colour magazine.

Hamilton had many good qualities; he was well read, could recognize talent and willingly gave young hopefuls their head. Unfortunately, this appeared not to apply to *The Times*; he seemed at first to have a low opinion of its journalists which might have explained why they were largely ignored in the early years. (One reason might have been that we did not have bylines, though this was quickly changed after he became editor-in-chief.) It took a little time for him to recognize that some of us were quite good at our jobs. Nevertheless, I came to like and admire him, concluding that the early mistakes were mainly due to ill health and overwork. The first was a legacy of the war; an ammunition dump was sabotaged when he was about to accept the surrender of a German panzer grenadier division. He was thrown some distance from his jeep by the explosions – his driver was killed – and was in hospital for months. His recovery was incomplete, and he fell ill when we were travelling with Thomson in China. He might have died had we not ignored his protests and rushed him to hospital.

The main trouble was that Hamilton had moved too quickly, probably urged on by Thomson, and had little time to think. The new business news section was an obvious example. It was a splendid idea if only because it could generate a great deal of advertising previously denied to the paper. The *Financial Times*,

which had largely cornered this market, was worried by its introduction, but not for long. About forty financial, industrial and
business journalists were hired within a few weeks. This kind of
specialist journalism did not then attract many bright young men,
and some of our recruits were not very good. They could be very
opinionated. Hamilton had another word for it; he complained
that they regarded the City of London as a class enemy. Business
news was an expensive flop, and at Bracken House the *Financial
Times* must have relaxed with relief between bouts of giggles.

The basic strategy had clearly not been thought out. Even if
the business news section had been successful, the readers it was
intended to reach did not want a newspaper that seemed to be
moving down market. It was also a mistake to aim for more sales
by flooding the market with extra copies. Although sales increased
the return of unsold copies from newsagents in the most unprom-
ising areas became a flood. Losses mounted with this indis-
criminate distribution until the alarm bells sounded, and
everybody was told to stop spending money like drunken sailors.

The commercial crisis more or less coincided with the White
Swan group's letter and, to use an old American newspaper
phrase, a row back was ordered. The layout was redesigned, much
of the old editorial content and character were reestablished; the
paper began to move closer to the objectives set by Haley, and
real circulation slowly but steadily increased. Bylines helped; I
discovered that my reputation was enhanced among the people I
reported as well as the readers. The thumbnail photograph which
accompanied my weekly column from Washington no doubt fed
my vanity – it had been kept under strict control during the
years of anonymity – but was nice; more important, the column
expanded my horizon. I had more space to explore the background of events, past or imminent, and the interplay between
men competing for the president's attention.

The period after the row back was one of the happiest of my
career. I should have known that it could not last, very little else
had since the change of ownership; and I was not unduly surprised
when a colleague phoned from London to say that I was due for
promotion. He said that the reason was obscure; some people said
that Hodgkin wanted to stop being foreign editor, and others that
Rees-Mogg wanted more old *Times* men in senior positions at

home. A substantial increase in salary went with the promotion.

I was not attracted by the prospect; indeed, I did not regard a return to London as promotion. As for a higher salary, my pay had been increased since the Thomson takeover, and with a generous living allowance and an expense account I was as well off as most of my American colleagues. American income tax was also comparatively low. Money was no longer a consideration, Washington was a wonderful job, and I felt at home in the United States. We had a wide circle of friends, and a pleasant house in Spring Valley. Ten years was a long time to be in one post; I agreed with the notion, in theory at least, that correspondents should move on before they became stale, but in the 1960s Washington was intellectually exciting.

The decade I spent there was one of the most exciting in American history. It began with the inauguration of President John F. Kennedy, and his promise of a new frontier appealed to me as much as it did to the American majority. Elspeth, the wife of Walt Rostow who was to become Johnson's national security adviser, put it better one evening. She said that the junior officers of the Second World War were taking over, and as one of them I thought about time too. They were heady days, probably because few of us realized that behind the inspiring rhetoric of the inaugural speech was an intent boding ill for the future. Nobody I met realized that Kennedy was to resume the arms race with the Soviet Union in conventional as well as nuclear arms. He had made much of the alleged missile gap during the election campaign; and although his defence secretary, Robert McNamara, quickly discovered that there was no gap, that in fact the Americans had as much nuclear might as the Russians, 1000 Minuteman ICBMs and 45 Polaris submarines were ordered.

Instead, we had thrilled to passages such as:

Let the word go forth from this time and place, to friend and foe alike, that the torch has been passed to a new generation of Americans – born in this century, tempered by war, disciplined by a hard and bitter peace, proud of our ancient heritage – and unwilling to witness or permit the slow undoing of those human rights to which this nation has always been committed, and to which we are committed today at home and around the world.

Let every nation know, whether it wishes us well or ill, that we shall pay any price, bear any burden, meet any hardship, support any friend, oppose any foe to assure the survival and success of liberty. . . .

And so, my fellow Americans: ask not what your country will do for you – ask what you can do for your country.

This was electrifying for Americans after the safe but dull Eisenhower years. A friend of mine, John Mecklin, a tough hard-drinking foreign correspondent, gave up a good job with *Time-Life* to work for the government. James Reston wrote in the *New York Times* that Kennedy had decimated Harvard for men to work in the White House. A little later Dean Rusk, the new secretary of state and a Rhodes Fellow, claimed that the new administration had more Oxbridge than Harvard men. Whoever was right, Washington seemed convinced that the best and brightest would man the new frontier.

I was carried along with this wave of enthusiasm despite my scepticism, long strengthened by experience, and a conversation I had with David Bruce in his house in Georgetown the evening before the inauguration. Bruce came from an old Maryland family, and by any standards was a patrician. He served with the OSS during the war, and as a confirmed Democrat had held a number of diplomatic posts abroad including ambassador in Bonn and subsequently in London. He was what was known as an in-and-outer, one of many wealthy men willing to serve in government for two or three years at a time. We had known each other well in Bonn, and he suggested a drink in order to put me in the picture.

Bruce reminded me that Kennedy had won the election with the smallest majority of the popular vote in history. The new president would have a rough time in congress; despite Democratic majorities in both houses conservative Democrats would vote with the Republicans if his programme was too liberal. He was actively disliked in the south because of his religion and his support for Dr Martin Luther King Jr, during the campaign. Business was suspicious in part because of the way his father, old Joe, had made his money. Like his father, Jack was also a notorious womanizer and this could get him into trouble.

Bruce mixed another martini, and said that he was worried for other reasons. Kennedy had not been a serious congressman. He believed that Kennedy had served in congress because his father had decided it was the best springboard for the presidency, and nobody knew if Jack had any fire in his belly. I was to hear that phrase again, but without any explanation Bruce suggested that I should approach the new president as I had approached Adenauer, only to be more careful. We knew what the old man wanted, and could judge his actions and speeches accordingly, but nobody seemed to know what Kennedy wanted – except to be president. Another thing, Bruce said after I had refused a third martini, do not be impressed by his Harvard academics. They may be bright, and they are certainly articulate, but they have no political experience; and always remember that politics here are more complicated, even more sophisticated despite appearances, than in Britain or Germany.

Bruce was a wise man, and had never misled me in the past. I wondered if he was personally prejudiced; he and his wife personified the old Wasp ascendancy, and he may have resented upstarts such as the Kennedys. Irish catholics dominated Boston, once the Wasp bastion; Kennedy had defeated Henry Cabot Lodge when he ran for the senate, and every New England child knew that the Lodges were so superior that they only spoke to God. The Irish catholics were now about to take over the country. I dropped this thought as unworthy, and trudged through a snowstorm which had suddenly smothered the city to find a cab. Georgetown was already celebrating the new frontier. Most of the houses lining its cobbled colonial streets blazed with light, and the door of one was open to admit a well-dressed young couple. The cheerful voices and the snow reminded me of Christmas. On M Street I squeezed into a crowded bus, and even the driver was in high spirits saying that it was just like the end of the war.

The west lobby of the White House was full of reporters waiting for advance copies of the inaugural speech. Many were elated, and they cheered when Pierre Salinger, Kennedy's press secretary, eventually appeared. His strong Gallic face, normally heavy and watchful, was split by an enormous grin, but he still managed to keep his cigar alight. Girls appeared with armfuls of copies, and after the agency men had scampered to the telephones by the door the lobby was hushed while we quickly read the embargoed speech with growing excitement. Pete Lisagor, the White House correspondent of a Chicago newspaper who was to become another mentor, whistled appreciatively. 'Well, Limey', he said to me. 'This almost beats Churchill.'

I had difficulty trying to remain the cool distant observer, especially the next day when Kennedy was sworn in on the steps of the Capitol. The storm had passed, revealing a brilliant blue sky and the vast crowds huddled together against the freezing wind were happy and excited. I was impressed by the simple but awesome ceremony which had marked the passing of power from one president to another for almost as long as *The Times* had been published. Jefferson, Jackson, Lincoln, Wilson and Roosevelt had stood there, and we had reported all of them. Lincoln had compared the power of the paper with the Mississippi; hyperbole no doubt, and our power had diminished, but I was confident I would get to know Kennedy as William Howard Russell had known Lincoln. I was very happy; this was the United States I had read and dreamed about, a country that had got closer than any other to the ideals of true democracy – and equally important, the best running story in the world.

I shall always remember that day; my report may have been unusually effusive, but as the historian, James MacGregor Burns, later wrote, the speech was in itself a decisive political act with unforeseen consequences. Nevertheless, Kennedy was a disappointing president, which is a polite way of putting it when one remembers the Bay of Pigs, the Cuban missile crisis which led to the first nuclear confrontation between the two superpowers – and one hopes the last – the involvement in Vietnam and the failure to help the blacks. I also failed to establish useful relations with him. As with many men of Irish origin, if you were not with him you were against him. I reported that the CIA had raised a secret army in Laos – Reagan was not the first president to mislead congress – and I was put in the doghouse; that is he refused to see me, and for some weeks I was *persona non grata* with his staff. A witchhunt followed, and there was an ugly scene in Salinger's office when I refused to divulge my sources. Only then did I remember that cautionary chat with Bruce. The paper again stood by me.

That said, Kennedy did inspire a generation, and his assassination conferred the nobility of martyrdom on his memory. Arguably he triggered the swinging 1960s. The vast majority of his admirers did not know that he was an enthusiastic swinger, and the few who did, including journalists, kept quiet about it; but after Eisenhower he was like a breath of fresh air which blew away many of the old social *mores* and conventions on both sides of the Atlantic. Certainly he was responsible for much of the strife which nearly tore the country apart, and made my assignment wonderfully newsworthy. I wrote nearly 5000 words about his funeral, and literally millions about racial strife in the south – all the more bloody because Kennedy had failed to meet the aspirations of the blacks – Vietnam and other upheavals. I became a confidant of President Lyndon Johnson, a devious politician eventually ruined by Vietnam. I spent hours in the oval office as he unburdened himself, seeking support as well as justification. I was in the situation room of the White House with Walt Rostow, his national security adviser, as the military reports of the Tet offensive poured in. Johnson was an unlovable figure, but he had fire in his belly. He, a southerner, did what Kennedy failed to do; his three civil rights acts swept away the last legal restraints and liberated the blacks. He was the last Rooseveltian, hence his war on poverty.

I was roughed up in the south, and tear-gassed in Chicago at the 1968 Democratic national convention. I slept about four hours and wrote more than 3000 words a day. Then there was Richard Nixon who carried on the Vietnam war until the Americans suffered ignominious defeat. I did not want to leave, and believed that I could continue to do well by the paper until I was put out to grass. My wife, however, thought that it was time to go home. Pat loved the United States as much as I did, but had followed me round the world for more than twenty years, and had borne me four children in four different countries. She was also unwell, and I reluctantly agreed to accept if promoted.

Rees-Mogg phoned soon afterwards, and said that he wanted to appoint me deputy editor (foreign). It was a new post, and he hoped that I would continue to write for the paper as well as run it. I accepted, which was just as well. We did not know at the time but Pat had become a victim of multiple sclerosis and had not long to live. We sold the house, said goodbye to our friends and sailed home in *Queen Elizabeth II*.

I found that at least one thing had not changed when I finally returned to Printing House Square in the autumn of 1970, or about twenty-four years after I had left for my first assignment. The endearing but occasionally infuriating habit of not being told what was expected of one had survived. Rees-Mogg gave me a distracted smile, but nothing more. Cudlipp, the other deputy editor, was no more communicative as he bustled about with a clipboard. My new secretary led me to my office, a large glass box with views of the square and the river to the right of my desk and of the editorial floor to the front. She said that it was very functional, but I sighed for the book-lined rooms of the old building.

The administrative officer phoned to say that my company car had been delivered, and an accountant arrived with the foreign editorial budget. I was baffled by the pages of figures, and asked what they meant. He was a nice Indian, a refugee from East Africa, and was delighted to explain but managed only to baffle me more. I sighed again, this time for the simplicity of making out expense accounts which was my only experience of bookkeeping. Apart from a few fixed items, I would divide the money spent under headings such as entertainment, cabs and newspapers. I soon gathered that a similar principle applied to the foreign budget of nearly £1 million, except that there were more fixed items, but the object was to avoid overspending. The company had lost £10 million in the previous year, and the executive board was determined to reduce that year's losses to £8 million. It seemed that at least one of the old management's deficiencies listed in the Cooper Brothers' report had been remedied, but it proved to be a futile exercise. The enormous losses were mainly incurred on the production side over which the new managers had little or no control.

The noon editorial conference was also different. The classroom atmosphere of Haley's editorship had gone; Rees-Mogg sat in a rocking chair, and the others sat or sprawled on sofas and armchairs. Most of them smiled a welcome, some had removed their jackets and loosened their ties, and a few smoked. Latecomers arrived without rebuke. The business in hand was conducted briskly, but punctured with the occasional joke or observation and one news item provoked a lively discussion. The afternoon conference was more disciplined, and was presaged by a change of atmosphere. The editorial floor was earlier more or less deserted, but by four in the afternoon some reporters had returned from their assignments and reports from foreign correspondents were spewing out of the telex machines. The copy tasters sorted out the overmatter from the previous evening and early agency copy. News schedules were distributed, including a list of when the various pages had to be completed.

It was an entirely new life for me, and not very satisfying. I was a reporter, a hack, and editing seemed to be dreary except when a big story was running. It always generated excitement; quick decisions had to be made and more pages changed through the night. My first big story, the death of Colonel Nasser, the Egyptian leader, was hardly typical. It broke late, but the words came in promptly from Cairo and the obituary was almost up to date. It was too late for a leading article, and I decided that we needed a feature article. The man to write it, the Middle East expert, was out club-crawling – club not pub-crawling – with a visiting foreign correspondent. Typical of *The Times*, I thought as I tried to track him down. He was eventually found, and he arrived red-faced but like a true hack wrote about 1000 very good words. My main contribution was to provide him with lots of black coffee.

More typical was the attempted assassination of Governor George Wallace of Alabama in that it demonstrated that the paper had lost none of its old efficiency. I was at home mixing a drink when the night editor, Michael Hardy, phoned and read out the news flash. The governor was in a serious condition, and the flash hinted that he was expected to die. Wallace was not as important as Nasser; but he was a racist who had the support of rednecks in the south and hard hats in the north, and was a Democratic presidential candidate. We decided that the assassination attempt would lead the next edition, and I put the martini in the freezer and drove back to the office. During the ten-minute drive I mentally composed a feature about the man, who I knew well, and in the office, after checking that the correspondent's copy was coming in and that the obituary was up to date, sat down to type it. I was completing my 900 words – each page was taken to the subs as it was written – when Iverach McDonald phoned from home to say that he had just dictated a 550-word leader to the copy takers. It would fit nicely in the space filled by the third leader which could be discarded.

Within the hour we had changed three pages, and the presses were printing the second edition. There was no fuss or obvious tension. In the composing room I stood behind the night editor and stone subs who oversaw the page changes, and watched the stonehands as they inserted the new headlines and columns of type. They worked quickly, almost nonchalantly, and one of them was pleased to show off his craftsmanship. Later I had a last cigarette with the back-bench subs, who control the flow of copy to the composing room, and one of them was already reading copy for the third edition. The others looked content, as if they had just finished a good round of golf. 'We need more late stories like that to keep us in trim,' one of them said when I left. Back home I took the frozen martini out of the freezer, poured more gin into the glass to loosen the ice, and switched on the BBC World Service to check if there had been more developments. The galley with the obituary notice was waiting on the stone in case Wallace died. I spoke to the night editor again, and only then realized that I had had nothing to eat.

Despite the functional architecture, Printing House Square in the 1970s occasionally reminded me of the old building when I was a lad. Nothing was allowed to shatter the cathedral-like calm. Nobody hurried, and on the free-standing stairs leading to the intelligence department was a sign with the legend, 'DO NOT RUN'. It was intended for the messengers; we were often excited by the news or the urgency of getting an edition away, but tradition and custom required that it must not be shown. For me it was the memory of Dawson's impassive face during the abdication crisis, but the external calm reflected the paper's aloof stance. Whatever happened in the world outside, our job was to get out the paper without raising the editorial voice or our own.

This must have explained the calmness that night during the blitz when the bomb fell on Printing House Square, and the first edition was delayed for only a few minutes. I was almost convinced that if the strategy of mutual assured destruction, or MAD to use the official acronym, failed and a nuclear exchange was imminent, we would still try to bring out the paper. The political staff and the Washington and Moscow correspondents would file their stories; the first leading article would recall that the strategy had worked successfully for many years, and while hoping that reason would prevail confidence would be expressed in life after death. The night editor would select the front-page picture, perhaps a choice of anxious crowds waiting outside 10 Downing Street or a nuclear submarine leaving Holy Loch; or on second thought he might select one of the paper's famous photographs of the English countryside with the caption: 'Peace or Holocaust'. Fantasy? Not entirely. During the alarums of the 1950s a mobile printing press was built and hidden in the country. Presumably an editorial team would have been detailed to write and edit the last issue.

The Times was a good newspaper in the mid-1970s; certainly better than it was under Dawson. We had a courageous editor who listened to his assistant editors and correspondents; the home news had been improved and foreign news was more extensive. The first edition went to bed much earlier – about 9.30 p.m. instead of 11.30 – but not because of any slackness in the office. All the Fleet Street newspapers had advanced their edition times; it was the price of progress which made the trains, the main system of distribution, run slower and less often. The last edition went at about 2.30 a.m., but was delayed for a big story.

The Times was still losing money, although less of it, in part due to the high cost of newsprint but mainly because of over-manning in all departments. The production departments were grossly overmanned, commercial were not much better and I suggested to Rees-Mogg that the editorial could do better with fewer men and women. We had about 300 at the time, and some did not have enough to do. My concern was not about money – there were more than enough managers in London and Toronto to worry about that – but I believed that journalists worked better when they got more in the paper. The *Guardian* proved that; with little more than half of our staff, and poorer paid, its journalists did well because they were published more often. Rees-Mogg disagreed, saying that we had to be fully manned to handle great stories well. We also had to have a large parliamentary staff because we were the only newspaper which published extensive reports of the debates. This was true, and I could hardly say that we could do with fewer assistant editors if he did not go home in the early evening.

It would have been unfair anyway, but comparisons with the past were hard to avoid. Ralph Deakin operated brilliantly as foreign news editor with the help of one trainee journalist and a secretary; the foreign news editor who answered to me had four trained journalists and two secretaries. They were good journalists and worked harder than many others, but mainly, until I stopped it, because they sent unnecessary messages to correspondents. Some of the others were lazy or put their outside interests first. One specialist writer had only five short stories published in a month. Other specialists were hardly more productive; they spent many hours a day at their typewriters writing, I discovered, for other publications. That said, we had many fine journalists, every bit as good as the giants of the past.

The Times was also a good paper to work for in the early 1970s; bylines and better pay helped, fewer of the bright young men left, and no more was heard of the White Swan group. Cudlipp resigned to launch the news service of the London Broadcasting Company, and I became sole deputy editor. I continued to write and travel, spending two or three months abroad every year. Rees-Mogg also travelled, and of course we took vacations, which meant that I was responsible for about one-third of the issues. Rees-Mogg was very good at delegating and never interfered. A few regular contributors to the features page complained to him when I rejected their copy, but were always told that I was editing and the decision was mine. The proprietor or advertisement manager never intervened. Ken Thomson called from Toronto one day and asked for a favour; an art dealer he did business with in London had died, and could I run an obituary? I told him that an obituary has already been prepared and that it had been in the files for months. Apart from that, neither he nor his father ever tried to get some editorial recompense for the millions they had sunk into the paper. Thomson Tours was given no more attention than other package holiday companies. I was eager to encourage political advertising because I thought it a legitimate part of the political process; but when I decided not to publish a four-page advertisement for Taiwan because it claimed to be the Republic of China, the advertisement manager only regretted the loss of revenue. There was no doubt that the traditional independence of the editor was still respected.

We survived the three-day work week imposed by Edward Heath during the miners' strike and the power cuts. Arrangements were made officially to guarantee power for the presses but not for office lighting. I had a couple of cases of candles flown over from Paris; some of the subs complained that they were perfumed, but at least they shed some light and the soft glow of candlelight made the editorial floor very pretty. Eventually Reg Evans, who was in charge of editorial services and was a born fixer, noticed that an office block on the other side of Playhouse Yard had power when we did not, and ran a cable across and rigged up temporary lighting.

We also survived the wrath of Downing Street when Harold Wilson was prime minister. His press secretary took exception to a joke made by Philip Howard in one of his articles on words, and formally severed relations with the paper. We laughed. Did he really believe that *The Times* depended upon lobby briefings? But we did depend upon Downing Street for the honours list, which we always published in full. Christmas and the new year were approaching, Rees-Mogg was away, and I decided to sue the prime minister and the head of the civil service. I did not have a watertight legal case – the honours list did not have to be distributed in advance – but went ahead. Affidavits were sworn, counsel retained and arrangements made to appear before the vacation judge. The day before the list was to be distributed I called Downing Street to tell the press secretary of my intention, but he only said that he would not be blackmailed.

This is it, I said rather dramatically; cars were ordered, and we were putting on our coats when the telephone rang. It was one of the prime minister's private secretaries, who asked what was the bother. He was a young foreign office high-flyer, and we knew each other well, but he called me Mr Heren. I explained, and he asked if I could give him a couple of hours. It was a reasonable request in that presumably he had to brief the prime minister, who was almost certainly unaware of the ridiculous situation his press section had got him into; but the judge lived on the other side of Wandsworth Common and the streets were clogged with

Christmas shoppers. I gave him an hour, and within that time he called back to say that we could have a copy of the list. I said that we normally had six copies, and after a brief pause was told that they could be collected the following morning. We cheered, although we had missed a good story. I could see the headline in the tabloids: 'Top People's Paper Sues PM'. Fortunately a messenger arrived with a bag full of Bollinger champagne, a Christmas present from an ambassador, and we celebrated or drowned our sorrow in paper cupfuls of champers.

Denis Hamilton had earlier decided to become chairman of the company, and Marmaduke Hussey was appointed chief executive. Duke or Dukey, as he was universally known, came from Associated Newspapers where he had learned the newspaper trade from the packing warehouse up to the boardroom. A tall bluff man who looked like a gentleman farmer, he had been badly wounded in the war and was often in pain when he hobbled about the office. His ruddy face could look grey, but he was invariably amiable. Hussey also knew his job, and successfully developed the classified advertisement columns which were our best source of revenue. In 1973 the expanding columns were still being set when the last of the news pages were ready for the foundry. The paper would have made its first trading profit in many years, but for one of the early senseless strikes which shut down the paper for about a week.

Apart from this demonstration of union indiscipline, the only other cloud on an otherwise clear horizon was the prospect of moving to Gray's Inn Road where the Sunday paper was published. The staff of the *Guardian*, which shared the premises, was to transfer to a new building in Farringdon Road and we were to take over their offices. The commercial argument was said to be irrefutable; most of the presses on which the *Sunday Times* was printed stood idle six days a week, and were more than capable of printing *The Times* and the *Guardian*. Overheads would be drastically reduced, ancillary services could be shared by the two papers, and the sale of Printing House Square would repay part of the debt owed to the Thomson Organization. That said, resistance to the move was considerable, and I was asked to inspect the premises. I was happy to report that our staff was too large to be squeezed in, and we had to wait until a new office block was finished next door. There were further delays, but we finally moved in the summer of 1974.

I organized a farewell party for the editorial staff in the board-room, and we drank champagne which management had decided not to take to Gray's Inn Road. The party became a wake, *The Times* had been printed in Printing House Square for 190 years and nobody wanted to go. Moreover, as we moaned into our glasses, the floors below the boardroom were being stripped of machinery, furniture, files and the library.

I had to admit that the move was well organized. It had to be done at the weekend if production was not to be interrupted, and completed in about twenty-four hours. When I arrived in Gray's Inn Road next day, the last linotype machines were being swung from a crane through a hole in the wall and furniture was being carried in. It was touch and go; the Post Office had failed to connect many of the telephones, and desks and chairs were still being delivered as the subeditors came in. I watched one of them emptying his pockets of pipes, pouch, matches and pencils, and then loosen his tie just as his chair was pushed into place. We were ready to begin work on the Monday issue more or less on time, but a printers' dispute over a disturbance allowance delayed publication. Nobody realized it at the time, but the dispute was the first of many in Gray's Inn Road and the beginning of the end of the Thomson regime.

11

In Limbo

Gresham's law is not restricted to money: bad workers can corrupt good workers, as we discovered in Gray's Inn Road.

Our production and clerical staffs had earlier been affected to some extent by the growing trade union militancy of the period. They had obeyed union orders and held one-day strikes against Edward Heath's trade union legislation, and in the 1950s *The Times* with other Fleet Street newspapers had been closed for a month by an engineers' strike. A few shop stewards, known in the printing industry as fathers of the chapel, had become less cooperative. A mother of the chapel was known as the red nun. But on the whole the production men had worked as hard as the journalists to get the paper out on time. The spirit of the old Companionship was not extinguished until the move to Gray's Inn Road where industrial indiscipline was endemic.

The main reason was the success of the *Sunday Times*. The presses had to be kept running for about ten hours to print the paper; delays or stoppages could mean the loss of thousands of copies, and this encouraged the casual labour, which produces most Sunday papers, to demand more money by stopping or refusing to work. It was sheer blackmail, and some of our men joined in. The numbers of copies lost (that is, not printed) from 1976 to 1985, but excluding 1979 when the plant was shut down, were as follows:

	The Times	*The Sunday Times*
1976	660,000	1,528,290
1977	4,231,915	2,550,587
1978	4,277,945	8,729,730

1980	2,999,244	5,262,159
1981	998,975	2,478,281
1982	4,044,320	890,744
1983	987,570	4,353,792
1984	4,803,197	6,601,625
1985	221,800	412,286
total	23,228,866	33,551,601

The excuses for the stoppages were invariably ridiculous. The Sunday paper was stopped one night because the cleaners had left a trolley between two lines of presses, while the company's attempt to appoint a clerical manager led to a seven-day strike for both papers. *The Times* lost a complete issue when the unions refused to print an article by David Astor of the *Observer* on Fleet Street malpractices. They demanded its removal, and struck when William Rees-Mogg refused. On another occasion when I was editing, we lost the complete issue because the proof pullers did not report for work. Theirs is the simplest of jobs, but union solidarity prevented other men in the composing room from doing it. Another complete issue was lost when the foundry workers failed to appear.

There was nothing management could do except pay Danegeld. Unlike other products, newspapers are totally vulnerable to industrial blackmail, for the simple reason that today's newspaper cannot be sold tomorrow. The loss of one issue can cost tens of thousands of pounds. Moreover, in those unhappy days newspaper economics, especially in Fleet Street, were unique. The indiscipline and grotesquely inflated labour costs would have ruined other industries, but the national press survived because there were always rich men to buy bankrupted newspapers.

Simon Jenkins described the Street as a market for glory in a book of that name. The former editor of the *Evening Standard* says that aspiring proprietors have always been happy, indeed, eager 'to derive non-pecuniary returns from owning newspapers'. They have been ready to lose millions of pounds for fame, honours, power, or just being part of the excitement of newspaper production. Northcliffe hungered for all four; and a prime minister, Stanley Baldwin, condemned Rothermere and Beaverbrook for aiming at 'power without responsibility – the prerogative of the harlot throughout the ages'. They did not achieve power; in fact, the newspapermen who have exerted the most influence have not been proprietors but editors such as Geoffrey Dawson of *The Times* and J.L. Garvin of the *Observer*. This has not deterred wealthy men from entering the market for glory, and huge financial losses have not reduced the number of titles. Three papers disappeared after 1970, but have been replaced by the *Daily Star*, *Today* and the *Independent*.

Union men who took advantage of the glory seekers were not primarily interested in higher wages after the linotype operators on the *Sun* broke through the £40,000-a-year barrier. Not wanting to share more of their loot with the inland revenue, they demanded a four- or three-day work week. This had the advantage of providing more time for leisure – many printers are enthusiastic golfers – or to promote profitable side lines. The FOCs also liked to show who was the boss. Thomson met them when he bought the *Sunday Times*, and said, 'I'm Roy Thomson, the new owner of this paper.' One of the FOCs replied, 'You may own it, but I run it.' It was no idle boast; they decided how many men and women were to be employed and were responsible for recruitment. To give one small example, I had to wait for three weeks for a temporary secretary. She was a nice girl, but could not take shorthand. I applied for a replacement, and after another three weeks a girl was provided who bluntly stated that she would only answer the telephones. A further three weeks passed before a trained secretary was allowed to report.

This was of no consequence although the clerical chapel committee probably enjoyed my assumed discomfiture. I could function without a secretary because I had few administrative chores, but the FOCs had more effective ways of showing their contempt for management. They had brutally demonstrated that over the years, which helps to explain their anger when the company dutifully observed statutory pay restraint. Elsewhere in Fleet Street various under-the-counter pay deals had been made in breach of government pay policy, and as a result they were relatively poorly paid. Marmaduke Hussey and the executive board had to be taught a lesson.

Previously, despite delaying editions and losing complete issues, they had not entirely abandoned the old standards of crafts-manship. The paper had invariably been clean, that is it had few typographical errors; but almost overnight it was full of them. George Vowles, the head printer, did his best to maintain stan-dards. He was a shrewd Cockney with the combative stance of a welterweight boxer, and had been a gunner sergeant in the Western Desert during the war. He ordered the linotype operators to correct their work without extra payment – traditionally they had been paid to correct their mistakes – and persisted in the face of growing unpopularity until the men in the reading room played the final card. They withheld corrected galley proofs until it was too late to make corrections. This was outrageous – the worst kind of industrial sabotage; and for management the final straw. At least, that is how it seemed to me at the time, but thankfully I was not involved in management. What is reasonably certain is that, like Astor before him, Ken, the second Lord Thomson, had had enough.

Ken had succeeded to the title in 1976, and it was said that the shut down of the paper would not have happened if his father had been alive. It was also said that he was not a chip off the old block, which was true to the extent that he did not enjoy being a lord, and preferred to live in Toronto as plain Mr Thomson. He was a modest man, almost self-effacing, and the eyes behind the large spectacles which had once been friendly came to look perplexed or painfully surprised. Presumably that was why some journalists had a low opinion of him, although he and his father had supported them for ten years. In fact, Ken had much of his father's business acumen, and despite appearances was a typical North American go-getter with few outside interests apart from his family and art collection. Most of the pictures were Canadian, which should have been an indication of national pride. Certainly he was rich enough to buy the best of European art. Later he bought the Hudson Bay company, which meant more to him than *The Times*.

Ken was a proud Canadian who felt like a foreigner in Britain. I think that he was conventional enough to accept the assumption that *The Times* was a great newspaper, but he could not under-stand why it did not pay for itself, and the depredations of the unions were beyond his comprehension. He was genuinely puzzled by their refusal to accept computerized photocomposition, known as the new technology. Knowing that I was the son of a printer, he asked me why they objected to progress, which for him was inconceivable. I pointed out that the new technology would make many men redundant – the system was designed for journalists and classified advertisement clerks to set their copy on computer terminals – and most of them would not be satisfied with generous redundancy payments. Their union cards were the most precious bequest they could leave to their sons. He was not impressed, and reminded me that the so-called new technology was only new in Britain. It had been used elsewhere for years, even in Third World countries. I had in fact seen it being used by a small newspaper in Brazil some years earlier. It had been so widely adopted that linotype machines were no longer made. Fleet Street could only keep going by buying old machines abroad.

All this explained why Ken Thomson had had enough. The jewel in his father's crown had cost the family about £16 million, and he believed that he had done his duty by *The Times*. When Times Newspapers, the parent company, became profitable he was determined to transfer it to the Thomson Organization and thus bring to an end the family's moral obligations to the paper. This could only be achieved by photocomposition, which would dramatically reduce production costs.

The omens were not good. An earlier industry-wide initiative led by Hussey had failed; but urged on by Ken Thomson and Gordon Brunton, the chief executive of the Thomson Organization in Britain, Hussey decided to begin negotiations with the national union leaders. He knew them well, they were on first name terms and often met for drinks; but it was one of many mistakes.

They met secretly in Birmingham in April 1978. Hussey complained of crippling unofficial strikes, adding that 'it is not an exaggeration that almost the total working hours of our board and senior managers are now occupied with trying to prevent disputes, solving disputes and repairing the damage they caused. Virtually no effort is going into improving the turnover and profitability of the company.' The company wanted urgent discussions on the following basic principles: absolute continuity of production; negotiation of a quick and effective disputes procedure; general wage restructuring based on new technology and systems; and efficient manning levels in all departments. There would be no compulsory redundancy arising from new technology, but negotiations must be concluded by 30 November 1978. If agreement could not be reached by that date, publication of *The Times*, the *Sunday Times* and the three supplements would be suspended and not resumed until the conditions were met.

The secret meeting was apparently friendly. The general secretaries of the unions may well have welcomed Hussey as a manager tough enough to discipline the Fleet Street chapels which ignored them, but they were not prepared to become involved in a long and destructive dispute. They made themselves scarce, and were not available again for some months when they complained that the company was not ready to begin detailed negotiations. This was not true as the exchange of letters subsequently published by one of the unions proved, but little progress was made before the expiry of the ultimatum despite a two-week extension. The main craft union, the National Graphical Association, even refused to discuss the key proposal that some journalists and advertisement clerks should set their own copy when photocomposition was introduced. Only four of the fifty-six chapels signed the new work agreements, and disruption continued to the end.

We lost 68,000 copies of the last issue before the shutdown because of trouble in the machine room.

There is nothing more infuriating for a journalist than when a strike or bloody-mindedness stops his scoop from being published, and it is doubly infuriating for the man sitting in the editorial chair when the efforts of his staff are wasted. This was why I supported the management. But most of the editorial staff were at best ambivalent. I thought I understood: as a young foreign correspondent I was more interested in my career than the problems of management or newspaper economics. But I was surprised when the the National Union of Journalists chapel refused to negotiate a new agreement. The editorial was the only department which was not a closed shop, and some of the men had refused to join a union. About forty belonged to the Institute of Journalists, which regarded itself as a professional body, but the majority were members of the NUJ, which was recognized by management as the negotiating body for pay and conditions. The father of chapel, Jacob Ecclestone, was, in the words of Rees-Mogg, a man of the Left. Nevertheless, the chapel was anything but militant – hence my surprise.

The meetings I held to keep them informed were always civil, but I soon discovered that there was little or no criticism of the unions responsible for the crisis. On the other hand, they did not support management. Even when I confirmed that they would not be dismissed if the paper stopped publishing for an indefinite period, despite their failure to reach a new agreement, the mood was resentful. To some extent I could understand the gentle moans; the paper had been blighted by poor managers for as long as I could remember. Hussey was better than his predecessors, but the buck did not stop in his office. He was answerable to Brunton, who in turn was responsible to the Thomson international headquarters in Toronto. Ken Thomson rarely came to London, and generally only to attend board meetings of the Thomson Organization.

Towards the end of November, Rees-Mogg met the assistant editors to decide what was to be done during the closure. He looked preoccupied as if he was mentally composing a leading article; but he was a member of the executive board, apparently an influential one, and I had the impression that he was more concerned about the power struggle between management and the unions. He had little to say although he was his usual confident self, and eventually I suggested that if we stopped publishing it would be useless to bring in the staff five days a week. I thought that one or two days would be preferable, and we also agreed that courses should be held to improve subediting and shorthand. It was an unhappy meeting; nobody was really interested, and it seemed that our corporate energy was already seeping away. I for one was ruefully aware that for all our professional vanity we had no control over the paper's or our own fate. It was not the first or last time, and this sense of helplessness may well have explained the resentment of the reporters and subeditors.

The last few days were awful. Outside the office appeals were made to the government to intervene and save a national institution. The vultures gathered to report its slow death, as I had once flown in to report crises; only this time I was one of the victims and had to deal firmly with the reporters and television teams. It was painful to feel the paper dying, and I was compelled to write a feature recalling the good times when we worked as a team – journalists and printers – and looked forward to our coming together again to produce even better papers. It was not one of my greatest pieces, but I sent it down to the composing room hoping that it was not too sentimental. When the galley proofs arrived, a message written on a piece of pink proof paper was attached. It read:

> Isn't it strange how despite the plethora of hostile publicity directed at the NGA, members of that Union in the Comp room continue to set and make-up feature pages like this.
>
> Thinks – perhaps NGA men are sensible, hardworking men concerned about *The Times* after all.
>
> [signed] Comps.

I had no idea who the writer was, but it was a reminder that most of the printers, although primarily loyal to their union, were decent men who had worked hard for the paper over the years. Later, one of the features' subs came in and asked if I had any corrections to make, and I went with him to the composing room. I thought that I recognized the author of the note, a youngish man who in happier days had been as chatty as the job allowed, but nothing was said. On the way home I met Jimmy, one of the drivers who ferried senior editorial men about town. He was a typical Cockney, quick spoken and fast on his feet. He was also a fast driver after years of driving one of the vans like a formula one racer to deliver belated editions of the paper to the mainline railway stations. The newspaper trains would wait for mass-circulation papers such as the *Mirror*, but not for *The Times* or *Guardian*. Jimmy drove fast even when taking passengers to lunch. One day I was lunching with a bishop at the Athenaeum, and foolishly told him that I was late. I realized my mistake when he shot off down Gray's Inn Road, overtaking a bus on the wrong side of the road and as always talking over his shoulder about his extended family in Southwark. It was a terrifying journey, and instead of driving round the Duke of York's column in Waterloo Place he ignored the no-entry sign and drove directly to the club.

For one awful moment I thought that he intended to drive up the steps and deposit me in the lobby. I declined his offer to collect me, saying that I would walk back.

That evening Jimmy darted across from the entrance to the *Sunday Times* building, and spoke so quickly that at first it was difficult to understand what he was saying. It seemed that he had heard about the feature, and said that it was much appreciated by the drivers. His conversation then went something like this.

'Well, Mr Heren, you understand, don't you. You've spent your life in the print as I have. Not like those geezers upstairs. I was only saying to my Auntie Nell that I wished old Lord Thomson was still alive. He was a gent, and wouldn't have closed the paper. He would have made a deal with us.'

We chatted for a few more minutes, and he was on the edge of tears. I said not to worry, that we would soon be together again, and would have a drink to celebrate. We shook hands, and Jimmy said, 'God bless you, Mr Heren, God bless you.'

When I returned to the office during the first week of the closure, Clifford Longley, the religious affairs correspondent, said that if we were willing to contribute towards the cost he would provide wine and something to eat at subsequent meetings. It was an odd idea, we had nothing to celebrate, but proved to be helpful during the months ahead. I would pass on any news of the efforts to bring the two sides together, and then we would drink white Italian plonk from paper cups and nibble the food available. The meetings were quite jolly at times, and helped to keep us together, but it was not all wine and canapés. The subbing and shorthand courses were held regularly, and the company paid for lessons in French and Arabic. The specialists, such as the defence, diplomatic and political correspondents, were expected to keep up to date in their fields. Reporters who had complained that they did not have enough time to research complicated stories were put to work on projects; but as the weeks went by morale was gradually dissipated. This did not affect everybody, one reporter admitted later that he had rather enjoyed being paid for not working, but some became depressed and used me as an unpaid psychiatrist. Most were content to talk, but one reporter, a very good one, appeared to be deranged. He was convinced that there was a sinister conspiracy against *The Times* in general and himself in particular. I arranged for a real psychiatrist to see him. I was also depressed. I had been conditioned to write or edit the paper five or six days a week, and the routine had suddenly stopped. It was the Pavlovian dog effect in reverse – the bell did not ring, or, to put it another way, working up to ten or twelve hours a day I had become a slave who loved his chains and did not know how to handle this unaccustomed freedom.

A respite came in the spring when the management decided to publish an international weekly edition of the paper outside the country. It would not be circulated in Britain to avoid further trouble with the unions. I knew a newspaper publisher with a large printing plant in Warrington, Virginia, about thirty miles south of Washington DC, who was prepared to print the weekly. A large number of potential readers lived in North America; the plant was near Dulles international airport, an ideal distribution centre; and there would be no trouble with American unions. *The Times* Washington bureau was equipped with two telex lines, and large enough to house whoever was required to subedit the copy sent from London and put the paper to bed. To my surprise, and not little annoyance, I was told that management had already decided to print in Frankfurt, a city where by West German standards the unions were militant and likely to cooperate with our unions to stop publication. I had worked in West Germany for five years but my advice had not been sought.

It was too late to remonstrate, and a small advance party led by Michael Hamlyn, the executive night editor, flew off. I organized the journalists who were prepared to write for the weekly – the chapel was split – and their copy was subbed and sent by courier to Hamlyn. A few days later, Rees-Mogg and I, accompanied by Charles Douglas-Home, the senior assistant editor, also left for West Germany. We first went to Darmstadt where a small jobbing printer was setting the copy. It looked very small for such a venture – the first issue was only sixteen pages, but we had plans to expand to twenty-four – but it was equipped with the new technology. The women operators spoke no English, but made very few mistakes. We then went to the Tercuman Press in Zeppelinheim, immediately behind Frankfurt international airport, where the initial print run of 30,000 copies was to be run off on Saturday. It belonged to a newspaper group in Istanbul, and was built to print a newspaper for Turkish workers in West Germany. The manager, a youngish Turk, was obviously a good man to have in a tight corner. I was relieved to be in such company, and the few pickets outside the plant seemed to be the usual rent-a-mob to be found in any industrialized country. The two men from the circulation department, who had arrived to supervise the distribution, were also in good heart. I was only bothered by the location of the plant, a *sacgasse*, or dead-end street. In the event of trouble, it would be difficult for the police to disperse a large crowd.

Alas, my foreboding was not unfounded. The mob grew during the late afternoon. Only 300 copies had been run off when the plant was stormed. The police charged, but the mob could not be moved because of the airport fence. Somebody stuffed flaming rags in the intake of a compressor, which would have exploded and wrecked the building but for the quick reaction of a policeman with a fire extinguisher. It was impossible to continue the run in such circumstances, and Michael Mander, the company's deputy chief executive who had negotiated the print contract, agreed to meet the police chief next day to decide what was to be done.

Rees-Mogg and I accompanied him to the police headquarters that Sunday morning, and I think that the editor was horrified by the armed policemen waiting in the courtyard. Certainly I was taken aback by what looked like an *Einsatz Gruppe* of the old Wehrmacht. The water cannon looked like an armoured fighting vehicle, and the troops – or rather the police – capable of storming enemy entrenched positions. We thoughtfully walked upstairs to a long narrow room filled with various officials and lawyers. The situation was reviewed in military fashion, and again I was reminded of the war. We could have been attending a brigade headquarters' order group before a battle. I was wondering if Scotland Yard held similar meetings when preparing for a potentially violent demonstration in the streets of London when the police chief gave his conclusions. He could guarantee that we could print and distribute the first issue, but not subsequent issues. He could not afford to deploy such a large force indefinitely. The decision was ours. After a short silence the young Turkish manager, who was flanked by senior executives who had arrived from Istanbul, turned to us and said that whatever happened he would honour the contract he had with us. Then Rees-Mogg, speaking as if he was deciding some matter at an editorial conference, courteously thanked the Turk and the police chief and said that it would be unwise to proceed. It would be asking too much of the Tercuman Press and the law enforcement agencies of the German Federal Republic.

The police chief was obviously relieved, and I thought that the young Turk, although expressionless, was disappointed that we were unwilling to have a go. As for Rees-Mogg, I was once again impressed by his ability to make decisions and by his dignified self-confidence. My mind was in turmoil; I did not like being beaten by a bunch of Trots and yobs, and said as much to the editor as we went downstairs. As I recall, he said, 'Louis, I have always admired your spirit, but occasionally, very occasionally, discretion is the better part of valour.' I supposed that it was, and then told myself that we could still publish in the United States. That evening I called the American publisher who confirmed that he was still willing to print the weekly. It was not to be. The management had lost heart; perhaps it was the NGA's threat to disrupt production of the Thomson regional newspapers, which were then very profitable. Whatever the reason, it was a great victory for the unions, and probably persuaded them to seek total surrender.

From the beginning of the dispute, the unions had been determined to defend their power and privilege in Fleet Street. Albert Booth, the minister for employment who tried to bring about a resumption of negotiations, later told me that not before or since had he encountered such intransigence. Moreover, the unions were well placed to do battle. The closure was not a lockout; instead, contracts had been terminated after due notice, which meant that every man and woman was given one week's pay for each year of service. This meant thirteen weeks' pay for long-term employees, a large minority, which gave the unions time to find alternative employment for their members elsewhere in Fleet Street. The other managements could not or would not refuse to accept them. Only the NGA refused to disperse its members employed in the composing and machine rooms, and mounted a picket in Gray's Inn Road. Each man was paid £80 a week, half from the union's fighting fund and the remainder from a levy on members working in other Fleet Street houses.

The union campaign was organized by an inter-chapel committee, whose skills I could not but admire although its purpose was destructive. I did not have Ken Thomson's unquestioning faith in progress, but thought that this ruthless exploitation of Fleet Street newspapers was morally wrong.

Hamilton said as much when he met the inter-chapel committee for the first time in June, albeit more diplomatically. He also seemed to admit that management had been out of touch with the shop floor. It was the first indication, at least for me, of growing differences between the chairman and Hussey, the chief executive. Hussey was duty bound to pursue the policy laid down by Thomson, and Hamilton, despite his military experience, was a conciliator. He was also a born journalist, and was tortured by the thought that he could be responsible for the death of the two newspapers.

The approaching summer vacations eased the tedium and frustration; seven months of idleness without the prospect of a negotiated solution was still, nevertheless, hard to bear. Some of us wrote books. Philip Howard, one of our four old Etonians and a classicist, occasionally worked as a butler. In an interview with the *New Yorker*, he said, 'One thing I learned is that professionals in that line of work always carry nutcrackers in their pockets. There's no better implement when you have to open a lot of champagne bottles with tight corks in a hurry. I also learned that receptions are usually more fun downstairs than upstairs.' Howard was one of the few men in the reporters' room who would have been at home in the old Printing House Square. He was appointed literary editor during the closure when his predecessor left to join a publishing house. John Gregg, the special numbers editor, started a bridge school. They remained sane, and loyal to the paper.

The dispute was costing the company millions in lost revenues and salaries for journalists and managers, and Thomson was the first of the two adversaries to waver. At the general annual meeting of the International Thomson Organization, he told the shareholders: 'We have regarded it as of great importance to the future of our publications that *ultimately* [my italics] this new modern equipment [photocomposition] should be used to its full potential.' In other words, the phased introduction of direct input to the typesetting computer by journalists and advertisement clerks would be postponed until after publication had been resumed. The NGA had won; its linotype operators, who should have been declared redundant, would operate the computer terminals.

An agreement with the NGA was reached in late July, but the other unions and the NGA machine minders' chapel also wanted their pound of flesh. Production was eventually resumed on 13 November 1979, nearly one year after the shutdown.

The management claimed that 70 per cent of its original demands had been won; but in fact the settlement in the eyes of the unions was unconditional surrender by management, and they were closer to the truth. Continuous production of the papers was not guaranteed and the *Financial Times* estimated that the closure had cost Times Newspapers £40 million.

Little attention was given to this on the editorial floor. The main thing was that we had a newspaper again. The first night was wonderful, like being reborn. I went across to the composing room and watched the front page being made up. It was a good newsworthy page, we obviously had not lost our old skills. There was a column-eight story written by Longley, the religious affairs correspondent. Under the headline, 'Vatican and Henry VIII bridge their official rift', it reported the granting of diplomatic rights to the papal nuncio which healed the breach that occurred between Henry VIII and the Holy See. (A television reporter later said that it was 'a typical *Times* story – quite obscure'.) As the stonehands locked up the page, Rod Macfadyen, a compositor, marched into the room in full Highland regalia playing a rousing march on his bagpipes. I assumed that he was celebrating the unions' victory, but it sounded good and we parted in a warm cosy glow.

Much more important, it was soon established that we had lost none of our readers. After an initially high sale, due to novelty interest, the circulation settled down to rather more than 300,000. We knew that we had to do better if we were to be profitable again, but at least we had a firm foundation on which to build.

The euphoria was also evident on the management floor,

although the senior men must have been exhausted by the negotiations with the chapels. There was much talk about a new
beginning, and in a well-printed report to the staff it was said that
teamwork would play a key role in the development of existing
and new titles. The formation of two executive committees, one
for *The Times* and one for the *Sunday Times*, was a vital ingredient
of the reorganization of the company. I think that Gordon
Brunton was responsible for the committees; he had discussed the
idea with me over dinner at Claridges. (Brunton was another poor
boy who had really made it; born in Hackney, he frequently
suggested that we should dine at an eel and pie shop in the East
End but we always finished up at Claridges.) He admitted the
mistake of placing the two papers under one management, and
hoped that eventually *The Times* would be moved from Gray's
Inn Road. The executive committees would be a start. Sipping
the Schloss Vollrad Auslese, a superb Rheingau I had been invited
to select, and then a very superior claret, it had seemed a splendid
idea.

The new beginning was formally launched at a two-day conference under the chairmanship of Lord McCarthy at a hotel near
Gatwick airport. Managers, editors and FOCs were divided into
syndicates to discuss various aspects of cooperation. My syndicate
produced very little, and I only acquired a hangover; Hussey had
asked me to 'talk with the chaps' at the bar after dinner and as
the drinks were free they went on guzzling until the small hours.
The staff report merely said that there was a commitment to
publish an internal newspaper to report on all matters relating to
staff, unions and the company, and that a regular pattern of
consultative meetings had been established.

I had the feeling that we, managers and editors, were being
indulged by the victorious unions. Certainly they were soon up to
their old tricks; once again the *Sunday Times* regularly failed to
complete its print run, and *The Times* lost about a third of its
classified advertising because of the failure to negotiate a manning
agreement, which should have been completed before resumption.
Apart from proving that they were the real bosses, the unions
must have assumed that Thomson could afford to ignore their
depredations. The staff report already mentioned contained the
good news that in 1979 the International Thomson Organization

had made a trading profit of £172 millions on a turnover of £699.6 millions. It mattered not that Times Newspapers was projected to lose about £13 millions; Thomson would continue to pay for the honour and glory of owning two great newspapers. He might well have done except that the unbelievable happened – the journalists of *The Times* voted to strike.

The strike was the first of its kind in the paper's history, and would not have happened but for the closure. Fifty weeks of inactivity had been unsettling; and I suspected that the handful of trade union activists, who had been associated with the inter-chapel committee during the closure, had been politicized. They had helped to defeat management, and probably thought that strong-arm methods could achieve another victory. The strike was over pay, but almost certainly one or two activists had other objectives. Trade union power had grown enormously under the previous government; it had become an estate of the realm, and there was talk of controlling the press which was regarded as a capitalist enemy. Some rank-and-file members of the chapel were probably attracted by the idea, but shorn of its socialist claptrap; certainly they were dissatisfied with their existing status. To resort to military comparisons again: young journalists, most of them university graduates, joined *The Times* as second lieutenants; some were promoted to captains but very few to field rank. Little or nothing could be done about this, it was the nature of journalism, but disappointing for the ambitious. Fortunately, a number were content to be good reporters and subeditors, but some of the middle-aged longed for a handle to their names even if it was only assistant news editor. It was understandable, and remembering my own progress from messenger to deputy editor I had tried to help. I had made at least six of them foreign correspondents, and helped others by ensuring that good jobs were not filled by outside recruitment. This had not always been possible, and no doubt some felt that they were at the bottom of the heap, as I did as a reporter in 1947.

In a way they were, but the social or class pyramid had long been dismantled. Rees-Mogg had established a consultative committee in order that their views could be heard. The members were chosen by the staff, but the meetings were rarely successful. They seemed to lose interest once the principle of consultation had been accepted. We tried to reward the best and brightest when they could not be promoted, but the NUJ chapel always insisted upon across-the-board salary increases. John Grant, who administered the editorial department, tried to set aside 10 per cent of the money available to reward merit, but generally had to be content with 5 per cent. This helped, but those without exceptional talent felt that they were taken too much for granted. They were convinced that they were the lowest-paid journalists in Fleet Street, but as far as the serious daily newspapers were concerned this was no longer true. The *Telegraph* paid no more and the *Guardian* less. Salaries on the *Financial Times* were higher, but it was a very profitable newspaper and demanded special skills from its journalists. Our journalists were well treated on the whole; they had six-week vacations plus sabbaticals, and working conditions were congenial. The pension fund was good by Fleet Street standards.

That said, some had been recruited during the early expansionary years of the Thomson regime, when standards had been lowered in the rush. This is not a blanket condemnation of the 1967 intake, but a number of them would have been happier on other newspapers. Expectations had also changed. In my early years we were attracted by the job despite the indifferent pay. We moaned about it, but the fun and excitement of journalism was sufficient recompense. In 1980 I had the impression that, for some, journalism was one of many careers proposed by advisers, and had been chosen because it seemed more interesting than banking or teaching.

I was in the United States during the salary negotiations. Returning on Sunday, 17 August, I went straight from the airport to the office; Rees-Mogg had left for California and I had to edit the paper. On my desk was a letter from Grant, who had also begun his vacation, warning me to be prepared for trouble. I should keep in close touch with Dugal Nisbet-Smith, the new managing director. Hamilton, the editor-in-chief, was in Italy and James Evans, who had succeeded Hamilton as chairman, was in Wales. I was sipping black coffee to overcome the usual jet lag when I opened the next letter. It was from Nisbet-Smith, and said that the NUJ chapel had rejected a salary increase of 18 per cent. This shocked me into wakefulness.

For the first time I regretted not keeping drinks in the office. I needed one badly. The paper was confronted with an unprecedented crisis, and all the top people were on vacation. I did not shirk responsibility, but as editor Rees-Mogg had more authority. Hamilton and Evans would have been helpful. Evans, formerly the legal manager, was a calm man and his unhurried voice and warm unlined face could make the irrational see reason. Nisbet-Smith was an unknown factor.

The next few days remained a nightmare for a long, long time. On Monday I called the reporters together, reminded them that Thomson had said that he would continue to meet losses as long as the journalists remained loyal and warned them that a strike could kill the paper. They were not impressed. They either thought that I was exaggerating, or like the printers believed that if Thomson did quit another wealthy man would be only too happy to become the proprietor. It was pointless to argue before I had seen Nisbet-Smith, and in any case I had to prepare that night's paper. I also wanted to phone the editor, and due to the time difference had to wait until the afternoon.

I called Rees-Mogg after the second editorial conference, and he was his usual calm and confident self. I told him that the chapel was in a surly mood, and that a strike was possible. This was received quietly, and after obvious reflection he said that I should try to get the paper out. We discussed the possibilities, and then I suggested that he should cut short his holiday. This time there was no pause for reflection. 'My dear Louis,' he said. 'I often wonder why I am,editor. You always do it so much better when I am away.' After he had hung up, I uttered a few good Anglo-Saxon swear words, then laughed admiringly.

Fortunately there was no aggravation on the editorial floor. If there had been surliness, it was not evident after that first meeting; everybody worked well, which was just as well because I spent a great deal of time on the top floor with Nisbet-Smith. He was a burly New Zealander, who looked as if he had spent his life on the rugger field. He always managed simultaneously to beam a broad smile and blow clouds of smoke from a large pipe. At our first meeting, he showed me the draft of a report for heads of departments, which said that the dispute had been referred to arbitration. Evans had testified at the hearing about the company's serious financial predicament; £18 million had been borrowed two months earlier merely to keep in business, and the estimated trading loss for 1980 was £10 million. The arbitrator had nevertheless recommended an average increase of 21 per cent, the burden of his argument being that the journalists should be paid the rate for the job irrespective of the company's ability to pay.

It seemed crazy to me, and Nisbet-Smith said that the recommendation would be rejected; according to the disputes procedure, the arbitrator's findings were not legally binding. He asked if the journalists would strike, and I thought that they would. The moderate majority would be reluctant, but would probably go along with the chapel committee unless the company could convince them of its inability to pay. I could produce the paper in the event of the strike with the help of about forty men who were not members of the NUJ, but I was worried.

I hoped desperately for some initiative from management. Nisbet-Smith seemed to agree; but we did not have the authority to act, and Evans would have to refer to the Thomson Organization. When told that the chapel was to hold a strike vote on Wednesday, I urged Rees-Mogg to return to London; but he decided that it was better to remain in California where he could keep in touch rather than be caught in mid-air during the twelve-hour flight. It made sense, and I began to plan to produce the paper with the help of journalists who did not belong to the union. This was met with varying degrees of enthusiasm, but when the chapel voted to strike from noon on Friday, 22 August, Nisbet-Smith told me that the company had decided not to try.

The strike lasted only a few days, but the consequences were devastating. Hamilton was the first of the top men to return from vacation, and on Saturday we dined in a restaurant beneath his flat in Victoria. We were both miserable, and in his Murdoch biography (*Barefaced Cheek*, 1983) Leapman says that we

felt betrayed by the journalists – their *journalists*, as both thought that they had a right to regard them. It might have been high-handed of the management to reject the arbitrator's award but all the same there was such a thing as loyalty; or at least there used to be, when Heren and Hamilton were young newspapermen. Things were not the same now and it was no use pretending they were.

Things were certainly not the same, but this time there was no pretence. Within a few days the Thomson board decided to sell Times Newspapers, although the announcement was delayed for two months. Rees-Mogg told the editorial staff on 22 October, and watching the silent group I wondered if they had finally realized the importance Thomson attached to loyalty to the paper. The questioning revealed very little except an anxiety about jobs and mortgages. Then one of them, who had joined the strike, had the cheek to propose that a letter should be sent to Thomson thanking him and his family for what they had done for the paper. The editor agreed.

Whatever Thomson thought about that letter – Rees-Mogg reported later that he was deeply touched – he abdicated the crown of thorns with dignity. He said:

> It grieves me greatly that in spite of the millions of pounds which have been provided to Times Newspapers over the years to enable these newspapers to survive, and in spite of the efforts of many loyal employees who have built the papers to their present eminence and to whom I express my deep gratitude, we have been unable to secure the cooperation of important sections of the workforce on a reliable and consistent basis. I believe that a change of ownership could provide Times Newspapers with the opportunity to create a new and constructive relationship with its staff. With their cooperation and goodwill Times Newspapers with its superb titles could be a viable and profitable business with excellent prospects for the future.

Brunton added that more than £70 million had been advanced from Thomson sources for investment and losses incurred. More funds would be provided to sustain trading losses until March 1981 when, unless new owners were found, publication would cease. The prime objective was to sell the company as a whole, but if necessary the titles would be sold separately. They would not go to the highest bidder. The national directors and editors would establish criteria, including the interests of employees, readers and advertisers, and the national interest; and they would be directly involved in assessing any proposals made concerning the future of the titles as editorially independent newspapers of high quality. Interested parties should apply before 31 December. If the sale was not achieved before the following March, the last dates for publication would be 8 March for the *Sunday Times*, 13 March for the supplements, and 14 March for *The Times*.

The atmosphere in Gray's Inn Road was dramatically transformed by the announcement. The print chapels stopped disrupting production, presumably to entice the next victim to place his fortune in their rapacious hands. The NUJ chapel committee demanded participation in the vetting of potential buyers, and representation of all chapels on the new Board. Other demands included participation in the selection and appointment of future editors, and no compulsory redundancies. The majority of journalists, dismayed by what they had done, had distanced themselves from the chapel committee. They had incorporated themselves as a limited company known as Journalists of *The Times* Ltd (JOTT) with the objective of helping to ensure the survival of *The Times* and its supplements, and to seek a shareholding in Times Newspapers or any successor company. It established its independence from the union by defeating with a substantial majority a motion moved by Ecclestone to refer to the chapel. More dramatically, Rees-Mogg decided to form a consortium to publish *The Times* separately, and left for North America to confer with Thomson in Toronto and look for backers in the United States. I was left in charge of the paper.

It would be misleading to say that we were moving into a fantasy world, but it seemed like that from time to time. I knew that Brunton wanted to sell the titles to avoid paying redundancies, estimated to total about £40 million; that should have been obvious even to reporters who had difficulty in totting up their expense accounts, but it seemed that everywhere – in the office, pubs and public halls – groups gathered to plan how they could take over the paper and run it. Readers formed the 'Friends of *The Times* Organisation'. For some reason, most of the sponsors were military men, ranging from Rear Admiral I.G. Aylen to Major General C.W. Woods, and they were opposed to the paper being taken over by foreigners. In a three-column advertisement, they also declared that *The Times* was the greatest newspaper in the world and part of the national heritage. Other outside groups became involved, again assuming that the paper was a national monument, rather like Stonehenge, and not a business concern. Few people seemed to realize that the consortium idea only made sense if Brunton failed to sell the paper, and Thomson was willing to give it away and pay the redundancies of printers, journalists and other workers.

Rees-Mogg, determined not to be the paper's last editor, left for Toronto accompanied by a BBC television team. He was a changed man, and before leaving London told the editorial staff: 'I do not believe that we should wait for the arrival of a new proprietor on a white horse.... In any case, it seems to me that if we are to secure the future of the paper we must do it ourselves.'

We talked about his journey – I began to think of it as a crusade – on more than one occasion before his departure, and he was his usual clear-headed self. This more or less is what he said:

> We could not go it alone, the working capital required was greatly beyond what journalists and managers could provide. We must plan a future for the paper in which journalists and managers could become joint proprietors with people of sufficient means to provide a strong commercial base to ensure that the paper could survive. One thing was certain; *The Times* and the *Sunday Times* were so different that neither paper was good for each other. The industrial logic which put the two papers together was mistaken, although the commercial and financial logic seemed to make very good sense at the time. The two papers with their industrial difficulties were seen outside as a financial black hole; any amount of money put into Gray's Inn Road just disappeared, and nobody was willing to accept that.

He sounded like one of his leading articles; I was impressed, in part because I had long thought that the move to Gray's Inn Road was a mistake, but said that we had to produce good papers while he was away or seeking capital in the City. I needed to know that I could do what I thought best. He agreed, and before his departure urged the journalists to support me fully, adding that for the foreseeable future he would be too busy trying to put the consortium together to be able to edit the paper properly. He would look in whenever he could, but I was in charge.

Rees-Mogg proved his shrewdness over the next few weeks. His trans-Atlantic visit produced few tangible results, Thomson was polite but noncommital and American publishers were not interested; but the publicity provided by the accompanying television team was free and very useful. A number of readers offered to help; many sent cheques and a few pound notes, and others expressed willingness to join the consortium. One wanted to invest £25,000. Rees-Mogg brought most of the journalists round to his point of view at frequent meetings, and in so doing got rid of the wilder ideas. Basically his position was that the paper could not be run as a cooperative, and that they must be willing to accept a minority share in the consortium; nor would it be able to afford to employ the printers who had earlier worked in Printing House Square. The consortium would launch a publishing company, and the printing would be done under contract in the provinces. He also disposed of an attempt by the NUJ chapel to dominate editorial representation in a new company; he was willing to work with JOTT, which had done its homework, and asked me to seek the opinions of the assistant editors.

Fantasy or not, I was more than half convinced that we could make a go of it if we were given the title, especially when Rees-Mogg said that he had the full support of Lord Weinstock, the chairman of GEC. Although I was acting editor, I became involved when United Newspapers, which later bought the *Daily Express*, told me that they could offer me a new printing plant in Northampton. It was equipped with Goss Metro offset presses and a photocomposition system. The editorial department could be located anywhere in London and transmit page facsimiles to the plant which was near the M1. Its capacity was inadequate, but the plant could be enlarged or, I thought, we could print in two places. I was mainly worried about installing the transmission equipment and overseas telephones in a new office in time to guarantee continuous publication, but Rees-Mogg said that Weinstock would take care of that. He also said in early December that he would be making a bid for the paper to Warburgs, the merchant bankers representing Thomson, before the end of the year.

This glowing future began to fade in the new year when Rees-Mogg told the assistant editors that Thomsons were confident of selling the company in one piece, and that Murdoch was the front runner. I was not surprised; a day or two earlier I had had a phone call from Bruce Rothwell who worked for Murdoch in New York. Rothwell was also Australian, and we were old friends. We had first met in Washington when he worked for the old *News Chronicle*, and later as one of Murdoch's men in London had asked me from time to time if Thomson wanted to sell *The Times*. He had called me in the small hours of the morning to ask if the senior editorial men would object to Murdoch buying the paper; journalists on the *Observer* had successfully opposed his bid for that paper, and he did not want to be embarrassed again. I assured him that there would be no trouble, and he then asked if I would write a memorandum on the paper for Murdoch. It was a tricky request, but I eventually agreed and went back to bed.

I must have dreamed about it because I awoke regretting my promise; bidders were supposed to get their information from Warburgs and not from individuals. Nevertheless, I wrote a five-page memo over the weekend and sent it off. I referred to recent history, and made a number of suggestions to improve the paper. I emphasized that the commercial benefits to be expected after improving the editorial content and cutting production costs would take time. Unlike the *New York Times* and *Le Monde*, we did not enjoy a monopoly. We had the *Guardian* on our left, the *Daily Telegraph* on our right and the *Financial Times* standing between us and all that lovely advertising in the City of London. We should avoid Thomson's early mistakes and prepare for a long haul. I estimated that he could be in profit within two or three years if he got the production costs right, during which time the Sunday could keep the company solvent. Murdoch replied, thanking me, within the week.

The announcement that Murdoch had bought Times Newspapers caused a commotion outside the office. That was only to be expected. He was not liked, in part because he did not behave as did other press barons. Above all, he owned the *Sun* and the *News of the World*, strange bedfellows for *The Times*. The worst was feared, including page three nudes desecrating the 'Thunderer'. Ecclestone objected in his capacity as father of the NUJ, but the other chapels were only too happy to have another rich man to squeeze. Stronger guarantees of editorial independence were written into the new company's articles of association.

William Rees-Mogg took his redundancy money, was knighted and joined the great and the good who are said to run Britain. He flourished, as was to be expected, and I was left with mixed feelings. He had been infuriating at times, but the consortium had been a great idea. We could have made a go of it. Later, admittedly in better circumstances, Andreas Whittam Smith, a journalist little known outside financial circles, successfully launched *The Independent*.

12

Murdoch and Evans

I was awakened by the steward before dawn, and went up to the top deck as *Queen Elizabeth II* steamed slowly through the Narrows. Manhattan looked as splendid as ever with the early morning sun lighting up the glass-clad towers. As always, it was good to be back in my second home again, despite the delays going through immigration and customs and waiting for a cab. I stayed with Bruce and Anna Rothwell for a few days in their uptown apartment on Park Avenue; Rothwell was then the editorial-page editor of the *New York Post*, and the page was the best written in the paper despite the right-wing views required. One evening he said that there were some very good jobs in Murdoch's expanding empire for men of my experience, and that I should leave *The Times*. My mind was more than half made up after five days at sea, but I still hesitated and at the end of the week flew to Washington to do some work. I wanted to do stories on Senator Jesse Helms and the national swing to the right, which then had not been fully reported, and on Reagan. The president was unfortunately shot before I had a chance to see him, but his staff was helpful as were Helms and other people on the right wing. I sent off the stories and a feature I had been asked to write on what went on behind the scenes, or bulkheads, of *Queen Elizabeth II*, and went down to Charlottesville, Virginia, to stay with friends.

On my return to London, I discovered to my dismay that not a word had been published; my enquiries were met with evasive answers, and it seemed that I was being squeezed out. Evans was entitled to get rid of men he did not want, but it was unpleasant. Being a director was no recompense, if a new experience. Murdoch was fascinating to watch. The other board members, including the Lords Catto, Dacre, Drogheda and Robens, comported themselves with well-tailored suavity and easy assurance, but Murdoch could behave like the proverbial caged lion. He could be charming, but made no effort to conceal annoyance or impatience. Crouched low in his chair and with eyes narrowed, he would bare his teeth which he tapped with his folded spectacles. His moods were mercurial, and I had to admit that he had much to be angry about.

The unions had behaved themselves at first, but were soon up to their old tricks again when they thought that another rich proprietor had been hooked. At least, that was my conclusion and probably Murdoch's. In September 1981 the board had to deal with yet another dispute, a classic example of how the chapels defended and exploited pay differentials. In the last few weeks of the Thomson regime the Sogat machine assistants had negotiated an agreement giving their senior members $87\frac{1}{2}$ per cent of the pay of NGA machine managers, whose chapel had then demanded forty-one extra shifts in recompense. This was rejected by ACAS, and the chapel then requested an independent manning study of the machine room. This seemed too good to be true, as was quickly proved. When the request was accepted with alacrity by the management, the chapel said that the study was dependent upon members being paid £700 each immediately to restore differentials.

This was infuriating; apart from trading losses, redundancies had already cost £7 million and the earlier demand for more shifts indicated that the chapel was determined to regain the jobs bought out at great expense. The Thomson board might have fudged the issue and settled for a couple of hundred pounds, but not Murdoch. He threatened to issue notices and close down both papers, and it was then that I decided to leave. I had had enough, of shabby treatment as well as union rapacity and threats to the paper's future. I wrote a 'Dear Harry' letter to Evans, saying that I was responding to his offer to pay redundancy to any member of the editorial staff who decided to leave the paper before the end of the month; and after referring to the NGA dispute went on:

Now let me try to explain why I think I should go. Obviously I was disappointed when I was not appointed as William Rees-Mogg's successor, but I was prepared to work loyally with you as I had done with earlier editors. As you know, I wanted to continue as deputy editor but for reasons, which I think I now understand and accept, you decided otherwise.

That was the second disappointment, but I still hoped that I could do a good job as an associate editor. It has not worked out, alas. I think that I have written some good pieces in recent months, but clearly I do not fit into the new team.

It took me a long time to realize that I was the odd man out, in part because, without being sentimental, *The Times* has been my life. But earlier this month aboard the *QE2* I had the opportunity to think things out and decided that with your new team of writers there was very little left for me to do ...

My departure was quite an occasion. I was invited to write a farewell article for the features page, and Murdoch presided over a grand luncheon. The assistant editors gave me a dinner at the Gay Hussar, and Victor Sassie presented me with a jeroboam of champagne. The editorial department bought me a Georgian inkstand with the inscription 'To Louis Heren, A Man of *The Times*', which was presented by Evans who said nice things. Readers wrote letters, and one of them sent me a box of cigars. A rare compliment was paid by George Vowles, the head printer, who had me 'banged out' of the composing room. This was an atavistic ceremony reserved for retiring printers, and I was even allowed to help in locking up the front page and slide the forme along the stone to the foundry. The linotype operators and stone hands armed with strips of metal banged the stone and other surfaces. The noise was deafening, and for me a reminder of the old days in Printing House Square when journalists and printers had worked together to produce good papers.

The next morning I collected my redundancy cheque from the paying cashiers, and one of the clerks suggested that I should have a security guard to accompany me to the bank. That should have been that, but Peter Hennessy, the Whitehall correspondent, arranged a lunch in a private room at the Garrick. I had hired some of the dozen reporters who attended, and expected a jolly meal. Instead, the conversation turned to the troubles in Gray's Inn Road; a few of them said that they were also thinking of quitting, and I found myself saying they should not quit, that they had a duty to stay. The Thomsons and the Murdochs could come and go, but the paper could not flourish without good journalists. No doubt the prolonged wining and dining explained the outburst.

When I had been thinking about leaving the paper, a friend reminded me of the advantages of working for *The Times*. Without the paper I would be just another chap with no pull or influence. I was not offended, having recognized almost from the beginning that presidents and prime ministers did not see me because they liked the colour of my eyes. I also knew that I was invited to too many luncheons and dinners because I worked for *The Times*; that I had also had enough smoked scotch salmon to last me a couple of lifetimes, and was relieved to know that I would not have to attend any more ambassadorial dinner parties and national days.

The loss of a generous salary – I was very well paid during the last few years – and director's fees should have been a blow, but I was confident that the golden handshake and freelancing would pay for the martinis. I was allowed to buy my company car for a reasonable price, and could look forward to a good pension. My tax accountant, Malcolm Slonims, another East End boy who had made good, kept an eye on me. To that extent I was more fortunate than many retired journalists. That said, the first weeks of retirement were worse than the months of closure; I was completely disoriented, unable to relax or use my time profitably. *The Times* had been my life, and suddenly I had ceased to be part of it. I still responded to news like that Pavlovian dog, and picked up information that could have been developed into front-page stories, but for no purpose. I missed the sudden eruption of wars and crises – and the delivery of the early edition at night. Life, it seemed, had little purpose beyond the family.

I adjusted gradually to the change when offers of work came in. I was asked to do a number of assignments, review books and write another book. I became editorial consultant to *The Straits Times* of Singapore, a country in which I had an almost proprietorial interest. It was exceedingly pleasant to return for two or three winter months to the warmth and friendliness of the tropics, and to work with a well-run and profitable newspaper. An extra advantage was that problems were not discussed in the office but over exquisite Chinese dinners. At home I rediscovered the pleasures of the theatre and reading books not about politics, foreign affairs and defence.

I was in Cardiff, beginning a series on provincial cities for the *Illustrated London News*, when Murdoch dismissed Evans, and was relieved to be beyond the reach of Fleet Street's search for comment although *The Daily Mail* did manage to track me down. I said very little, mainly because of my surviving loyalty to the paper and in any case knew little or nothing of the immediate background. It was also difficult to believe; I knew that Gray's Inn Road had become a very unhappy place, but Evans had recently been proclaimed Editor of the Year by Granada Television. Murdoch also had a reputation for firing editors but it had been a reasonable assumption, after the furore over his purchase of the paper, that he would not have invited criticism so quickly.

Later, much later, Rees-Mogg said of his successor that 'you can't fight the staff and the proprietor simultaneously'. Remembering my own experience it seemed to explain half of the predicament Evans had created for himself.

I had admired Evans as the crusading editor of the *Sunday Times*, and apparently he regarded me as a fellow professional. Certainly when Frank Giles, his then deputy, was thinking of early retirement, he asked me if I was interested in becoming his deputy editor. In the event, Giles remained to succeed him as editor of the Sunday paper; but sitting together at the top table of a large dinner party in Claridges I had thanked him and declined. Apart from my attachment to *The Times*, I said that I was a daily journalist conditioned to respond to news, and did not think that I could adjust to the weekly cycle of a Sunday newspaper. The enquiry was presumably serious; Giles had been our Paris correspondent for many years, and I had assumed that he was considering replacing him with another *Times* man to take care of what could be described as the more conventional side of the paper. Evans had a flare for investigative journalism, and campaigns such as the Thalidomide story and the subsequent legal action must have taken a great deal of his time.

That was one reason why I offered to continue as deputy when we had lunch at the Garrick soon after his appointment as editor was announced. McDonald had made a similar offer to soldier on to Rees-Mogg in 1967, who was grateful enough to acknowledge that the older and more experienced man had been a tower of strength. It soon became evident that Evans did not want me as his deputy, which was his right but he did not say so at our first meeting.

Evans trashes me, to use the US army expression, and most of my former senior colleagues in his book, *Good Times, Bad Times*. The book was published in the year following his dismissal, and reflects the shock and resentment. One reviewer said that he should have waited, but the shock was understandable. He had had a brilliant career. The son of an engine driver, he had begun in newspapers after leaving his Manchester central school. To that extent, our beginings were remarkably similar, but after his national service he went to Durham University and then joined the *Manchester Evening News* and became a leader writer and assistant editor. A Harkness fellowship took him to the United States for two years, and he became editor of *The Northern Echo*, which had once been edited by the great Victorian campaigner, W.T. Stead. Evans followed in his footsteps, and his campaign for an official enquiry into the hanging of Timothy Evans for the mass murders committed by John Christie attracted the attention of Denis Hamilton, who invited him to be his chief assistant.

Evans was appointed editor of the *Sunday Times* the following year when Hamilton became chief executive and editor-in-chief of Times Newspapers, and continued the good work of his mentor. His Insight team did superb work under his leadership, including the Philby exposé; and he became nationally famous when he published the diaries of Richard Crossman, the Labour politician, which had not been submitted to the customary official censorship. It was a famous victory against an arcane law of confidence and government secrecy. I for one regret that he was not in a position to contest the banning of Peter Wright's *Spycatcher*. He went on to investigate and expose the cause of the DC-10 crash in France in 1974, which with the Thalidomide case helped the victims and their families to challenge great corporate power. Evans was also an inspired production journalist; he wrote a number of books including five volumes on editing and design, and achieved international recognition with his work for the International Press

Institute. There was a period when he seemed to be everywhere; the incarnation of modern journalism, battling mightly with institutionalized resistance to the public's right to know and at the same time personifying the upwardly-mobile men and women of his generation. He wrote a book about skiing, played table tennis and rode a ton-up motorbike; and when Times Newspapers was closed down in 1979, and I went home to get gently drunk, he attended a party at Langan's, where people went to be seen, and TV cameras ensured that millions saw.

The editorship of *The Times* was to crown this extraordinary career. He was 53 at the time, and signed a contract with Murdoch for seven years; and it was confidently expected that despite the failure of previous editors he would return the paper to its old pre-eminence before its bicentenary was celebrated in 1985. To be fired by a man such as Murdoch after only one year must have been a bitter blow.

It must be said that some people in Fleet Street thought that he was the wrong choice; the editor of *The Times*, it was suggested, should not career about town on a motorcycle and wear denim. That was silly or snobbish nonsense, but others were aware of the enormous difference between editing a Sunday and a daily newspaper. I had said as much to Evans when he earlier enquired if I would like to join the *Sunday Times*. To revert to military comparisons, the Sunday was a cavalry unit raiding behind enemy lines. Because of my American experience, I once compared Evans with Stuart, the great cavalry commander of the Civil War, immortalized in the song, 'Riding a Raid'. A daily such as *The Times* is an infantry corps; it has outriders such as foreign correspondents and the better journalists at home, but most of the troops are foot soldiers. The reasons are obvious. A Sunday newspaper has the cavalry's freedom of action because a) generally there is little news to report on Sunday, and it has to be created by investigative journalists, and b) it has a week in which to choose its objectives. A daily such as *The Times* is in the trenches for six days a week, going into battle as the enemy shows itself and necessarily being prepared to change its dispositions nightly on the run.

There was yet another reason why some thought that he would not adjust easily to his new command. The *Sunday Times* had been very successful and profitable most of the time under his and Hamilton's editorships. Hamilton had transformed the once stuffy newspaper – it did not have a reporting staff when he took over – and in so doing had revolutionized serious Sunday journalism. Evans had carried on the good work, building on Hamilton's sure foundations and adding his investigative flare. They must have been wonderfully exhilarating years, and as the profits rolled in Thomson happily increased the editorial budget which made their new journalism possible. The editorial staff was relatively small, and there were few foreign correspondents and fewer subeditors. Evans recruited some very good journalists, and they responded to his enthusiasm. Those I know remember Evans' editorship with affection.

The Times was very different; it was a daily and a newspaper of record. News that would not sell a copy, and probably deterred new readers, was published as part of the nation's record. The editorial staff was much larger, and worked in shifts. I rarely saw some of the late men. The political and parliamentary staffs, the arts critics and some of the sports writers hardly ever came into the office. I only met Bill Mann, the music critic, once, and that was in Bonn. The crossword editor apparently never came to London, and his puzzles arrived in the morning post. The élan of the *Sunday Times* was impossible. *The Times* had been losing money for years, which was bad for morale. The collective pride in the paper had been weakened by the journalists' strike.

Arguably Evans was the man to pull the staff together, but looking back things did not go well from the beginning. On the day the national directors confirmed his appointment, Murdoch called me to his office and complained about Bernard Levin; the columnist, among other things, wanted to be paid more which enraged the new proprietor. He asked for my opinion of Hugh Stephenson, the editor of business news, and Margaret Allen, the features editor; and before I could answer said that they were no good and would have to go. He angrily waved that day's issue of the paper as he spoke, and did not listen when I tried to defend them.

His anger surprised me. Stephenson had rescued the business news section from the mess created by his predecessor, and had recruited some good men who were devoted to him. He was a private person who said little at the editorial conferences and always looked tense. His professionalism was beyond doubt; he had been a member of the Wilson committee on financial institutions, and was the brain behind JOTT, the staff group formed to keep the paper going after it was put up for sale. Stephenson was an obvious product of Winchester, and had been president of the Oxford Union – he was one of three on the staff – and a diplomat for four years. He had also been a Labour member of the Wandsworth borough council, and subsequently voluntarily left the paper to edit the *New Statesman*. Margaret Allen, like Evans, belonged to the first working-class generation to attend university, and had started as a financial journalist. She was a handsome, bouncy lady, full of northern grit, and a former member of the Equal Opportunities Commission. She was the paper's first successful woman executive, and I thought a good features editor. Murdoch did not get rid of Allen, she accepted voluntary redundancy, but conditions of employment and the hiring and firing of journalists were none of his business. I attended my first board meeting with some foreboding.

The first item on the agenda was the finalization of the sale of Times Newspapers, and Murdoch showed no elation or satisfaction as the lawyers did their work. It was extraordinary. He had acquired two of the best known newspapers in Britain against considerable opposition in and out of parliament whereas his earlier attempt to buy the *Observer* had failed. I supposed he was already thinking about the tasks ahead, or the next stage of expansion in the United States. Admittedly he was well supported; his lawyer was a youngish Australian QC who had plenty of experience of buying newspapers and television stations, but it was chillingly impressive. At one stage Murdoch raised his eyes to the ceiling and yawned.

The next item, the appointment of the editor, took very much longer. Murdoch proposed Evans, who under the articles of association had to be approved by a majority of the independent national directors. They moved to another room to deliberate, and were absent for more than an hour. One of the Australians looked at the portraits of former proprietors, and seemed particularly interested in the painting of John Jacob Astor, Dawson and Lints Smith, the then manager. It was unusual in that Dawson sat somewhat imperiously behind a desk staring over the heads of the proprietor and manager, who sat each side of the desk with the humility of subordinates. The Australian looked puzzled, and probably thought that in any future painting Murdoch would sit behind the desk glowering at his editor and manager. Coffee was brought in, and to pass the time another Murdoch man asked me about *The Times*. I obliged to relieve the tedium, and was running out of anecdotes when the national directors finally returned.

They looked unhappy, even cross, and they confirmed Evans as editor without comment. He was not a popular choice; Lord Dacre – the historian, Hugh Trevor-Roper, before his elevation – had opposed the nomination. He preferred Charles Douglas-Home, my successor as deputy editor, as did Hamilton, but they could not nominate another candidate. Only the proprietor could do that, but their discussion had dragged on until Dacre had to get back to Oxford.

It was a bad beginning. The national directors were not required to reach a unanimous decision, but Evans' authority was weakened on the editorial floor; or to be more precise, the senior journalists who did not want him were careful to distance themselves. While acknowledging his success with the Sunday paper, some of them thought that he was the wrong man for *The Times*. Michael Leapman, who later left the paper, said that the Sunday had two basic techniques. One was to make accessible the difficult but important stories of the day by dramatizing them and bringing out the personalities involved. The complementary skill was to use hard reporting methods on essentially soft stories – probes by the Insight team into antique buyers' rings and phoney wine labelling. By contrast *The Times* had traditionally treated serious events seriously and trivial news trivially.

That was a bit unfair, but others regarded Evans as a usurper. The majority had long assumed that Douglas-Home was the heir apparent. Rees-Mogg had groomed him for the job, steadily advancing him from defence correspondent to features editor and then to home editor. At my suggestion, he became foreign editor and I took over the home side apart from my other duties.

Dacre, or the Dacre faction, was also angry because Murdoch had appointed Sir Edward Pickering to fill a vacancy as the sixth national director, and he was assumed to be a Murdoch man and therefore not independent. Pickering was in fact a second choice. Murdoch had first approached Oliver McGregor, but the Advertising Standards Authority demurred on the grounds of possible conflict of interest. Pickering had been a distinguished journalist and successful newspaper executive, and arguably was better equipped for the job than the objectors. He had been executive editor of the *Daily Mail* and *Daily Express*, and editor of the *Express* for five years. When he and Beaverbrook parted company – it was said that the loquacious lord was unnerved by his silences – he became editorial director of the Mirror group, and eventually chairman. In retirement he was associated with the Commonwealth Press Union and the Press Council. That said, Pickering and Murdoch were old friends. When young Rupert came down from Oxford his father had asked Beaverbrook to teach him the journalist's trade, and Pickering took him in hand. They worked together until Murdoch returned to Australia to claim his inheritance.

The other national directors decided to exclude Pickering from some of their meetings, and this led to an angry scene at a board meeting. They became more suspicious, as did Evans, when he was given an office. Pickering had asked for it because he was frequently in London for meetings of the CPU and the Press Council and had no place to leave his papers. He also told Murdoch that he would have to acquaint himself with the editorial and production departments if he was to be of any use in a crisis.

Rees-Mogg had occupied an office big enough for editorial conferences, and it was a mess. The sofas and armchairs, worn and with cushions missing, had been brought from Printing House Square, to which had been added two large and ugly tubular chrome settees with over-soft cushions bought at a Heal's sale. He was probably unaware that the office looked like a second-hand furniture store. Understandably Evans threw out the junk, but then enlarged the office and called in an expensive interior decorator to create an executive suite. It was much too posh for a working journalist, which was probably why he did much of his work and held the editorial conferences in a room in the far corner of the floor.

I assumed at first that this was why he was always in a hurry;

he rarely sauntered, and more often than not broke into a trot; this deterred people who tried to talk to him. Indeed Evans, who had freely and profitably communed with his *Sunday Times* colleagues, seemed to isolate himself from most of the *Times* men.

Men were brought in from outside who had more loyalty to him than to the paper. Some were of high calibre, especially David Hopkinson, formerly editor of the *Sheffield Telegraph* and the *Birmingham Post*, who was an amiable man and worked well with the subeditors. Anthony Holden had worked on the Sunday, and was brought back from Washington where he had been the *Observer* correspondent to be features editor. He was also likeable, but had little or no interest in politics. The appointment of Bernard Donoughue as an assistant editor in charge of policy raised eyebrows in and out of the office. Alan Watkins wrote in the *Spectator* that Donoughue 'was not a journalist but an academic who had turned to the political advising trade'. He had in fact worked briefly as a reporter, but Evans first met him when he was a lecturer at the LSE. He then became senior policy adviser at 10 Downing Street for Harold Wilson and James Callaghan. Evans thought highly of his political judgement, and after Labour's defeat in 1979 had invited him to spend one day a week at the *Sunday Times* as his political adviser. He continued in this role on *The Times* to the annoyance of leader writers. Other men were also brought in, but Holden and Donoughue were closest to Evans. They were not cronies in the derogatory sense, but they became a protective screen when things began to go wrong, and were loyal to the end.

Edwin Taylor, an internationally known designer, was brought in to help make the paper more readable. To my regret they restored the royal coat of arms to the title, which Haley had dropped in 1966 largely because it gave the paper a misleading official character. He had been congratulated by Sir Anthony Wagner, Garter King of Arms, for getting rid of what he described as an eighteenth-century solecism, but readers apparently welcomed its restoration. Otherwise I welcomed his improvements and innovations, including the printing of news on the back page. I had vainly recommended it to Rees-Mogg, but he was loth to put the classified advertisements on an inside page.

The honeymoon was brief, due in part to the alienation of some of the old *Times* men. Evans also seemed incapable of making up his mind. At least, that was the general view, but I thought that he strove too often for perfection; a condition difficult to attain anywhere and impossible on a daily newspaper. The introduction of computer typesetting with NGA men at the keyboards had slowed down production, which meant earlier deadlines. It was annoying, but even under the best possible conditions editions have to be completed on time. Trains and planes have to be caught, and a less-than-perfect early edition in the hands of readers is better than no paper. Changes can be made between editions, and the second is always better than the first.

Evans seemed not to understand this, perhaps because on the Sunday paper he had had most of the week to prepare stories, and once the presses began the longest print run in Europe it was foolhardy to stop them to make changes apart from football scores and major disasters. One incident comes to mind. The perennial story of Sir Roger Hollis, the late director of MI5 suspected of being a Soviet mole, had popped up again; and Craig Seton was asked to do the story and then write a short feature explaining the complicated web of suspicion. Seton, a very good and meticulous reporter, spent about an hour going through the cuttings prior to writing the feature. I thought that it read well, but although the deadline for the features page had long passed Evans and one of his men on the back bench demanded rewrites. The production schedule was once again seriously delayed.

Soon afterwards he asked me to lead an investigation into a military coup allegedly contemplated in 1968. The story was not new. Lord Cudlipp, then editorial director of Mirror Newspapers, had suggested in his book *Walking on the Water* that something very odd had happened when he and Cecil King, the chairman of IPC which published the *Daily Mirror,* met Lord Mountbatten on 8 May, 1968. The reason for the meeting was obscure. Cudlipp wrote that he was invited to Broadlands, Mountbatten's country house, where the last viceroy of India expressed disquiet over the state of the country; but he did not explain why Mountbatten agreed or asked to meet King. The press lord's dissatisfaction with the Wilson government was well known, and was potentially embarrassing for somebody in Mountbatten's position. According to Cudlipp, the meeting broke up when Lord Zuckerman, who had been Churchill's scientific adviser, said that it was rank treachery. 'All this talk of machine guns at street corners is appalling. I am a public servant and will have nothing to do with it, nor should you Dickie.'

Evans asked me to investigate after the *Sunday Times* had published an interview with Lady Falkender in which Harold Wilson's former political secretary referred to Mountbatten as a prime mover in a plan to overthrow the government by military coup. I was happy to oblige; I had known Mountbatten in India, and considered that his political ambitions certainly went beyond being the last viceroy. A senior general on his staff in Delhi had described him in conversation as Tricky Dicky – this was before Richard Nixon emerged from congressional obscurity – and quit in disgust. I could imagine him being tempted to become involved, and Falkender's version certainly demanded further investigation.

I sent Dan van der Vat, a former foreign correspondent, to interview King in Dublin where he had retired, and three other reporters interviewed Cudlipp and others who had been in Mountbatten's country house when the meeting was held. I concentrated on Zuckerman, who I knew would talk more freely to an editor. It was a difficult story to write, but we did rather well. We established that Cudlipp had published Mountbatten's version and not his own of what was said, which diminished its importance. King showed us his diary, which contained a long account of what had happened. We plumbed the depths of unease which had pervaded Whitehall at the time; and were told some disturbing stories and rumours, including one that King was a key figure in the alleged preparations for a *putsch*. Some may have been nothing more than 'loose talk by gin-sodden generals', to quote a former director general of MI5, but they had been taken seriously enough to be investigated by the security service. Mountbatten's role remained unclear, but many years later Philip Ziegler wrote in his official biography that Mountbatten had hankered for strong leadership and a government of national unity. He recorded that after our investigation Zuckerman had written in his diary that 'the fact of the matter is ... that Dickie was really intrigued by Cecil King's suggestion that he should become the boss man of a government.' Zuckerman had also remarked to Cudlipp after the meeting: 'I wonder what Dickie would have said if I hadn't been there.' Ziegler added that nobody at the meeting said anything to suggest that a *coup d'état* was necessary or even possible, still less that steps should be taken to make it more likely.

That was our conclusion, blazed over six columns, and we wrote what we had learned without suggestion that where there was smoke there must be fire. We might have written differently if we had known at the time that according to Peter Wright's *Spycatcher* King had worked for MI5. I doubt it; King might have spoken to those 'gin-sodden generals', but men with grudges as big as Wright's are rarely to be trusted. In the event, we strictly observed the old *Times* disciplines. One of the younger reporters was possibly disappointed that we did not reach a more dramatic conclusion, but in getting as close to the truth as we could suspicion of machination in high places was allayed.

It was a long story, about 4000 words, and I took it into Evans about five in the afternoon. He was busy as usual, and after reading only the first three or four paragraphs he sat down at a typewriter and banged away furiously. When asked what he was doing, he said that he was rewriting the lead. I was astounded, and said that he should first read the story which was complicated and some of the quotes contradicted each other. We had written the lead with great care so as to strike an honest balance, and it would be dangerous to make changes before reading the supporting evidence. Van der Vat said that he wanted his name deleted from the joint byline if the lead was to be changed.

The story was published more or less as we had written it, but these two relatively minor incidents are typical of Evans' editorship. He wanted to do everything, and frequently on the spur of the moment. I came into the office one Sunday afternoon and found him subbing galleys of university results, a chore normally given to a down-table and inexperienced sub. He seemed rarely to give himself time to think, and was the exact opposite of Rees-Mogg.

This is not to suggest that Evans' predecessor was the perfect editor. In my opinion, Rees-Mogg did not involve himself enough in the news. He delegated too much – he liked to say that he practised a cabinet-form of government – and control was diffused. That said, the paper was well organized to deal with sudden crises, and while accepting the decision of whoever was in charge the men and women I had worked with were accustomed to making their own contributions. They expected to be heard, if not to win the argument. Above all, there was little or no fuss. I was acting editor when some great stories erupted – Black Sunday in Northern Ireland and the resignations of Harold Wilson and Richard Nixon come to mind – and we produced good newspapers on time because we worked together. Good manners and mutual trust always prevailed. It was their paper as much as mine.

It can of course be said that we were too set in our ways, and that a new editor with the responsibility to make the paper profitable could not preside over a newspaper written by gentlemen for gentlemen. I accept that changes were necessary, I would have made some if I had been appointed editor; but if papers such as *The Times* are to flourish an orderly routine is fundamental. Alas, it disappeared, as Leapman illustrates in his book when President Sadat of Egypt was assassinated:

> Rushing, shouting, frenzied telephone calls, wild ideas put up and shot down – such signs of incipient panic intensified throughout the late afternoon. Evans and his chief advisers gathered in groups by the foreign desk, the back bench, the features department, all trying to talk at once. Then Evans would march away, leaving a half-formed idea in his wake, and a clutch of people would follow him, waving pieces of paper. As the time for the first edition approached, nobody was at all clear how the front page was to look. The first edition, by general consent, was a disaster – and a late disaster at that.

Evans was no doubt seeking perfection again, but his own book reveals that he was unaware of the effect of his behaviour on the staff, and there was a steady haemorrhage of talent. The departure of men such as Marcel Berlins, Roger Berthoud, Peter Hennessy and Dan van der Vat was as much a loss for the paper as the men who, for very different reasons, left when Haley was editor. Others retreated into themselves.

Evans believes that he was the victim of Murdoch and Gerald Long, the new managing editor. Both must have been unsettling, in Long's case perhaps because he was too big for the job. He was an extraordinarily gifted man, famous for his pioneering work in information technology. We first met in Bonn in the 1950s when he was bureau chief for Reuters. He was a large man with a black bristling moustache and a cropped head. He loved food and wine, and if he then looked like a caricature of a well-fed German, he was a highly intelligent man and a natural linguist who, as I recall, spoke Turkish and Romanian as well as the usual languages. He was the master of many subjects, from lexography to Zen Buddhism, and a formidable man. After ten years abroad, he returned to London in 1960 and eventually became managing director. He soon transformed Reuters and made a fortune for its larger shareholders, the Fleet Street newspapers.

Reuters had always been in the forefront of communications, from Baron de Reuter's pigeon post to the electronic girdle it put about the earth in the late fifties. Its international communications system became more extensive and flexible than any of its competitors, and realizing the potentials of visual display terminals and retrieval systems Long developed it by taking an apparently regressive step. He took the agency back to its origins as a supplier of prices and business news and revolutionized information technology. When he left to join *The Times* about 90 per cent of the agency's profits were generated by the business information services, and the news agency had become the poor relation.

Why Long accepted Murdoch's invitation to join *The Times* remains a mystery. Had he remained at Reuters the stock given to its executives would have made him a millionaire and he would certainly have been knighted. Presumably he could not resist being managing director of *The Times* although he had a poor opinion of its correspondents, including myself. He cleared the office of his predecessor, and installed only a white shag carpet and a couple of chairs. When I remarked on the absence of a desk, he said that he was paid to think and did not concern himself with details. This sounded strange; in those days newspaper managers spent most of their time fighting a losing battle with the production unions instead of thinking deep thoughts. He went on to say that his task was to save a once great newspaper which had lost all claim to greatness.

I thought at the time that he meant only to make the paper financially secure, but I may have been wrong. At Reuters the line between management and editorial had never been clearly defined, and Long had reorganized the agency's executive committee, removing the editor who subsequently reported to him. Whatever Long's intention, he was soon seen on the editorial floor standing behind the back bench or in the glass-walled office of Brian Horton, the new foreign editor. They had been colleagues and friends for many years; I had first met Horton in the Reuters office in Bonn, where Long had quickly promoted him over the heads of more experienced men. Long had also proposed him for the foreign editorship of *The Times*, and paid him considerably more than the other assistant editors. One thing was certain, Long did not accept the traditional role of a *Times* manager.

Evans did not seem to recognize the danger. Only later, in his book, did he complain that Long interferred in the formulation of editorial policy and editorial appointments. If this was the case, he could have silenced Long by appealing to the independent national directors. No editor in Fleet Street or elsewhere was better protected against managerial and proprietorial interference, by tradition and the company's articles of association. His position was impregnable.

Evans also complained that he was not given an editorial budget. This was true, but we had not had a budget since we resumed publication after the closure. The original reason was trade union bloody-mindedness. The budget was monitored by a unit known as management accounts, and after resumption no agreement had been reached on manning and its functions. Two clerks had been dismissed for hiding invoices, which the clerical chapel treated as a declaration of hostilities and acted accordingly. We had survived; John Grant, the editorial manager, had taken the last budget as a base line and had allowed for inflation.

It was not an ideal system, but it worked and could have gone on indefinitely, as seemed possible because of Murdoch's reluctance to discuss finance even with the board. At an early meeting he had produced figures which were clearly inadequate, and Lord Drogheda had said as much in polite but firm terms. The former chairman of the *Financial Times* was accustomed to having his way, and a fuller financial statement was produced at the next board meeting. It was not a reassuring read; even to my untrained eye it was clear that the company was still in a bad way. Hence the redundancies demanded in all departments, including editorial, but redundancies cost money and economies were necessary.

This was almost certainly the cause of much of the friction between Evans and Long. Murdoch had said at a board meeting, and presumably to Evans, that the dead wood – his expression – must be got rid of. I had retorted that it would be difficult, that the inefficient and time servers would not quit while they had the protection of the union, but was only glared at. Sure enough good men went, confident that they could pursue their careers elsewhere, and much of the dead wood remained. Evans was obliged to recruit new talent, but rather overdid it. At the end of 1981 the editorial strength was marginally larger than at the beginning of the year despite the hundreds of thousands of pounds paid to reduce it. What is more, many of the new recruits were given salaries above the average.

The most famous was Bevis Hillier who had joined the paper in the 1960s, then left for the British Museum and later became a successful freelance specializing in art and antiques. Evans hired him to replace a man who he hoped would go but did not; Hillier became an assistant to Philip Howard, the literary editor, and discovered that he was paid more than Howard, one of the most respected men on the paper. Hillier left after less than four months, with six months' pay in lieu of notice. Long was not amused, and Murdoch was furious when the *Spectator* published an article listing some of the senior people who had left the paper, most of them with tax-free redundancy cheques.

Apart from the difficulties Evans had with *The Times*, it did not make commercial sense to move him from the *Sunday Times*. Both titles had lost circulation and advertising because of the uncertainty as to their future, and only the Sunday could be expected to become profitable quickly. To transfer its editor was quixotic, but Murdoch was primarily interested in the daily. The Sunday was rarely discussed at board meetings I attended. The appointment of Frank Giles as its editor appeared to be an afterthought, and was disposed of without discussion. Murdoch was determined to return *The Times* to its former glory and commercial viability as quickly as possible, despite my memorandum.

I had said that we should be prepared for a long haul; that it would take two or three years to get the paper right, during which time the Sunday could keep the company solvent. But Murdoch and Long were impatient men, and they had urged Evans to keep running costs to a minimum. The impatience turned to anger when they steadily increased. This became evident at an editorial conference when Evans lectured us about the expensive production delays. I mentioned mildly that all we had to do was to observe the 'off stone' schedule, which listed the time, reckoned in minutes, when the various pages were to be ready for the foundry, but was ignored. By then I was accustomed to being treated as an invisible man, but Murdoch could not ignore the extra costs of delayed production. The overtime bills were said to be horrific, and the delays affected distribution and circulation. Its growth was inevitably more modest than Murdoch had expected when the paper failed to reach the wholesalers and newsagents on time. Advertising was also disappointing. Evans blamed Murdoch for this. The paper's advertisement salesmen had been dismissed and their opposite numbers on the Sunday were expected to sell space for both titles. Evans had a point; a similar combined effort had failed in the past, but poor circulation figures were mainly responsible. The hiring of more journalists had also infuriated Murdoch.

I still thought that he was wrong to expect instant improvement, but of course he saw it differently. What passed between the two men could not have been pleasant for Evans. Murdoch had a reputation for treating his editors harshly, and even with contempt. Giles also suffered, but refused to be agitated.

His performance as editor of the Sunday was competent but not brilliant, and he was the kind of Englishman ridiculed by Australians. He was very much the gent, which probably explained why he had not intended to be a journalist. Due to ill health, he had been an ADC to the governor of Bermuda and a Whitehall warrior during the war, and subsequently failed the entrance examination for the foreign office. *The Times* was the next best thing, and after marrying the daughter of an earl he served in Paris and Rome and mixed largely with top people. Murdoch nevertheless complained that he had turned the Sunday into a nasty radical paper staffed by a bunch of left-wing layabouts. He was said to have fired imaginary pistol shots at the back of his unsuspecting editor, but Murdoch had finally met his match. Giles remained unperturbed; or as a colleague remarked, he treated the proprietor with cool arrogance. Giles eventually retired with his dignity and equanimity intact – and his good manners. In his autobiography, *Sundry Times*, he merely says, 'I took leave with mixed feeling. The beginning had been friendly, the middle rough, the end outwardly friendly again. He and I were different sorts of animals, as he would readily agree'.

Evans did not have Giles' composure. The end came suddenly, and was brought about by the disaffection of two of the old *Times* men. By this time they had assumed the significance of the old black friars who had fought Northcliffe in defence of their inherited standards. Very few of them remained, and their departure would have reflected badly on Murdoch and Evans.

At the beginning of 1982 Charles Douglas-Home, the deputy editor, returned from his sabbatical and was told by John Grant, the editorial manager, that he had had enough and had decided to resign. Douglas-Home, who was in poor health, was also unhappy and had had five weeks to ponder his own future. He was appalled. Apart from Owen Hickey, the senior leader writer, Grant was the last of the senior men who had worked with Haley and Rees-Mogg. He was a phlegmatic northerner with reddish hair and a very red face, who after war service and Oxford had worked for the old *Manchester Guardian* before joining us as defence correspondent. I learned to respect him when in the 1950s he came to Bonn to help me cover a NATO defence ministers' conference. We became good friends, and when I resigned he said that he was going to be very lonely.

Apparently Douglas-Home felt much the same when he heard that Grant was determined to go. There would still be Hickey, but he was a very private person who seemed to avoid the company of his fellow assistant editors, and said little or nothing at leader-writer conferences. When we were in Printing House Square he would lunch alone in the railway buffet at Blackfriars, and his lunch was said to consist of a British Rail sandwich and a cup of tea. He was a sterling chap, who had won a good MC in the war and wrote beautifully, but not a colleague to provide comfort and support; and Douglas-Home decided that he would also ask for redundancy.

Sir Edward Pickering, the national director, heard about it and told Murdoch, who asked him to persuade Douglas-Home not to resign. They had a lunch at the Garrick, and in the same week the two of them met Murdoch at breakfast. Enough was said to persuade Douglas-Home and Grant to stay on for the time being. On budget day, one of the busiest in the year for *The Times*, Murdoch asked Evans for his resignation, and Evans refused.

According to *Good Times, Bad Times*, Murdoch said that the place was in chaos and the senior men were up in arms, and Evans accused Murdoch of putting pressure on him through Hickey and others. Later that evening Evans discovered that the place was indeed in chaos. He had extended the budget report to eight pages, and stories about the reactions of industry, business and the banks had been squeezed out of the paper. In Evans' words, there was an incandescent glow at the back bench; it emanated from the home news editor who was furious that his specialist writers had wasted their time. Evans had not told him that, contrary to established practice, reaction stories would be published the next day.

Evans then went to Douglas-Home's room, and told him he had behaved despicably in colluding with Murdoch. He had no integrity, no honour; how could he betray his editor? According to Evans, Douglas-Home said that he would do anything to edit *The Times*. He then said that Evans was too close to Murdoch, too desirous of his approval and too ready to do his bidding. As evidence, he referred to a memo Evans had written to Murdoch asking if he agreed to producing the budget special as a separate section. It had been a long night, and both men could not have been themselves.

Douglas-Home had long aspired to the editorship, and must have been disappointed when it went to Evans. He was only 44, but had a bad back after too many riding accidents. He was frequently in pain, and often could not sit. At one editorial conference he had to kneel on the floor. Unbeknown to us, he was also suffering from a debilitating disease, and was probably aware that he did not have long to live. For this reason he might have acted out of character when the editorship was finally in his grasp, but I would not have expected it.

Charlie, as he was always known, was a relaxed and modest

man. He was a sprig of the nobility; his uncle was the 14th earl of Home who unbelted himself to become prime minister, and he was related to Princess Diana. He'd been a King's Scholar at Eton, was commissioned to the Royal Scots Greys during his national service and was ADC to the last governor of Kenya, but nevertheless had come up the hard way. He sold encyclopaedias in Canada and was a general reporter on the old *Scottish Daily Express* before joining the main paper in London in 1961. It was a hard school, and he ruined his liver – he became a teetotaller and vegetarian – before joining us as a defence correspondent.

Charlie was a very good journalist, but painstaking rather than brilliant: as features editor he ran a series on the armies of the world which ceased to be compulsive reading after the 16th or 17th. He was probably a better editor than I could ever be. Reading other men's words was a chore for me, whereas Charlie willingly read thousands of words, and seemed to find pleasure in them. He had a passion for putting everything down on paper; I probably dictated three or four letters a week, but his secretary always seemed to be typing letters and memoranda. This passion caused considerable embarrassment when a reporter discovered files on members of the home news staff detailing their personal and professional weaknesses and strengths. I would have fired the reporter, for he had unlocked a cabinet and purloined the files; but Charlie was a kinder man, and a rumpus with the NUJ chapel was the result.

We got on well together despite our different ages and backgrounds, and he often lent me his cottage in the Borders. We occasionally lunched together, and at his club, the Caledonian, he generally insisted that I begin with haggis soaked with a tot of whisky while he sipped some vegetable soup. He had no side, and wore threadbare shirts, worn jackets with split elbows and cracked shoes that had belonged to deceased uncles. Somebody remarked on the meanness of the Scots, but he was saving to send his two sons to Westminster. Everybody liked him, and his face, with the tight skin of the Douglas-Homes, smiled easily. I could not recognize him in the two-faced character that stalks through Evans' book.

Douglas-Home was honest and straightforward; and his conversation, somewhat similar to mine, had military parallels. He was more profuse in the use of military phrases; but we both thought of the paper as a good regiment and the editor as a commander to whom one was always loyal. These qualities were apparent when he became editor. Evans' contributions to the paper were publicly recognized; and the men he had brought with him and remained – only Donoughue and Holden left – were treated as *Times* and not Evans men. The staff was reunited, and the paper flourished. During his few brief years the circulation rose from under 300,000 to about 460,000 without loss of standards. 'Portfolio', the stocks and shares game for money prizes, helped; it was derided by critics, and a few on the staff, as top people's bingo, but was enjoyed by readers. A former permanent head of the foreign office told me that he always played 'Portfolio' after reading the front and foreign pages. The last time we met I asked Douglas-Home if Murdoch interfered; he said that he showed more interest than the Thomsons, but no interference. (Incidentally, Giles also said in his autobiography that Murdoch did not try to interfere.) The political position of the paper shifted to the right, but Douglas-Home had always been more to the right than his uncle, the former Tory prime minister.

Philip Howard, another of the paper's old Etonian scholars, wrote that Douglas-Home was the hardest news man since Thomas Barnes to become editor of *The Times*. Unlike all the editors who came between them, Barnes and Charlie had been up at the frontline with a notebook, reporting the real news. When working in Scotland, if there was a runaway heiress to be intercepted at Gretna, or documents had to be bought from somebody arriving by plane, those working for opposition papers had an uneasy feeling that Douglas-Home would have got there first. He usually had. In conclusion, Howard wrote, 'In the long eye of history the principal achievement of Charles Douglas-Home's two years as editor was taking over in a raging storm, with mutiny and panic below decks, and the ship in danger of foundering, and to steer it into calmer waters.'

His obituary in *The Times* said:

He liked to say that he was an orchestral conductor, creating a harmony in which integrity, authority and accuracy blended. But whether the metaphor should be a military one or a musical one, he succeeded in rejuvenating a paper which had been disconsolate and discordant since the industrial dispute of 1978–9, and through the first year of the Murdoch regime.

Many people who liked and admired Evans wondered why he failed to create such a harmony. Some blamed Murdoch, and refused to believe that he did not interfere despite the experience of Giles and Douglas-Home. For many of them he was the dirty Digger and the tits and bum artist. Murdoch was not another Thomson or Astor, and undoubtedly was a difficult man. His method of conducting meetings was unconventional, to say the least. He was impulsive and fidgety, and Richard Searby, his Australian legal adviser, once described his regime as episodic autocracy. In other words, there were times when he wanted things done his way. The restraints of the articles of association must have been irksome, and he was not prepared to show the exaggerated respect to which successive editors of *The Times* were accustomed.

The fact remains that Evans and Giles were the best protected editors in Fleet Street. Evans could have emulated his former deputy editor, and ignored Murdoch's irritability and temper. He did not have to write to him about increasing the size of the paper for the budget coverage. Rees-Mogg and I had always tried to maintain the agreed balance of editorial and advertising, but had never asked permission to go up in size to cover a big story. I would notify the production editor, who would tell the production department to prepare another unit in the machine room. At least, I assumed he did, but did not bother to ask.

Above all, Evans could have complained to the independent national directors if he felt that his authority was threatened or undermined by management. Their sole purpose was to guarantee the editorial independence and integrity of the two titles, but they could not act in isolation. Similarly with Murdoch's demand for his resignation. If he believed that it was improper, he should have appealed to them. They could have asked Murdoch to reconsider if they thought he was unfair, and resigned if he had refused. This would not have saved Evans his job, but Murdoch's reputation, and the paper's good standing, would have been damaged, perhaps irretrievably. This was the ultimate power of the national directorate; but Lord Robens, who was a friend of Evans and privy to his thinking, later said, 'He never asked us'. Instead, he called in a television crew to announce his departure, and forgot to tell the night editor. *The Times* was scooped on the resignation of its own editor.

Evans was of course under immense strain, and it must have seemed that his world was coming to an end. He might have survived this first major crisis in his professional career if Hamilton had still been editor-in-chief. As the man who had recognized his talents as a provincial editor, and had brought him to London to be his successor, Hamilton would have helped and guided him in his first year as editor of *The Times* as he did on the *Sunday Times*. To suggest that Evans needed guidance is not to denigrate him. He was, and remains, a brilliant journalist; but Rees-Mogg was right when he said that an editor cannot fight the staff and proprietor simultaneously.

Evans was terribly vulnerable. The hurt is apparent in his book, and he did himself an injustice by writing it when he did. His good nature and generous spirit, which endeared him to the staff of the *Sunday Times* in happier circumstances, are rarely evident in its pages.

13

Escape from the Past

I have met men, and women for that matter, more unlikeable than Murdoch, but very few who have generated as much hostility. On both sides of the Atlantic critics regard him as some kind of antipodean misfit directly descended from the original convicts, but he is not a dirty Digger who with a tube of XXXX in each hand shambled out of the outback in search of a page three nude. His grandfather was a Presbyterian minister from Scotland and his father a successful and respected newspaper publisher. Young Rupert attended Australia's most exclusive boarding school, and read Politics, Philosophy and Economics at Oxford where he was converted to socialism. He learned the craft of subediting at the *Daily Express*, which probably explains his interest in layout and production.

Murdoch was only 21 when his father died, and had a lifetime before him to expand the family business which had been reduced to two small newspapers in Adelaide. He made a flying start, and before he was 50, when he bought Times Newspapers, controlled the world's largest media conglomerate with newspapers, magazines, television stations and much more in three continents. The youthful socialist had become a conservative, which would have pleased his father, a pillar of the old Australian establishment. But Murdoch, by his own choice, remained an outsider more comfortable in the first-class cabin of airliners than in gentlemen's clubs in London, New York and Sydney. He constantly circumnavigated the globe visiting his properties and on the lookout for others to buy. Unlike other large corporation bosses, he had no centralized managerial structure; instead, he travelled with a briefcase, admittedly bulging, and a secretary. At one time he had a permanent booking for two seats on the first Monday of the month on the Concorde flight from London to New York. He entertained and conducted business in restaurants.

Murdoch's ruthlessness is legendary; for instance, he hired and fired one editor within 48 hours. Americans are supposed to admire success and rugged individualism, but many were appalled when he bought the ailing *New York Post*, a liberal newspaper, and took it down market in search of hard-hat readers. The *Columbia Journalism Review* said that he was doing the devil's work by appealing to the basest passions and appetites; the *Post* was no longer a mere journalistic problem but a social problem, a force for evil. In fact, the *Post* had been a fifth-rate paper stuffed with syndicated columns; and arguably Murdoch returned it to the lusty origins of American journalism, when Wilbur Storey of the *Chicago Times* said 'print the news and raise hell'. Alas, he also said to his reporters, 'when there is no news, send rumours'. No, I am not an admirer of Murdoch's *Post*, but I doubt that his critics admired it before he arrived. Murdoch, who appeared to be genuinely puzzled by the critics, dismissed them as elitists and wondered if there was any other industry in the country which 'seeks to presume so completely to give the customer what he does not want'.

Murdoch remains an enigma in Britain and the United States, but not in his native Australia, long known for buccaneering press barons. Unlikeable no doubt, but just the man to take on the Fleet Street unions.

The move to Wapping was in fact in the tradition of *The Times*. In the early nineteenth century, when John Walter II made it the first independent newspaper, the old hand presses could still only print 250 sheets an hour. Circulation growth was hampered by old technology, and even in those days printers were resistant to change. Then in 1814 Walter heard that a German, Friedrich Koenig, had invented a steam press and had failed to interest his countrymen. The press was smuggled piece by piece into Printing House Square and secretly assembled to avoid Luddite interference. On the night of 28 November the printers were told to stand by for a late foreign story – a not uncommon occurrence – while the issue was run off in the new press room. He then announced to the astonished printers that '*The Times* is already published – by steam'. The first Koenig press printed 1100 sheets an hour, and with the help of Augustus Applegath and E.A. Cowper, two English inventors, this was raised to 4000 within a few years.

Newspapermen everywhere owe a debt to Walter because he initiated the age of mass-circulation newspapers; and one of these years other Fleet Street proprietors will thank Murdoch. Eddy Shah, who challenged the monopoly power of the National Graphical Association in Warrington, was the first man to plan the launch of a national newspaper using the new technology; but Murdoch risked more in that he owned four established titles and not a new paper with an uncertain future.

Only a ruthless gambler such as Murdoch would have made the move to Wapping. He must have seen on television the union's heavy mob trying to storm Shah's Warrington plant, and knew that it would be very much worse in Wapping. He made the plant as impregnable as a fortress to withstand the sustained assaults of outraged trade unionists and Trotskyist groups. A nationwide distribution system was created to circumvent union blacking in the wholesale houses and on the railway. Members of the electricians' union were trained in the provinces to man the new equipment. All this had to be done in complete secrecy, and with the knowledge that failure would cost him dear.

Perhaps because *The Times* prospered as a consequence of his audacious move, I could not understand why Murdoch was condemned. About 5000 men and women lost their jobs, but they brought it on themselves. They did not have to follow union leaders like sheep. Other trade unionists had rejected their leaders; 'Red Robo', who helped to bankrupt British Leyland, was an obvious example. They did not have to strike in support of claims for more pay and employment for life; they were already the highest-paid workers in the country and enjoyed enviable guarantees of employment. The *Sunday Times* was required to employ casual workers who were in their eighties; in other words they could continue to work even when they had a company pension. Work was the wrong word. Many arrived by taxi, tottered up to the cashiers on the first floor, collected about £85 for the night's shift, and were then solicitously helped to the waiting cab.

Other printers had more than one job before retirement, or could supplement their income by dubious means. There were the so-called ghost shifts notionally built into manning levels in case production was increased. As Simon Jenkins says in his book (*The Market for Glory*, 1986), it mattered not that many more men than necessary were already employed. The unions had obstructed the introduction of the new technology for years; *The Times* had been closed for fifty weeks, and they had resumed their plundering when it reappeared. They stunted the growth of the Sunday paper by refusing to print larger issues, and were no less cavalier with the daily. They misused their monopoly power as cynically as the old American robber barons. Indeed, their arrogance was such that when the Wapping plant was built to print new titles one union leader told Murdoch that he might as well burn the place down because he would not be allowed to use it. Some of the chapel officials achieved tycoon status, both for their wealth and the number of jobs they controlled; and Jenkins' book establishes that they were not confined to Gray's Inn Road.

> In the late 1970s the head of the *Sunday Times* machine assistants' chapel, Reg Brady, doubled as NATSOPA (Sogat '82) boss at the *Evening Standard* with hundreds of 'shifts' theoretically at his disposal. Part of the *Observer* machine room was under the patronage of chapel officials from the *Daily Mirror* ... For villainy perhaps nothing has compared to the machine room at the *Mirror* building in the 1960s, when it became a notorious place of criminal resort, especially on a Saturday night. Blue movies were shown on the company's premises. The *Mirror* building poker schools had stakes as high as in any West End club, reputedly operated under the wing of the East End's Kray twins. Management at one point protested to the machine chapels for being expected to employ two convicted murderers at one time, one of whom was terrifying the staff.

Such people were a disgrace to the trade union movement. During the paper's closure I had a long conversation with a very senior TUC official at Congress House who expressed support for what the management was trying to do; it was not only the introduction of new technology, but management's right to manage. He was especially critical of Brady, who, he said, was bad for the movement. He wielded too much power, and refused to share it with the men he represented or to seek their opinions. The movement could not prosper while such men dominated the shop floor; they were not interested in his efforts to make trade unions responsible. That official was not alone. Jack Jones, when he was a general secretary of the Transport and General Workers' Union, said to me that Fleet Street newspapers were critical of the movement because they thought that their own unions were typical. Even the provincial branches of the print unions disliked the Fleet Street chapels, and Sogat '82 eventually refused to continue its financial support for the men who were sacked by Murdoch.

A man such as Murdoch was required to bring such people to heel, and subsequently the chapels of other Fleet Street houses behaved with circumspection. They accepted the new technology and large-scale redundancies when their proprietors decided to follow Murdoch to docklands. Moreover, Murdoch was not the hard-faced capitalist he was said to be. He offered to give the sacked workers the plant in Gray's Inn Road, complete with computers, visual display units and rotary presses. It was said at the time that the equipment was worn out, which was not true. The presses were later moved to Wapping where he planned to use them to print more titles. The reason why the chapels refused the plant was obvious; they knew that it could not be used profitably with the old methods and manning levels. An opportunity for the trade union movement to publish its own newspaper was missed; and they preferred to accept the generous redundancy payments subsequently offered.

Allow me to make a suggestion although it is unlikely to be accepted. Northcliffe's contribution to the newspaper industry earned him a memorial on the outside wall of St Dunstan in the West at the top of Fleet Street. At the bottom of the street is St Bride, the parish church of the newspaper fraternity. Caxton's apprentice, Wynkyn de Worde, who brought the first printing press to Fleet Street, is buried there. When Murdoch goes to that great news room in the sky, it would surely be the appropriate place for a memorial to the man who more than 450 years later was responsible for the removal of the last press from the street, and in so doing gave the national press a new lease of life.

Has Murdoch been good for *The Times*? Not an easy question to answer, but first consider the good he has done. I doubt very much that the paper would have survived had it remained in Gray's Inn Road. It is now better managed and profitable; to that extent the senior editorial executives who thought that he was the best of the bunch who wanted to buy Times Newspapers have been proved correct. The circulation has been increased by half as has the size of the average issue. Advertising is no longer a problem. The journalists are now among the best paid in the industry; and are treated well apart from doing without wine, beer and spirits in an otherwise excellent canteen used by everybody from editors and managers to cleaners and messengers. Moreover, they know that industrial action – an extraordinary misnomer – is unlikely to keep their stories out of the paper.

It is true that many have left, and not all of them were militants. A few were shocked by Murdoch's ruthlessness or were unwilling to walk through hostile and frequently violent pickets for a year. Others could not accept the change of political direction although Douglas-Home was responsible. The labour editor and his staff obviously could not remain; they would have been blackballed by the people they were paid to report, but they might have had other reasons. The remainder were probably convinced that he would ruin the paper, or could not bring themselves to work in the same complex with the *Sun* and *News of the World* people. In many instances their going was a loss, but not irreparable. The majority remained, and some very good men and women have since joined.

The prediction that Murdoch would ruin or vulgarize the paper has been proved wrong. It has certainly changed, and is said no longer to be a journal of record. I have never understood what such a journal is supposed to record. The *New York Times*, a much larger newspaper, boasts that it carries 'all the news that's fit to print', but no daily newspaper can do that. It employs more foreign correspondents than any other newspaper, but its foreign coverage is spotty. For instance, its news about Britain is at best sporadic, and it does not attempt to cover debates in Congress. They just might improve if it did. *The Listener* tried to define what a journal of record actually is – a useless task in that value judgements are involved – and complained that *The Times* no longer published every official report. It never did in my time.

The magazine seemed relieved that the Court Circular was still published, but I am not convinced that the circular is essential reading. Does it really matter if readers are not informed that the queen is still at Sandringham or that Princess Anne has attended a dinner? With all respect to the royals, those who need to know have access to the circular. Parliament is still reported extensively as are party politics and conferences, and international and national events. The letters columns are still the best daily forum for the exchange of views and opinions, and the op-ed page still provides space for left-wing as well as right-wing writers. The standards of the arts coverage remain high, no other newspaper reports European and American drama, music and dancing as thoroughly; and the obituary notices and law reports are still unrivalled.

The Times is said to be no longer authoritative, and I agree that it is no longer regarded as part of the establishment. That can only be applauded. Haley tried to dispose of that libellous assumption, although I suspect that Rees-Mogg occasionally liked the idea. A newspaper is authoritative when sufficient readers trust the veracity of its news and the soundness of its judgement. That was not always the case during the first year or so in Wapping, but that was understandable. Previously the paper was more often than not in turmoil due to changes of ownership, indifferent management, strikes, industrial anarchy, the closure and then the sudden move to dockland. Fortified offices surrounded by angry men were not ideal for the production of a good newspaper. Too many senior people retired or died in too short a period; few if any of the men who replaced them had my good fortune to be given time and opportunity to gain experience in and outside the office. The early death of Douglas-Home was doubly tragic. His successor, Charles Wilson, looks like one of Glasgow's hard men, but some of Britain's best journalists have come from that city and arguably they had to be hard to excel at the job. Like Haley, he believes that first and foremost newspapers must be concerned about news. Wilson has a larger editorial budget than any of his predecessors, and is determined to make *The Times* the pre-eminent *news*paper. It now publishes more home news, and foreign coverage has been steadily increased. This is most noticeable in news of the Far East and Latin America, which I had to restrict when the unions turned Gray's Inn Road into a black hole.

The paper has changed in other ways, but due to changes in readers' interests and tastes that was essential for survival. The *Guardian* recognized this some years ago. The transformation from the old *Manchester Guardian*, which reflected the stern morality of C.P. Scott, to a national newspaper reflecting the interests of feminists and groups who question or reject conventional standards and assumptions must have dismayed many old readers; but it has flourished. For decades the success of the *Daily Telegraph* was assured by its attention to readers in the armed services and extensive coverage of home news and police court cases; but a declining and ageing readership persuaded the new proprietor and editor to recognize the necessity for change. Haley recognized it thirty years ago, but apart from managerial resistance he could not bring himself to report the likes of Marilyn Monroe. Commercial success since getting rid of the print unions now makes it possible to provide a more extensive news service and serve the new interests and tastes. The formula may still be less than perfect, but there is nothing to prevent further improvement.

These changes do not mean that *The Times* cannot be a great newspaper again. If it had recognized the fundamental change brought about when the stamp tax was revoked in the 1850s, its subsequent decline could have been avoided. It has had more than one bad period. Northcliffe went mad, and Murdoch's compulsion to own more newspapers and television stations may seem to be another madness. He saved *The Times*, but has yet to prove beyond reasonable doubt that he is a good proprietor. Arguably he owns too many newspapers to run any of them properly, but that could be an advantage if the staff remains free to uphold and extend the paper's traditions. And if they are looking for an immediate objective, they could do no better than remember Haley's objective: to play a useful part in helping to run the country by producing a balanced, interesting and entertaining newspaper for intelligent readers for all ages and classes.

I wish them well, and admit regretting not being one of them – especially since the move to Wapping. It must be wonderful to write and edit a newspaper knowing that it will be published and distributed – but I have another reason. A few yards from the entrance to *The Times* is the Caxton, a pub once known as the

Artichoke where my mother was born. A couple of hundred yards down the Highway was the City of Dublin dining rooms, the coffee shop where I first saw the light of day. It would be like going home.

Chief Proprietors of *The Times*

John Walter	1785	Hon. Gavin Astor	1964
John Walter II	1812	Lord Thomson	1967
John Walter III	1847	2nd Lord Thomson	1976
Arthur Walter	1894	Rupert Murdoch	1981
Lord Northcliffe	1908		
John Jacob Astor, later Lord Astor	1922		

Editors of *The Times*

Thomas Barnes	1817	R.M. Barrington-Ward	1941
John Delane	1841	W.F. Casey	1948
Thomas Chenery	1877	Sir William Haley	1952
G.E. Buckle	1884	William Rees-Mogg	1967
Geoffrey Dawson	1912	Harold Evans	1981
H. Wickham Steed	1919	Charles Douglas-Home	1982
Geoffrey Dawson	1922	Charles Wilson	1985

Index

299